CHURCH IN SOCIETY

PERSPECTIVES OF AN ANABAPTIST PASTOR

LESTER TROYER

FOREWORD

Thus saith the Lord,
"Stand ye in the ways and see,
and ask again for the old paths,
where is the good way, and walk therein,
and ye shall find rest for your souls."

_____

Jeremiah 6:16

I t is with great pleasure that we get the opportunity to introduce you to our friend and brother in faith, Lester Troyer. He is one of those people you come across in life who leaves you inspired and encouraged to grow in your faith and wanting more of Jesus. A man of passion, tempered with genuine humility, he has spent decades serving the Lord and the church, with a zeal for reaching out to unbelievers. His Amish-Mennonite background flavors his language with an emphasis on honoring God, developing genuine character, avoiding temptation and sin, living plainly, and holding God's sovereignty with confidence.

Led by the light and resolve for the mission of Christ, Pastor Troyer believes in seeking truth and living obediently according to the Word. _The Church in Society / Perspectives of an Anabaptist Pastor,_ is a collection of challenging essays grounded in Scripture that reveal this truth and provide timeless wisdom for a complicated world of mixed messages, spiritual apathy, and lukewarm Christianity.

In each section of the book, we ask that you read with an open mind and time for thoughtful immersion. Many of the concepts may seem foreign or even, to a degree, uncomfortable. Faithful to the principles of Scripture, these concepts resound an eternal perspective that will provoke an internal examination of oneself and the world around us. This book should be judged not in the light of prevailing opinion, but in the light of God's Word. "The word of God is quick and powerful, and sharper than any twoedged sword, piercing even to the dividing asunder of soul and spirit, and of the joints and marrow; and is a discerner of the thoughts and intents of the heart." Hebrews 4:12.

It is our prayer that your heart will be quickened, renewed, and revived so that at your crossroads, you will look, walk in the good way, and find rest for your soul.

—Kevin and Heidi Bordenave

INTRODUCTION TO THE CHURCH IN SOCIETY

This book reflects sixteen years of essay writing for the quarterly Mennonite periodical *Reaching Out*. It also includes material developed through many years of pastoral experiences, and ministry within our culture at large.

You will find this to be serious reading by design, in hopes of stimulating equally serious questions and discussions about the status quo of both the church and the society in which we live. This book is aimed at revived interest and commitment to truth, in hopes of rejecting the serious deficiencies that corrupt our manner of life, our freedom, and even threaten our existence.

It is necessary to cover a broad range of subject material for an overview of issues that should command the attention of all Americans, because we have been caught up in an almost unprecedented cultural shift. Thus the material is for those who profess Christian faith – and, for those who do not profess Christian faith. Whoever you are, pastor, theologian, politician, economist, lawyer, scientist, broker or businessman, and whatever your belief system – from Christian to atheist, there is material here that you will connect with.

Yes, Christian responsibility does come first. That's why the material on salvation is presented as the life-changing event that it is, a true regeneration of life. It is a call to wholeness of character, biblical morality, and Christian living to magnify the grace of God to the rest of the culture. It reveals that the biblical line of demarcation between believer and unbeliever, lies not in what we profess, but in whether we fulfill the will of God. This is a call to righteousness that exceeds both self-righteousness and unrighteousness. Because evil always contaminates, this material is a call to high alert, refusing to indulge in the decadence of a corrupt culture. In this interest this book repeatedly calls us to repentance.

The material focuses much on apologetics and science, not as a replacement for faith, but to present lots of compelling evidence against the growing monolith against the claims of God, against divine creation, and against the Bible. It exposes the sweeping cultural reverses that blindly dismiss integrity and absolute morality as keepers of the culture, only to replace them with tin soldiers of pleasure and materialism.

If there is one thing I dread in word processing, it is the window that opens up with the declaration that –"*This program has become unstable and must be shut down.*" Will my worst fears be imagined? Is this the crash that takes out all these days and hours of labor, forever? Then I ask whether God would not have ample cause to look down on America, (a nation that knew him and now refuses him), and saying, "*This program has become unstable and must be shut down*". . . These essays explore moral, political, social, economic, and environmental issues, with the cause of their instability firmly in mind.

I had expected to present this material, separated into neat categories, only to conclude that "neat" categories were merely a dream, and perhaps not even desirable. So, as with eating habits, as you read, expect variety in your diet, or check the index to select your next reading. Where you find some similarity of content, I trust that it will expand and clarify the subject material.

I'm not a prophet, nor a scientist. Neither do I claim to be an expert in every subject addressed herein. However, I do claim to live my life committed to God, and my understanding to biblical authority. This means that I take biblical instruction seriously, and that I expect biblical authority to illuminate a depth and breadth on any subject worthy to be addressed.

All thoughts are not created equal, and all ideas are not equally valid, and all religions do not lead to God. The sincere quest for truth yields clear, non complex answers. Blurring the lines of truth yields confusion, and complex problems that defy solution. Christian faith is a classic case of the tortoise winning the race against the speed and skill of the hare. The reason? The rabbit is self-obligated to explore every dead-end bunny trail, because he can't accept the truth that there really is only one way to the finish line. So he never does arrive.

Thus Christians and churches in society who buy into popular inclusiveness (imagining validity in many other religious forms) are doing double damage. They surrender the Way, for the confusion of culture without God, even while failing to be responsible as salt and light in a darkening world.

There is but one faith, even as there is but one Lord Jesus Christ. ***To God only wise, be glory through Jesus Christ for ever. Amen*** (Romans 16:27).

Lester Troyer

INDEX and APPRECIATION

This book could use a heritage section. But lacking that, I would at least acknowledge my indebtedness to former generations of great men and women of God. My own father and mother, along with seven older siblings provided an excellent place of incubation for my growing up. I heard a lot about my grandfather Robert M. Troyer (I was too young to know), and his almost legendary, and far-reaching ministry, especially for an Amishman. But I reaped tremendous blessings, first hand, from the examples of my uncles in ministry, Levi, Robert, and Noah.

There is no second hand faith in God. We can't build faith on our forefathers, but we can see how they built character upon their faith. So I expect to be eternally grateful for the long reach of the Anabaptist heritage tracking back to 1525. Most of this comes through writings, but there has been before my eyes, the evidence that faith in God, and in the authority of Scripture, does beam a shining light down though the corridors of time.

It is only fitting then, that I am passionate that the readers of this volume receive something of the vision of a decidedly biblical worldview. To this purpose, any positive results from reading this book are forwarded to God, for Jesus' sake.

This first section is fittingly dedicated to my wife, Katie. She has been such a wonderful help through these forty-five years, being there for me, in countless ways. She has reviewed many of the articles in this book, for suitability of wording and content, and has served as an honest, much needed (and much appreciated) critic. (Katie joins me in dedicating other portions of the book).

This particular article is written to my friend, Dr. Thomas Fritz, a man who asks difficult and sobering questions, because he really wants compelling answers.

We dedicate this section to our children, and their spouses, Allen and Brenda Troyer, Jerry and Ivy Troyer, Mark and Margaret Troyer, Conrad and Kristen Troyer, Linwood and JoAnn Hershey, and to all our grandchildren (sixteen and counting). We pray everyday, for their understanding, and for their faithfulness to God, and to his service.

My appreciation goes to Dr. Damian Vraniak. He sparked this discussion by requesting an analysis of the question, "Are boys becoming men in our community?" This does not assign any responsibility to him for the content herein.

We dedicate this section with heartfelt appreciation to Kevin and Heidi Bordenave. They reviewed much of the material, joyfully, willingly, and on their own time. Their's was a specialized focus, and does not obligate them to the overall content of this book. Their help and their insights were truly amazing, just what we needed to reach toward our publishing goal. Then again, timing was everything, but that's another story. We pray for them, and their children, with great thanksgiving to God for them.

This may seem rather unusual, but the critics in this case were serval inmates from the Sawyer County jail. They served as sounding boards as I developed the material, with both good advice and confirmation. My thanks to them.

WE CAN KNOW

THE BEGINNING OF CERTAINTY

Elsewhere in the book, is an article entitled, *The End of Certainty*, noting how Darwinism ultimately answers nothing, and gives no basis for any system of belief. (That is so in the same sense that the reality of Santa Claus breaks down somewhere between the North Pole, and the soot in your chimney. In the final analysis, Darwinism is not a sufficient answer, even for Darwinism).

This time the focus is on the basis of certainty. The evidence whereby men may know God is so compelling, that those who do not believe and therefore do not know, really are left without excuse. Call it willful ignorance. Call it denying the presence of the elephant in the living room. The problem is not the lack of external evidence for God. The condemnation of not knowing comes from a heart that rejects compelling evidence for the personal preference of living without accountability to God. This is the process whereby men change the truth of God into a lie, They refuse the worship of God, and choose rather to promote their own desires. However, in the process, they also choose their own condemnation.

What God has done is to provide ample evidence for the truth, through which those who are open to truth can indeed know with certainty. Another way of saying this is that we may know the validity of faith, without being force -fed the faith.

I was in Hollywood with an evangelism group on *666*, that is, June 6, 2006. We hadn't known that this was slated as a special time of Satan worship. Satanists had gathered from all over, dressed in all black, in honor of the devil. Now is there sufficient evidence to believe in Satan? They are right on that part. (But how is it that they know Satan is real, when so many want to claim that there isn't enough evidence to believe in God?) Ironically, and by the admission of several I engaged in conversation, the Bible is a primary source for believing in the devil. But Satan worship is a dead end. The fact that people will devote their lives to the one who destroys their souls is beyond comprehension. Their devotion and service gains them nothing. They will never win his love. Satan will hate their lives even unto death.

This is the condemnation revealed in Scripture, *that light is come into the world, but men loved darkness rather than light because their deeds are evil.*

Thus we must understand that the evidence for God is compelling enough for those who are willing to accept the truth, but not so compelling, as to overcome an obstinate will. *"It will never happen."* That is the easy answer to the man who insisted that if God is real, God needs to confront him to his face, His unbelief is not a problem of "cannot know," but one of "will not know."

Ultimately, the certainty pertaining to God is faith based, which doesn't weaken the reality of knowing.

I've heard faith described as though it were a kind of fluff to fill the gaps in missing information. But in fact, faith doesn't build sand castles. Faith builds on the utter reliability of God, and the evidence of what God has already done, as the tool to understand the greater picture of what God can do and will do, based on his record of faithfulness. It is not a blind leap into the unknown. It is more like connecting the dots. Faith in God is reasonable, while supplying understanding in what otherwise would not be known, beyond the realms of hard, natural evidence.

Some Christians try to make the case for faith in God as a parallel to faith in your car, in an elevator, or in some other mechanical invention. Personally, I see that as nonsense. With mechanical things, it's simply expecting the mechanicals to do what they are built to do. Your car has started 50,123 times. You think that it probably will again. But if that is faith, then what are those jumper cables doing in your trunk? Again, if that is faith, someday your faith will let you down. That is always the nature of the temporal. The brand new starter in the brand new car, is already on the way to its own demise. Faith in God is not like that. What lets you down is not faith, or at least not valid faith.

But again, the religious faith of some may indeed be like that mechanical faith. Faith may indeed be misplaced. Such faith will let them down someday. Faith is validated only in the truth of what is believed. It is not faith in faith. It is not faith in any form of a false belief system. The question is not even whether faith will get you through life, but rather whether it will get you through death, and on the blessed side of the judgment of God.

So how can I know for sure? The Bible blends two lines of evidence. One is nature. This universe is evidence for God. This evidence can be misinterpreted. Many have believed that the universe, or parts of it, are actually God, or gods. That is how ancient idolaters came to worship the sun, or other aspects of the hosts of heaven. But these idolaters have missed the most important factor.

This decisive factor can, in fact, be illustrated with the new starter, in the new car, but from the other direction. If you would follow the pagan logic of nature worship, then this shiny new model is actually a god to be worshiped. But that simply means that you have never known the bigger picture of what happens prior to the assembly plant. Behind that new model, is a long history of designers and engineers contributing their skills before the parts are ever manufactured, and long before the first new model comes off the assembly line. The fact that you never saw these people at work doesn't negate the certainty that it happened. But again, it does allow you to connect the dots. The new car in the showroom equals untold hours of designing and engineering by people you don't know. But that's your position because you never had the opportunity to meet these people. There are others who actually know these expert instigators of new models. Your position is one of faith. Their position is one of sight. Either position is one of *knowing*. The first is one of totally credible theory. The second, removes every doubt.

Do you **know** the truth of the universe? The origin of the universe is based on the same principle as the one we accept for the origin of the "new model" out of Detroit. This is the inherent truth that the evidence of nature reveals the fact that God is. Unless your reasoning powers have been hopelessly diminished by the strident calls of the high priests of the altar of Darwinism, you will need to confess that there exists a designer and engineer par excellence. But this fact that God exists, is as far as nature can guide you.

That is where the second line of evidence takes over. It is the "paper trail". The divine engineer has left copious notes that dovetail very well into the first line of evidence. Whether creation, the coming of sin into the world, the Genesis flood, the giving of the Ten Commandments, or the coming of Jesus Christ into the world, the historical documentation is all in place. And to what purpose? *"That they might **know** thee, the only true God, and Jesus Christ whom thou hast sent"*.

So again, **you can know**. It begins with accepting the evidence that *"God is"*, and finds fulfillment in the fact that God rewards the faith of *"those who diligently seek him"*

There are reasons why one would pursue such a personal relationship with God. There is the discovery that finally the endless rounds of earthly pursuits and pleasures, will never satisfy.

Then there is the matter of guilt. This intuitive knowledge that we really do come short on some unyielding scale of measure will either drive us into further denial and deception, or to the point of *truly knowing God.*

ALL PEOPLE ARE DIVIDED
INTO TWO CAMPS

Let me explain. The Bible says, *In the beginning God created the heaven and the earth.* There have always been people who staked their lives on this statement.

"God created" makes a tremendous statement about God. It shows him to be a super genius as an architect, an inventor, a chemist, an engineer, a microchip designer (DNA), a linguist (communications between living things) plus a host of other attributes beyond description. This divine being would be outside of the universe and have an eternal existence. His could, in his power, create everything that exists, out of nothing at all. When he made living creatures, he would have already provided the right atmosphere, including air, light, heat, and energy, and the right food supply in place, so that they might thrive and fill the earth. Furthermore, since each kind of living thing, from plants and trees, to incests, to birds, to mammals, to people, would have been created but once, their survival would depend on a fully functional means of reproduction. Those systems could not evolve. They had to be perfect from day one. And last, but not least, if God created us, he would certainly have had a purpose in doing so. It would mean that we really are not own, but that he owns us by creation. All this describes an incredible God. Right? This view holds, that though creation is not testable in a science lab, it is in perfect harmony with science.
But let's pick up on the other side.

Another group of people believes that *God did not create the heavens and the earth.* They would claim that we are without divine purpose, guidance, or absolute morals in this world.

This group typically rejects anything supernatural, as unscientific. Now, if you are anti-creation, then you have taken care of the incredible God. However, you now face a greater dilemma. What astounding mechanism accounts for a universe teeming with life and intelligence, with its countless orderly living systems, fully dependent on non random sequences? If we could put the universe into random mode, swift and sure destruction would surely follow.

Yet this group expects that given enough time, anything is bound to happen. This means that random mindless nothing produced something, and mindless something produced everything. Now I live 400 miles from Chicago. So go ahead, blindfold me, spin me around until I'm disoriented, then put me in my car, and tell me to drive to the Chicago Field Museum (since they are great believers in the accomplishments of time and chance). Given enough time . . . Sorry!

There is a colossal scientific problem here. The chance of making Chicago is resolved in the first two minutes. Millions of years add no new information. Likewise, neither time nor chance, are on the side of evolution. For lack of information, both are on the side of degeneration and death. Life can thrive and reproduce only on the intelligent programing of DNA utilizing a sufficient, renewable source of energy.

Here is what most people fail to realize. There is only one valid avenue of scientific inquiry into the possibility of an evolutionary history. That one thing is the fossil record. It is the only material connecting link between the distant past and the present.

The fossil record is very extensive, containing fossils by the millions. If evolution were true, fossils should reveal all kinds of creatures in various stages of development, and defying neat classifications. Fossils of intermediate stages should far outnumber clearly defined species.

Only such evidence could give scientific credibility to evolution. In other words, the evolutionary scientist would do more than insist that evolution happened. He would show us that the belief in evolution is at least consistent with the fossil record.

However the fossil record does not support an evolutionary beginning (*"Where Darwin Went Wrong"; Reader's Digest,* September, 1982). Even the limited claims of "missing links" have shrunk considerably under the glare of scientific inquiry.

The reason that the fossil record is the only scientific inquiry into a possible evolutionary past, is in itself very telling. It is because there are no known scientific laws presently in effect, to lend credibility to evolution. This failure in relation to science, has reduced evolution into a highly biased belief system. Evolutionary scientists have merely traded belief in the miracle working God, for the much greater miracle of life without God.

The Biblical teaching of creation is indeed worth another look. Unlike evolution, it aligns well with scientific inquiry in many fields.

- Genesis one (the first chapter in the Bible), declares that the world was made by God. This concurs with all scientific observation that nothing ever produces something, and with the science of biogenesis, that life begets life. Life is never the product of non-life, and chaos never produces order.
- Genesis one underscores the point of intelligent design. Every invention and innovation is planned and carried out by intelligence, matched by the means of accomplishment (energy). Where is even one museum, dedicated to inventions and artifacts of unintelligent design?
- Genesis one shows us that the earth, and the planetary system were made for their particular place and purpose in the scheme of the whole. We find this to be true with clockwork precision. Survival of life on this planet depends on this accuracy in nature. If the laws of nature were the product of chance, we should expect them to change by chance. For example, why would the earth stay in a chance orbit around the sun?
- Genesis one declares that living things reproduce only after their own kind. This is both observably true in the present, and is totally consistent with the fossil record.
- Genesis one describes the good work of the good God. This accounts for the beauty of nature, and pro-

vides the only consistent explanation of meaning and morals in this world.

- Genesis one reveals the inventive genius of God. This is very consistent with the inventiveness and resourcefulness of the human race (made in God's image.)
- Genesis one shows us a universe of order and predictability that is friendly to the complex needs of all living things. This is the law of nature. We should then anticipate another law, which, though unseen, would dictate a system of moral law, prescribed by the same God, directed to the human race. That is exactly what follows in the Bible.

Understandably, Darwinists and atheists do want to claim a slice of the moral pie, (who wants to be known as being without morals?) To be sure, these "morals" may take some strange twists. But this is an area not inherently theirs. Whatever they claim in morals, is borrowed from outside their box. **This is our point.**

The denial of the Creator God has left humanity without meaning, without purpose, and without morals. Without God as anchor, who needs permission for anything? Who is to judge any sort of behavior?

Fortunately, it is not the nonexistence of God, but the denial of God that causes the problem. He did not forsake the world which he had made. Look around you. The signs of his intelligence and power are with us, revealed everywhere in nature every day. *He is not far from every one of us, seeing he gives to all, life and breath and all things.*

A BRIEF INTRODUCTION TO THE BIBLE

The Bible is literally a book of books, really 66 books, rolled into one. It is an ancient book, written over a span of 1600 years. It is also an ancient book, in that it has had nothing added to it for close to 2000 years.

The Bible was penned by men, and contains the elements and characteristics of human authorship.

It is a controversial book. This all times a best seller, has been spoken against, outlawed, banned and burned (many times with its owners), as no other.

Yet the Bible is relevant as no other book. It is the one perfect book. It is *given by inspiration of God, and is profitable for doctrine, for reproof, for correction, and for instruction in righteousness*, (2 Timothy 3:16). The men who penned the words *spoke as they were moved by the Spirit of God,* (II. Peter 1:21).

The perfection of the book is more than a creed. It is right because the one who rightly put the universe together is also perfect and right in his character. The Bible reveals this rightness of God (otherwise called holiness). The moral law given to man, for man, flows out of that same rightness of God. People can ignore it, argue about it, or disobey it, but they cannot change it. *The Word of the Lord endureth forever.*

DEADLY MISCALCULATIONS

I saw the wreck. But I never knew the man. Not in life. Not in death. I don't even know his name, though I'm sure I had seen it in the news following the accident. No, I remember him only for his reported last words to his bride of a few days: "I can still make it."

Why did he die? First, consider the obvious. His pick-up truck was hit broadside by a log truck. But going beyond that, he died for his wrong calculations. His last words indicate that he was aware both of the intersection ahead, and of the log truck, in a blind pursuit of its own right-of-way from the left. Stupid miscalculation, wasn't it. But frankly, I have done some very stupid things myself (both in and out of traffic), yet I'm still here to tell about the other man's mistake. After all, people do err in judgment, and we all know it.

Finally, it was really not miscalculation that led to his senseless death. That intersection was clearly marked with a stop sign. Had he not chosen to run the stop sign, he would not have needed perfect timing. Simple obedience would have saved him.

Some folks see traffic signals as nuisance interference with personal freedom. Not so. They are designed to minimize the perils of human error. In this case the stop sign, taken as a command would have saved his own life and spared the new bride the anguish of new widowhood. Thus, the twisted steel of the wreck stood as a monument to folly worse than miscalculation.

The Bible shows that we face similar problems in things that are of a spiritual and eternal nature. And frankly, our tendency to miscalculate in spiritual things is not our greatest threat. God himself has fully surveyed the spiritual landscapes and traffic hazards of the soul, and has given his Son for our deliverance. If we would but renounce our arrogance in thinking we know better than God, along with our reluctance to obey, we could be safely delivered from the spiritual perils that come our way. And it's not just outside the church that we encounter this problem. Let me discuss a few of the miscalculations that plague church people:

1. Professing to believe the Bible, yet not bothering with its teachings. That's like believing in traffic signals without knowing whether to stop on red, yellow, or green.

2. Being satisfied with knowing what the Bible teaches with no intent to obey. Can you imagine the chaos and destruction if most people would behave that way in traffic?

3. Blind sincerity."It doesn't matter what you believe, so long as you believe." What? That, my friend is patently false. The value of sincerity is limited strictly to what is factual. Believing what is untrue is mere delusion.

4. "It must be O.K. because many Christians are doing it." Well, just how many vultures eat carrion? Does that mean you should join them? Besides, the Bible teaches that it is the broad way that leads to destruction, and that many travel that way, even while claiming to know God (Matthew 7:13,22,23).

5. "I know I'm a good person because I do many good things." Perhaps you do many good things, but that can be like salve on a deadly wound, or a Band-aid on a tumor. God is looking for the kind of good (from sin to righteousness) that happens only in repentance from sin, and faith in Jesus Christ.

6. Feelings of well-being. Yes, it may feel good to give God a whole hour of church on Sunday. The cathedral has a religious feel. The music stirs the soul. The service is uplifting. It feels so right to drop a few coins in the offering. Feelings are important. But they can also be deceptive. Mere good feelings cannot be trusted to determine whether we are right with God.

7. "My church accepts what I am doing. It must be all right."
   Sorry - the church has no authority to decide moral
   issues - only to accurately apply moral issues as already
   established in the Scriptures. Many Christians have been
   taken in with ungodly trends of our society, even as these
   trends are in outright contradiction to biblical teaching,
   and prove to be detrimental to our culture

When life is finally over, the Word of God will only show
those wise unto salvation who are saved through faith in
Jesus Christ, in obedience to his word. "I think I can still
make it" actually means you won't.

BREACHING THE FREEDOMS
OF AMERICA

Americans seemingly revere their great twin freedoms - Freedom of Religion and Freedom of Speech, even while setting the course for their destruction.

Our historic Freedom of Religion has evolved into an enlightened tolerance toward all religions. This new religious freedom offers a red carpet welcome to most any kind of belief system, and makes room for the promotion of the same in America. In this politically correct age, who would be so narrow minded as to think one belief system better than another, or that the nation wouldn't do just as well under many gods, rather than an entrenched but outmoded Christianity? Thus many news commentators are drawing friendly parallels between religions (Christianity and Islam for example), as though vague similarities should render the jarring differences moot. This also includes an appeal to the notion that various world religions really do worship the same God, but under different names. Nothing is offered as to what to do if the friendly spread of Islamic Centers, and the growth of the Muslin population doesn't turn out as expected. (Actually, there is no need to. It would be too late anyway.)

Meanwhile, freedom of speech has expanded its territory unchecked into unimaginable debauchery. We pride ourselves on the idea of accepting whatever self-expression one can imagine, and parade our shame for the whole tech world to see. Yet by focusing on "free" without regard for what is being destroyed in the corruption of speech, appearance, and behavior, the rising sewer has contaminated our very well springs of freedom. This is true in politics, in education, and in entertainment. It corrupts the morals of the young and dims the vision of the aged. It has polluted the foundation of law and order and perverts our courts of justice.

Perhaps most disturbing, is the dumbing down of theology in the church (in a remarkable parallel to education.) As a result, the average person in the pew has very limited knowledge of the Bible and Christian living. This means that not even God can tell us how to live. (That is as though the sewage has inundated the very control room of the purification plant (the church in the world).

Americans have forgotten that freedoms without boundaries are sure to self-destruct. Such destruction proceeds right before our eyes. The "woman's right to choose" has shut the door to the rights of the unborn, and marked millions of them for death. The favoring of the homosexual agenda has covered for risky behavior, and has facilitated the deaths of possibly millions, around the world. We may save a few people from death through myriad health and safety regulations, yet fail to warn them away from an early grave by endorsing perverted sexual practices.

Our past failures in not allowing the truth to limit our freedom brings serious questions about any collective wisdom we might bring into our current debates on free speech and religion issues. It appears that our so-called freedoms trump even our own survival.

The real question of the present Islamic/ mosque building debate is whether America should extend religious freedom at the price of surrendering that freedom. Islamic governments are diametrically opposed to freedom of religion. Among those who come through our borders are some who are quick to claim every legal right of speech and religion extended them in America. However, their idea of returning the favor would be to eradicate us from the earth. You don't go into Islamic nations, passing out Bibles and building churches. Proselyting is not tolerated, and conversion to Christian faith often comes with a death warrant. Muslim converts to Christianity are often disowned by parents, spouses and families. A violent mix of beatings, persecutions, and killings ensues.

Here it is profitable to consider the history of freedom of religion in America. Doubtless, many European settlers came to our shores for rugged challenges and boundless opportunities. But a goodly number came for a far different reason - to escape persecution, imprisonment, and death, under the steam roller of religious tyranny in the various "Christian" governments in European nations. A given nation's particular version of Catholicism or Protestantism was imposed on every citizen. The reformation leaders themselves, Martin Luther and Ulrich Zwingli, showed no mercy and gave no room for individual conscience. Thus the Protestant Reformation spawned freedom of religion only negatively - through those whose conscience was not for sale, and who were willing to pay the price for their faith, in persecution.

These Quaker and Anabaptist groups believed that coercion and Christian faith were incompatible, that one's standing with God is an individual, voluntary matter. (Interestingly, every protestant group that I know of, came around to embrace this same concept. I would be grateful to any protestant leaders who would update me on when, why, and how this shift came about).

How did our government come to embrace such a radical departure from established practices of Europe, embracing the cause of the religious outcasts? I can only speculate. For one thing, there was no prevailing denominational preference among the framers of the Constitution. Those leaders were themselves of varied Christian persuasions (a few of none.) Also the stalwart, peace-loving Quaker, William Penn loomed large, both in England and America. Above all, I choose to believe that God was pleased to have it so.

Today this freedom is under threat, not primarily from without, as with Islam, but by the internal abuse of that freedom. We have banned the basic tenets of Christian faith as the checkpoint of freedom. Thus the Christian faith, which once breathed life and substance to our freedoms, is eyed with suspicion as though being the cause of our present dilemma.

The "Wall of Separation" which Jefferson invoked to assure the Danbury Baptists of protection from government meddling, has been turned on its head, to banish biblical truth from the public square. Children brought up in such an environment may receive more teaching on the "evils" of fossil fuels and homophobia, than they do against lying, cheating, or sexual immorality.

The modern take on religious liberty that lauds all religious views as having equal merit, has nothing in common with the price of freedom with which brave people settled our shores. Not for a moment did they embrace the equality of religions. They didn't come to toss their religious meat into a common kettle. They came because they were not expected to do so. In fact, the strength of America has always been with strong churches and families who respected government, but needed no government regulation to lead lives of integrity. Both their trust and their reverence were toward God. Christians can never be the light of the world and the salt of the earth by being stirred into the stew of the common culture.

Ironically, it is these same Christians, willing to die for their own beliefs, who would never consider coercing others in matters of faith. They believe that only the gospel of Jesus Christ can change the hearts of men, and that force has no power to extend the kingdom of God. They love their enemies. Thus they will suffer torture, prison and death for their beliefs, but they can never build prisons for those of other beliefs, even dangerous ones. (Does the general reader of this article have any clue of how much faithful Christians are suffering, under regimes of terror around the world, and that churches and homes are ransacked and destroyed, Bibles burned, pastors imprisoned, and thousands of Christians put to death every year?)

The tragic but inevitable rewrite of religious freedom comes from an America that is rejecting the biblical God of our creation and the Jesus Christ of our salvation, and is now riveted with the claims of Eastern Mysticism, the religion of Mohammad, or of Marxism, and atheism. This is the embrace of a conglomerate of errors that contribute nothing to our souls or our bodies. Thus have we shredded the nourishment of biblical morality into a religious stew devoid of truth. If this mix was only deficient in nourishment we would not be so concerned. But alas; there is poison in the kettle.

God is dishonored when people turn from the truth they had known. Exchanging absolute truth for multiplied error is bound to introduce error in response to both foreign and domestic challenges to our freedoms. In the abuse of these freedoms, we have put them on borrowed time. Finally, unless God is pleased to defend our borders, the best laid plans of men are vain.

A BIBLICAL WORLDVIEW

What is a worldview? The term comes from the German "Weltanschauung," literally, "beholding the world." Everyone has a perception, a basic set of ideas about life as though looking at the world through a particular pair of glasses. Worldview than, translates into the way people respond to surroundings, the goals that they set and the values they pursue. The outcome can be radically different. For example, in the abortion debate, one worldview seeks to destroy the very lives that the other is seeking to save. This also demonstrates how wildly worldview can swing, even in fifty years. Thus, cultural stability and cultural change are dictated by the particular worldview of societal and political powers.

There are religious worldviews of great diversity. For example, in the Middle East, a young Christian believer and a Muslin suicide bomber might live practically side by side. Both believe their own faith worth dying for. There the similarity ends. Why? Because their views of who God is and what God is like are polar opposites. As a result, the Christian believer would rather die than deny the faith. His neighbor though, would die for the promised reward of killing "infidels."

Religious worldviews are taught. This is so because they include spiritual teachings of unseen realms. This explains why people of charisma and dynamic personality can quickly gain a cult-like following, even when their teachings promote error and deception. In contrast, the biblical worldview (our subject), is firmly entrenched with thousands of years of historical events, including God's interaction with our ancestors, all the way back through Noah and to Adam. Unfortunately, this vital point is forgotten in today's mad rush to equalize all worldviews.

On the other hand, a secular worldview may be simply caught, rather than taught. I still remember suggesting to a successful Mexican businessman that he had probably carefully established his belief system. He admitted that he had not. In fact, he had given little thought to what he believed.

This would indicate a worldview mired in temporal advantages, such as marrying his lovely wife, and building his beautiful estate. In this he would join multitudes of Americans whose basic worldview begins and ends in the pursuit of the "good life," otherwise known as the American dream. This often dictates a bigger house, new places to which to travel, weekends on the lake with a new boat, and goals for his offspring to excel in sports, and to graduate from college.

This temporal worldview bypasses searching questions such as: Why am I here? To what purpose is my existence? Where am I going? How do I know, or why don't I know the answers?

Worldviews are changeable. If they were not, there would be better things to do than to write this column.

SO WHAT IS THE BIBLICAL WORLDVIEW?

1. The biblical worldview must be revealed from God. It can be sought after. But it cannot be invented. The notion that people are capable of inventing anything other than phony religion has about the same probability of success as a team of brilliant scientists and surgeons fashioning a living, breathing, fully human, two hundred pound man from nothing (or even from two hundred pounds of clay). It doesn't happen because both human life and a relationship with God are acts of God. Both are beyond the reach of human skill and invention.

The fact that the Bible is the revelation of God and from God assures the generational sameness of the message of God to man. After a thousand years, it is still the same. Rather than the message becoming old, it is forever new to all people of all times. But people, even those with a Christian worldview, are still inclined to deviate from the revelation of God. However, the unchanging Word of God assures a return to the centrality of truth to the sincere seeker. *Men seek him and find him when they search for him with all their heart.*

2. Thus the biblical worldview is God-centered. It is focused on the Eternal, Almighty one, who made everything that ever was, is, or will be. This is the one who ordered the events of

history, wiped out the world of Noah's day with a worldwide flood, brought the confusion of tongues into the plans of men at the tower of Babel, and etched divine law into tables of stone in the days of Moses. In due time he sent his Son, Jesus Christ into the world to save sinners. These are things that have happened in history, with the great climax yet to come. *For we must all appear before the judgment seat of Christ.*

This view is forever, unapologetically exclusive. Why? Let me ask you some questions. How many gods created the world? How many gods continue to uphold all things by the Word of their power? How many gods have provided the perfect sacrifice for sin? How many gods for the historical testimony of rising from the dead? How many gods will judge the world? To attribute the work of the God to "gods" is like crediting the outcome of the civil war to George Bush, Barak Obama, or even Fidel Castro.

3. The biblical worldview is one of a fallen world because of sin entering into the once-perfect creation, and death through sin, catching up with every person alive. Thus the biblical worldview carefully evaluates the difference between the temporal values of this world which are soon to pass away, and the spiritual things which abide forever. In many ways the world is a wonderful and even beautiful place to live - thanks to the God who created it, and continues to load us with benefits. Yet it is also a dangerous place, where Satan trips people up through the lust of the flesh, the lust of the eyes, and the pride of life.

4. The biblical worldview defines the truth of the power of God unto salvation to everyone who believes, whether Jew or Gentile. It defines conversion, morals, and manner of life out of the principles taught in Scripture. Though conversion does not yield automatic perfection, it does deliver here and now from the bondage of sin. A healthy diet of continual feeding on the Word delivers from being swallowed up in ignorance and sets the believer on the course of righteousness.

One of the greatest needs today is to biblically define what it is to be a Christian. The Christian walks in the light, embraces the truth, keeps his own word, confesses his sins, loves his brother, blesses his enemy, and opens his heart and wallet to the needy. He professes with his mouth the Lord Jesus. He lives in obedience to authority, and lives in fidelity with the wife of his youth. He forgives others, and suffers adversity graciously. He becomes like his Master. In short, the life of the Christian is defined in learning the teachings of Scripture, and then doing them, thus fulfilling the will of God.

One of the great tragedies of evangelicals is in switching the focus from what a Christian is, to how to become one. The deceptive result is "Christians" who continue in their sins quite unaware that they face the same condemnation as their non-Christian counterparts. To such Jesus says - *Depart from me, ye that work iniquity* (Matthew 7:23).

BENEFITS OF THE CHRISTIAN WORLDVIEW

The most important benefit is the personal knowledge of the Truth. *Ye shall know the truth and the truth shall set you free.* This is to know God through Jesus Christ, and to be known by him. This meets the Bible definition of eternal life.

This is not about finding an easy way through life. It is about following the narrow way, which leads to life, with life in the very presence of God to follow.

But the Christian way is also about the way we live in this world. If we Christians will exemplify the grace and the Spirit of Jesus Christ in this world and in our culture, we will by influence (not by force), be a light and an example in a dark place. This is the atmosphere where God works conviction and regeneration in the hearts and lives of others. God draws the line of demarcation between righteousness and wickedness. People will either accept or reject his great salvation.

CHRISTIAN CONTRIBUTIONS TO THE STATE

Ye are the salt of the earth, but if the salt hath lost its savour, wherewith shall it be salted? It is thenceforth good for nothing, but to be cast out, and trodden under foot of men. (Matthew 5:13)

A casual reading of this text will hardly convey the cutting edge of its message. As an example, let's consider food preparation and preservation, which is a matter of either life, health, and plenty, or, on the other hand, of famine, starvation and even death by poisoning.

Food preservation is hardly the challenge that it was in history. Methods include refrigeration, freezing, canning, drying, and vacuum sealing. So with a minimum of care on our part, the perils of food going bad is practically nil.

Not so in olden days. Some foods could be dried. But before refrigeration, the basic preservation of meat was salt. Meat not properly preserved, went beyond assaulting the taste buds. Health and life were at stake. Even kings and presidents couldn't totally avoid food on its way to spoilage.

But there is another developing peril of the modern day that has nothing to do with preservation, but has everything to do with sanitation in production and processing. For all the sophistication of modern methods, from equipment to inspections, there is an underlying loss of integrity among producers and processors. Sanitation is shortchanged by the profit motive. The result is seemingly unending recalls of vegetables, meats, eggs, and other products that pose a threat to consumer health. (I'm not picking on agribusiness here. These people certainly don't have a monopoly on greed and rule-bending).

These issues become the point of our message. Cutting corners is perilous. What a safe and nutritious food supply is to public health, so is the salt of righteousness, to the preservation of the culture. It is always true that *righteousness exalts a nation, but that sin is a reproach to any people.*

Contamination in the food supply is like sin. It is always culturally degrading, and unless it is checked leads to further chaos and disintegration of the culture.

If statistics are of any use, the state of our own culture is in that deadly way. The television culture and the online habits of typical Americans, and the prominence of violent and morally kinky behavior, can only be a mirror to the heart and soul of America.

Most Americans still identify with Christianity, and have some connection to church life. But regrettably, this majority fails to embody the truth of Christianity in practice. They do not portray significantly higher standards of morality and integrity than the rest of culture. They have very significant incidents of unwed parenthood, divorces, abortions, and even homosexuality. They piggyback on the sleaze industry for entertainment, and demonstrate the same musical preferences as the ungodly.

It is to this segment that I especially address this message. The Bible does not give room for some middle ground where we are merely forgiven sinners, still free to feed in the germ infested recesses of a fallen culture. We are either for Jesus Christ, or we are against him. If we are for him, then it follows that he is our Lord. He would have us to do his will, and use us to fulfill his cause in this world. This is the salt principle. The holiness that sets us apart for God, is at the same time, a tool of God, to reach the ungodly with the knowledge of sin sickness, and to lead them on to repentance, forgiveness, to change, to hope, and to challenge.

The point here is for nominal Christians to get off the fence. God despises lukewarmness. He would have us hot or cold. If we will not surrender the love of sin, then let's not live under the guise of Christianity. But on the other hand, let's accept the challenge of humbling ourselves before God in repentance, and take personal responsibility for what is wrong with us.

I appreciate opportunities to sense the heartbeat of the evangelical front of our day. It is for that reason that I recently attended three hours of lectures from a few of the foremost thinkers and Christian leaders of the day. I heard much about the problems across the world, and of the impact of ungodly philosophers and men of influence and who turned the world toward the moral abyss (Darwin, Marx, and Dewey come to mind). I also heard much about bad policies and bad politicians corrupting our nation. Yet in three hours, sitting among a cross section of two thousand Christian people (with the responsibility of being the salt of the earth), I don't remember even a single word of introspection, that perhaps there are certain changes that first need to happen among us (*judgment must begin at the house of God)*, or that the words of Scripture might apply (*Be afflicted, and mourn and weep; let your laughter be turned to mourning, and your joy to heaviness. Humble yourselves in the sight of the Lord, and he shall lift you up* (James 4:8-10).

In contrast, the imperative Christian contribution to the state, is to be Christian. That is where the heart of God is. With all due respect to the laws of the land, and to support those laws, The fact remains that the U.S.A. never is, was, nor will be, Christ's earthly kingdom. *(If his kingdom were of this world, then his servants would fight for it).* This then is the great mystery. From over the past hundreds of years, I am not aware of a single Christian group taking a position that arms and killing is justified to advance the kingdom of Jesus Christ. Our Commander clearly disallows the practice. The Christian calling is to serve unto death, not to carry out a death warrant against others. How is it then, that practically all evangelicals bless the practice of Christian soldiers going into carnal warfare, and maiming or killing the enemy?

A very similar dilemma faces us in Christian / political involvements. First, as a matter of New Testament teaching and early church practice, Christians live in the obligation of a decidedly higher kingdom, with a higher code of conduct, and a higher calling.

Secondly, I've had the privilege of watching the conservative Christian involvement in politics from the time of Jerry Falwell's "moral majority." This turned into a powerful force

THE MOST IMPORTANT QUESTION

What then shall I do with Jesus which is called Christ? -
Pontius Pilate (Matthew 27:22)

I am the Way, the truth, and the Life. - Jesus Christ (John 14:6)

Some of you will see this as just another of those religious questions, and since you're not religious, or because you pursue some other religion, you think it doesn't pertain to you. Pontius Pilate wasn't religious either, but he was forced to decide what to do with Jesus anyway. Because he was unprepared for the pressures of that hour, he had Jesus crucified. He didn't know he would have a resurrection on his hands. If Jesus had stayed dead in the tomb, Pilate's wrong choice would have been nothing to worry about. Now some day Jesus will have Pilate on his hands. Then what?

Today, you have a decision about Jesus on your hands. Being nonreligious doesn't change that. You may ignore him, or seem to do nothing. Even so, and without even realizing it, you face choices every day that determine what you are doing with Jesus - entering a shady business deal, a negative report about an innocent person who just happens to be in the way of your success, under reporting your income, or illicit sexual relations. If Jesus had stayed dead, you would have nothing to worry about. But some day, at the judgment, he will have you on his hands. Then what?

Many of you reading these lines say you are Christians. You go to church. You do good deeds. You read the Bible. You consider yourself a good person. Now sometimes I ask others to tell me how to become a Christian. The answers I get are not always reassuring. So I ask you; do you know how to become a Christian? What do you say? Read the Bible? Pray? Do whatever the church says? Do the best you can? Sorry, these things may be involved, but they are not sufficient for the day when you face Jesus Christ at the judgment.

If the claim of being Christian hinges on us having been, or trying to be good people, we obviously don't even know ourselves, let alone the Christ who died for our sins. Jesus didn't come to make us a little better. He came to raise us out of the spiritual death of trespasses and sins. What to do with Jesus needs to begin with the understanding of the dire need that confronts us.

Though we were created in the image of God, that image is corrupted by the sin nature through which all are defiled. The sin of Adam back in Eden led to the curse under which we were born. We may not fully understand the process, but the results are painfully clear, even as the Bible says. *There is none righteous no not one* (Romans 3:10). *For all have sinned and come short of the glory of God.* (Romans 3:23). Now add to that the penalty for sin. *The soul that sinneth it shall die* (Ezekial 18:4). *The wages of sin is death* (Romans 6:23). There is no solution and no remedy for the sin problem starting from ourselves.

The second aspect of deciding what to do with Jesus comes from heaven where a tremendously costly plan was put in place whereby we may be saved. *For God so loved the world that he gave his only begotten Son that whosoever believeth in him, should not perish, but have eternal life* (John 3:16). Thus Jesus Christ, the sinless One, by his own blood, became the sacrifice needed to deliver us from our sins. In paying the price to save us, he provided the only name under heaven whereby we must be saved. And in rising from the dead three days later, he became positive proof that sin and death could be defeated through the love and mercy of God. The historic fact of the death and resurrection of Christ is the guarantee that after we have died, we will live again.

So does this gospel of salvation make the difference? In essence, it is the only thing that does. Without it, personal faith in Jesus would be a vain exercise. This sets Jesus Christ and Christianity an eternity apart from all the religions and isms ever invented among men. The fulfilment of prophetic Scriptures concerning Jesus Christ, also assures us that other matters of which he spoke will surely come to pass. This means that indeed he will come again with the holy angels with power and great glory. This is the coming day of judgment (when he has us on his hands), the day when he severs the righteous from the wicked eternally, claiming the righteous for his kingdom and casting the wicked into hell.

There is a final aspect of salvation that comes back to us. God has made us with free choice. Though only the Spirit of God can move us to salvation, we are not forced to accept. God has not made us to be robots. But consider carefully. We are hopelessly, eternally lost unless we respond to God through his Holy Spirit. The Spirit works unseen, yet very persuasively to convince us of our sin, our lostness, and our need of a Savior. This usually occurs in conjunction with exposure to the Word of God.

The way to heed this call is through repentance. This is a godly sorrow for sin, with a willingness to confess and forsake every known sin, clearing the slate with God and people. (It is possible to be sorry about certain sins or consequences without the kind of surrender that is effective for salvation. Further, we must allow Scripture to define sin. Sadly, even many churches condone behavior that God condemns.)

Finally, repentance alone cannot save. It conditions us to receive salvation from God. It is the sacrifice of Jesus Christ on the cross, wherein God can remain just, and yet forgive our transgressions. The forgiveness we so desperately need, comes through faith in Christ, wherein his blood washes away our sin. In surrender, we yield to him the position of Savior, Master, and Lord of our lives. We deny ourselves, to take up the cross and follow him. The salvation which may well have begun in secret, is followed with water baptism. This puts you publicly and unashamedly in the camp of Bible-believing Christians, living out their faith in the One who died for them and arose again.

This is truly a life - changing faith. It turns us from the condemnation of sin into the peace of forgiveness from God. It breaks up the old sin patterns and produces the righteous-

LET HEALTHCARE REFORM BEGIN

(This was offered before the healthcare bill was signed into law. But the principles for actually controlling costs, remain the same).

The real tragedy in health care is not that millions of us are uninsured (some of us by personal choice), but the continued shrinking of the collective American spine. We tank among the jellyfish, lured by promises of painless ways of doing things, seemingly never learning that "free" ends up costing the most. We didn't used to add trillion - dollar deficits to the budget, because we couldn't fathom the cost. Now we just may add another trillion, to make health care "affordable." Is this because we still can't fathom the cost?

I wanted to compare health care expenses to buying a house or a vehicle. Need a house? You work, you skimp, you save, you budget, then you buy. Need a car? Hit the repeat key. If you want health care? Buy the services. What's the difference? A few hundred to a few thousand a month for house and car, or monthly payments for medical expenses incurred? But now even that argument is being seriously undermined in this new and glorious day of *Cash for Clunkers*, and *Tax Credits* for *First Time Home- buyers.*

To be sure, the drain of medical costs does impede status in a generation that believes life really does consist of the abundance of things possessed. There's not much glory in buying appendectomies, or surgical repairs, or blood pressure meds, but as long as we are in human bodies, we will be hit with these things from time to time. And we will pay, either directly or indirectly. The fixation on entitlements and insurances helps generate skyrocketing costs and then attempts to conceal them.

There is a larger picture here as well. The lack of personal accountability, in the context of easy credit, encourages living beyond our means. For example, in homebuying, actual need, and family serviceability might call for a three-bedroom ranch. But that's a long shot from what is actually being built in most new developments. Further, a newly purchased used car, can represent financial smarts (not the same as status), and excellent value. But again, that scenario, seems almost rare in suburban driveways. These reality-based family purchases reined in to need and ability to pay, could, to a large degree, also accommodate a family budget that includes healthcare.

So let's take another look at true health care reform? The system is broken for lack of overall integrity. (This really does run in parallel with our broken economy). So let the debate begin over the practice of seeking a pot of gold (through litigation), in every medical slight or misstep. The honest miscalculations of doctors and other medical personnel should not drive malpractice insurance costs through the ceiling. Second, restore personal accountability between the medical provider and the patient. This step calls for less insurance rather than more. For example, in 2008, we paid $2600.00 for a medical procedure. We had two other quotes for $8000.00 and $10,000 respectively. The present trend of behemoth medical conglomerates does nothing for cost control, and probably not even for patient care. (That's why I would hope that smaller, competitive clinics could be the wave of the future). Finally, how is it that we debate health care coverage, with little regard for unhealthful and even dangerous, lifestyle choices?

The tools to make healthcare affordable for most of us, are in easy (not painless), reach.

But what about those truly caught up in medical dilemmas and emergencies beyond their means? In the first place, "beyond their means", is often lost in artificial highs. So what we need is a deflation of the medical balloon itself. (There really are some medical facilities around the country that are trying to do exactly that, with package pricing, catering to the uninsured with cash pricing, etc.).

We also need a refocus on entitlements. A public official who refused to redirect stimulus money into payments for organ transplants for the poor, was accused as running a "death camp." I crossed that bridge years ago. I can't afford a heart transplant, nor is there any person or agency on earth that owes me one. Thank You.

"Owes me," is a cancer on the system. It needs to be replaced from the opposite direction. It is the generosity principle. This simply means that we ought to open our hearts and our wallets. Indeed, there are people who through various tragedies, are in way over their heads. Despite the entrenched affliction of the entitlement mentality, we could give local examples showing that the generosity principle is still alive in our community. Great things can be accomplished, and much greater would be to come, if, under God, we will cultivate that great command, *Thou shalt love thy neighbor as thyself.* Giving and sharing does build character, and is a vital part of healthy and happy lifestyle choices.

UNDER COMMAND

"Let every soul be subject to the higher powers. For there is no power but of God: the powers that be are ordained of God" (Romans 13:1).

The most powerful people in the world still find that their position of authority is conditional. Presidents can be impeached. Dictators may be tried and executed. Popular generals can be fired. General Douglas MacArthur of World War II fame, stepped over the line of insubordination, and was promptly fired by President Truman. The same recently happened to General Stanley McChrystal, who just last year (2009), was advanced to command the war in Afghanistan. When his comments, critical of the Obama administration were made public, he received a quick summons to Washington and an equally speedy release from his duties.

Apparently, McChrystal took the chastisement in humility and straight to his heart. Unrepentant rebels care about themselves. They will do as much damage as they possibly can. Their speciality is not to build, but to destroy. They excuse their rebellion, bemoan the injustice of their situation, condemn their superiors, and try to gain sympathy and support on their way out. Like devils' advocates, they despise the worth of authority over them. To his credit, McChrystal did nothing of the sort. He showed honor to his boss (the President), in tendering his resignation. He didn't blame anyone else. He didn't claim he was overworked or that his nerves were frayed. He didn't claim he'd been misrepresented or that his words were taken out of context. He didn't say, "everybody makes mistakes." In this he showed more virtue than many who are called to account across the churches.

Now we'll move from the top rung of the powerful to the bottom where this whole theme has its birth. Reportedly, studies have shown that children with a literal fenced-in play area enjoy maximum freedom and security - right up to the fence. On the contrary, the lack of clear boundaries brings insecurity and confusion. It stifles both freedom and creativity, and actually inhibits their range of play area. The fence stands as a twofold barrier against harm. It keeps the child from straying into danger, but it is also a security issue by serving as a barrier against harm, such as vicious dogs, or men with evil designs.

To be sure, there is more involved in happy child play than physical barriers against being crushed by a truck. More important boundaries need to be established inwardly. Babies are born with countless foolish and hurtful traits. The worst of atrocities carried out by men, and the darkest deeds of history, bear witness to an unlimited capacity for evil. The toddler that once played safely inside the fence, may grow up to be the very one who would, granted the opportunity, prey on the innocent ones within the fence. It is still true that *the child left to himself* (and his own nature), *will bring his mother to shame* (not to mention making her the gazing stock of the local supermarket). This failure of boundaries, may well be an initiation into a life of crime.

The "under command" principle is the authority vested in the parents to define what the child may or may not do. It is a call to forcibly interfere with the makings of dishonest, immoral, or violent behavior. It's no less than taking parental control, until such a time as the child knows and accepts the will of the parents. The child is being trained up and prepared for a healthy self control, giving respect of the authority of teachers, employers, church leaders and government officials. This method is not merely approved, but actually ordered of God as the way to train the next generation. Parents are themselves "under command" to God, to take command of the child. To summarize the biblical principle: *Thou shalt answer to thy God for the character training of thine own children.*

This also exposes the overlooked perversion that dominates our abortion culture. Abortion says "no" to the birth and the of training of offspring, choosing to dispose of responsibility and personal integrity through the garbage dump. We have taken the heritage of the Lord (the fact that children are gifts given from God), despised the command principle of parentage, and turned it into an issue on a level of whether or not one chooses to buy a puppy. We would be hard pressed to come up with a greater insult against the sovereignty of God of the universe.

But for the moment, welcome to the storied world of today's teens and adults where "doing as I please" is the only rule many people know. My personal contacts and experiences of the years with the criminal element would produce quite the lineup of people who escaped being under command. These would include the bank robber, the arsonist, the murderers, the sexual offenders, the thieves, and the much more common trove of those addicted to drugs and alcohol. For these, the court system is a revolving door. They get caught with an amazing degree of regularity. In the name of freedom, many of these are now behind bars.

Whether in or out of prison, self-ruled people appear not to find life very fulfilling. American teens are among the most likely in the world to get drunk, to do drugs, to be sexually promiscuous, and to get arrested on felony charges. But besides this, they are also among the most likely to commit suicide. Not being under command does indeed leave a vacuum. Those who reject the lineup of legitimate authorities such as parents, teachers, officers of the law, and employers, are easy fodder for entertainment and sports heros of the day. Elvis Presley and Michael Jackson can't shake their tenacious fans even in death. These deluded worshipers of fame, have nothing else to keep alive the illusory sense of being connected to greatness.

It really comes down to two options. We all really do have someone over us. Either we will respect our ties to legitimate authority over us, or we will be turned into hero worshipers and idolaters, trying to run on the fumes of some unworthy's greatness.

As we will see, being under command is not an unhappy but necessary option, nor a mere human invention. It's not like parents or employers decided one day that it would make their day much more pleasant if they could just command their children, or their employees what to do.

God is clearly identified as the author of the chain of command in the Scriptures. Children are to obey their parents. Wives are to submit themselves to their own husbands. Servants and employees are to obey their masters in all things. All of us are called to be faithful to the mandates of government. This is the tie that binds, the means to unity, harmony, and peace among people. We cultivate the depth of good character when we *love the brotherhood, fear God, and honor the king.* This is the culture blessed of God, by being under his authority.

To the uninitiated, this looks like the end of freedom. Indeed, it isn't. This time it is God's fence, defining our personal sphere of freedom and productivity. Heeding God -given authority to be followers of what is good delivers from following after persons of vain or evil intent. It provides the power to fulfil the common goals and objectives of those in charge. For example, by coupling the authority of the husband with the submission of the wife, the children of that union are not conflicted with opposing directions.

Are we suggesting that it is easy to subject our will to the authority of another? That this is not the case, is shown by Jesus Christ in the most trying hour of his earthly ministry. Shortly before his death on the cross, in the garden of Gethsemane, Jesus committed his own will to his heavenly Father and so continued on the road to crucifixion and resurrection, so that we might be saved.

In asking our obedience God is showing us by example what it means to be like his Son. *"Though he were a Son, yet learned he obedience by the things which he suffered; And being made perfect, he became the author of eternal salvation unto all that obey him"* (Hebrews 5:8,9)

ALCOHOLISM – A SADD ENDING

A number of organizations have tried to separate drinking from driving (surely a worthy goal), Students Against Drunk Driving (SADD), and Mothers Against Drunk Driving (MADD). Today, the efforts to keep drinkers from driving have been greatly enhanced through rigid law enforcement. This is as it should be, since alcohol is a factor in a high percentage of fatal accidents. Yet, the concern for impaired driving is still a minor part of this great social problem.

It is one thing to recognize the folly of driving drunk. However such wisdom is too high for those who have voluntarily made fools of themselves by drinking. To be sure the effects are usually temporary. Most people get to go home and sleep off their self-imposed stupor. But not always. The accident, or the crime committed, or the fight stops the whole scene in a timeless frame of folly.

So where are the pastors and churches to teach us that the problem is not drinking plus driving? The problem is in the drinking.

Alcohol does two things. First: alcohol is always its way toward bringing the imbiber under its influence. Some can handle more, some less. But the most intelligent people become half-wits under the influence. Getting behind the wheel doesn't change the fact. The failure of driving skills merely marks the dangerous incompetence of the inebriated person. That individual is in a position to harm himself, his family, is friends, his enemies, in whatever context he happens to be. You cannot name a single atrocity, but that some drunken person hasn't committed it. These are things he would never do in his right mind.

"The influence," has been behind the abuse and murder of many innocents, not only on the highway, but also in the home. It has been the major cause of broken homes, hungry children, and ruined careers. Alcohol is probably greatest single investment Americans make in crime. And it certainly "pays." It has been the major contributor in countless prison sentences. Alcohol lubricates the revolving door, for an end-less stream of people through the court system.

Drinking promotes a life of sin. It carelessly dismisses the timeless standards of morality and decency, and makes one easy prey to sexual immorality. One cannot imbibe the dark secrets of alcohol and remain a respectable, depend-able, and godly individual. When you purchase at the bar, you barter your own soul. So let's heed the biblical warning. The drunkard has lost his way with God. He will not inherit the kingdom of God.

Even as a person drinks away at his sanity, he is inviting slavery to demon alcohol. We call it alcoholism or chemical dependence. The means that what the person does vol-untarily with alcohol today, he may be doing involuntarily tomorrow. We call it sickness. The Bible calls it sin. So obvi-ously, the place to stop can't be anywhere close to the point of no return. That would be like trying to talk someone out of suicide, only after one has pulled the trigger, or after he has jumped off the bridge. What? Will we expect him to put the bullet back in the chamber? When people get together in drinking parties are some living in sin while others are not? Thus, the first drink of that teenager, is neither innocent, nor is it fun. For many, it is more like Russian roulette – bound to get to the loaded chamber.

Certainly we abhor the mixture of alcohol, blood, and steel. But until we get to the bottom of our personal and social permissiveness toward alcohol, we will continue to reap every tragedy that mixes so well with this deadly potion.

It is time to flush this stuff out of our houses and churches, down into the city sewers where it belongs. Let us teach our children the truly safe level, not the one mandated by law for driving, but the one that finds peace and fulfillment of the soul – zero. If they drink a little, they will want it. If they don't drink any, they will never will.

Section II

THE TEN COMMANDMENTS

THE FIRST AND GREAT COMMANDMENT

"Thou shalt have no other gods before me" Exodus 20:3. This negative commandment (thou shalt not), is stated positively (you shall) in Deuteronomy 6:5. *"Thou shalt love the LORD thy God with all thine heart, and with all thy soul, and with all thy might."*

A PARABLE OF BETRAYAL

James was a fine young man. Unlike most of the young men his age, James had high moral standards. He took his Christian commitment seriously. When the time came, he would approach his marriage commitment with equal seriousness. So the few girls he had dated, he treated with utmost respect, just as he would want his sister, Rachel, to be treated.

James was also intelligent and a skilled worker. He really did want to find the right girl and get married. Supporting a wife and children should not be a problem. And now at 23 he was sure he had found the right one. Just a year ago, Nancy had moved into the area with her parents. And that is when he had seen her at church for the first time. Nancy was very attractive, friendly, without being flirtatious, reflected maturity, and appeared to fit James's expectations exactly. She never actually expressed the same high ideals, but then she never tried to get him to compromise his.

James didn't waste a lot of time. This was certainly the girl of his dreams. He knew he was in love. He just wanted to be with her. So three months ago, James had proposed and Nancy accepted. He could not have been happier. Now today had been the big day. By mid - afternoon, most of the guests were gone, and by 4:00 P.M. they were on the way. Just the two of them. James had it all planned out. A hundred and thirty miles away was a restaurant with a cozy, relaxing atmosphere, for a quiet evening together. A bit pricey? Sure. But what could be better than having his own beautiful bride in such a lovely place?

But as the miles slipped behind them, James became puzzled. That Pontiac Bonneville seemed to be tailing them. Their destination called for a few route changes; 63 to 35, to 94. But the Bonneville always stayed in sight. However, when they reached the restaurant, the Bonneville was nowhere in sight. So much for the coincidence. Yet, ten minutes after their arrival, a tall handsome young man slipped into a booth adjacent to James and Nancy. When James glanced his way, the young man offered a wide smile, and a wink (what could that mean?) Nancy had seemed rather quiet, but now she was nervous, and totally distracted. But not for long. It was soon obvious. The other young man had her full attention.

It only gets worse from here. The other fellow stood, came across to their table with a polite request, "May I sit with you?" When James had regained a level of composure, he replied, "I would prefer you didn't. We were just married today, so we would like the time to ourselves." To which Nancy coldly injected, "James, if that is the way you're going to treat Phil, then I'll go sit with him. With that, she stood, gave "him" her hand, and the twain headed for a table in the far corner of the restaurant, chatting and laughing like old friends, which, obviously, they were.

Now what should James do?

We introduce the first Commandment with this parable for several reasons. For one, God himself refers to his relationship to Israel as a marriage, *Turn, O backsliding children, saith the Lord; for I am married to you* (Jeremiah 3:14). In fact, the Scriptures frequently draw parallels between the marriage relationship, and the relationship with God.

Secondly, most of us can relate to an all consuming affection for that girlfriend or that boyfriend, and as in the parable, with the new bride. This relationship has a way of making us deliriously, perhaps even insanely happy. Now it was God who formed that girl or that young man, put a human face to your affections, and made possible your heartthrobs for that person. Why then does it seem so foreign to us to find that God himself could and would actually satisfy every aspect of our lives, in other words, that we would truly love God?

The third is the matter of exclusivity. Married love and faithfulness is utterly contrary to a cheap spreading of affections. Where there is true love and commitment on the part of one, the discovery of unfaithfulness in the other brings utter devastation and intense jealousy. Though jealousy may be misguided or unreasonable, marital jealousy really is rooted in a righteous cause, one that rests close to the heart of God. The intensity of betrayed faithful love is visited with intense pain. Godly jealousy is not only about personal loss. It broods over the wreckage of the unfaithful life. Jealousy will not allow you to share your mate with another. As in the relationship with your spouse, so the relationship with your God is fulfilled only in being exclusive. This then is both a commandment and a plea, *You shall have no other gods before me.*

Finally, as unreasonable as the girl in the parable appears, the spiritual side of her story is all to common. We are utterly without excuse in relation to other "gods," whether these are actual false religions, or the displacement of God in the pursuit of worldly fun and fulfillment in material things. Also, like the girl in the parable, even in our evangelical circles, our hypocrisy and the shallowness of commitment is so readily exposed. So we run off, leaving God alone in his booth. May I say that at least the temptation to this problem is not far from every one of us. *Nevertheless I have somewhat against thee, because thou hast left thy first love* (Revelation 2:4).

FIRST THE NEGATIVE: THEN THE POSITIVE

The bridge from - *Thou shalt have no other gods,* to - *Thou shalt love God,* is a gulf the carnal man can never hope to span. As strange as it may seem, the God who created the world, in all its glory and all its beauty, and for all his benefits to man does not rate in our affections. The sinner has no software, no programming from which he might love God. His carnal mind is at enmity against God, because it is not, and cannot be subject to the law of God.

There is however a ray of hope in awakening the soul, however godless, to a sense of utter lostness and hopelessness apart from God. "Thou shalt not" carries a certain warning to the flesh, a bit like a *"high voltage"* or *"bridge out"* sign.

Let's cite another illustration. You have vacationed in Mexico for years. Every time it all went exactly as planned. Sure, you'd heard of bandits, and robberies, but only as things that happen to other people. Now this time as you're driving in Mexico, another tourist couple passes you on the highway. They wave as they pass. Your paths had overlapped on other vacations here. Some miles later their Land Rover sits abandoned and bullet riddled, just barely off the road. You are suddenly horrified, knowing that you too could be ambushed and killed at any moment. For the first time in your life, you live in fear of Mexican bandits. And you suddenly awaken to the fact that you had ignored every warning about rising violence in Mexico. You also know that if you get out of this one alive, you will never again risk your life against the pleasures of a few days in Mexico.

Now obviously, there is a huge difference between God and Mexican bandits. But we are considering few similarities. Both wield great power. And yes, God too can inflict tremendous damage. In fact, the apostle Paul was motivated with all his strength to warn sinners against the awful judgment of God. He knows the God who in flaming fire takes vengeance on those who know not God, and obey not the gospel of our Lord Jesus Christ. These are they who will be punished with everlasting destruction from the presence of the Lord, and from the glory of his power (from Second Thessalonians 1:7,8). So in knowing the terror of the Lord, he persuades men (II. Corinthians 5:11).

The Bible says that men everywhere ought to fear God. It says that the fear of God is the beginning of wisdom, and that by the fear of the Lord, men depart from evil (and so escape the judgment of God).

So why fear God?

- Because we are his by creation. We live our lives and all our works in the confines of his universe. This is not our world, and we are not our own boss.

- Because God knows everything. He has the complete record of all that we have ever said or done. Many people complain bitterly that a good God should not allow so much sin and evil in the world. But, in fact, sin and evil dominate the world in direct proportion to the failure of the fear of God.

- Because God will allow you to do as you please, even if it destroys your soul, and harms other people. Here's the irony of it. We are guests in God's universe, yet for now, Jesus himself behaves with the meekness and gentleness, of a guest. He may stand at your door and knock. But he will not force entry within. We ought to fear lest he withdraws from us, and we meet him unexpectedly, in our lost estate. (The Bible says he will come as a thief in the night, to the unprepared).

- Finally, we ought to fear God because there is coming a day when he will set everything that has gone wrong, at right again. We shall all stand before the judgment seat of Christ to receive a just recompense for everything we have done, whether good or bad. Out of this judgment come only two possible verdicts. "Come, ye blessed, inherit the kingdom prepared for you," or, "depart ye cursed, into everlasting fire prepared for the devil and his angels." It is not the love of God, but the judgment of God, that usually drives people to come to terms of surrender with God their Maker. The sinner coming to God, has usually come to an overwhelming sense of being lost, and of being subject to the righteous judgment of God upon his wickedness.

This fear of God, working a personal sense of danger (of what good then, are the pleasures of the sinful life), becomes a powerful tool of transformation. It brings on the powerful reality of the condemnation of sin. This in turn is key to a godly sorrow for sin and complete repentance before God. This repentance coupled with faith in Jesus Christ brings forgiveness of sin and cleansing from all unrighteousness. A new creation is formed in you, now in a relationship of peace with your God. Now you will indeed love him, because he first loved you. The love of God is shed abroad in your heart by the Holy Ghost given unto you.

Suddenly, the positive command to love God with heart and soul and mind, and strength has a channel out of your own life. It is the same channel in which the love of God came in by his Holy Spirit. This love to Godward, is also openly manifest in loving your neighbor as yourself.

THE SECOND COMMANDMENT
Exodus 20:4,5

THOU SHALT NOT MAKE UNTO THEE
ANY GRAVEN IMAGE

Are modern cultures too enlightened to bow before idols? Is an image, or a picture, really worth a thousand words? How would you draw a picture to convey this popular slogan about pictures? Then again, could the Ten Commandments have been effectively communicated to Moses through pictures rather than speech? In fact, this dusty old commandment about graven images is as pertinent today as it ever was. So read away! Ignorance of this commandment effectively shuts us off from the lessons of history, including God's judgment upon idol worshipers in the Old Testament.

God's way of creating the universe was by the power of his word. The Bible shows that it was language based. God commanded what was to happen with words, *and it was so*. Likewise his communications with men were spoken and then recorded in writing (The Word of God.). Sin came into the world as Eve despised the spoken commandment of God, (You shall not eat), in favor of the image (the tree looked good for food).

Though Jesus came in the very image of his Father, that is not what why he was crucified. He didn't die for what he looked like. He died because of what he said. He gained a following by doing miracles, and feeding the hungry. But he died for verbally challenging their sin, and provoked them with their condemnation before God. They could not forget this, nor forgive him. That is why he died. The verbal method of turning sinners toward God, and the resultant regeneration of the same, through repentance and faith in Jesus Christ remains the same. It is by the Holy Spirit of God convincing us in heart and conscience with the Word of Truth.

In contrast, every historical attempt to reach God through idols, has had the opposite effect. The graven image concealed the truth of God, and idol worship typically descended into shameless sexual debauchery, and even to human sacrifice.

Today our love affair with image-based communication is leaving our culture factually challenged, and wide open to deception. For starters, there's nothing like four or more hours of television imagery a day to stifle creativity, and leave the brain trailing the body (may even have something to do with the increased body mass index). This replaces the reception of truth into the mind, with the bodily appeal of imagery. It leads otherwise intelligent people away from sound thinking, into a zombie - like parroting of image-based appeals. This then lowers the bottom line of accept-able behavior into trash culture. Thus the debased and perverted become the newly embraced normal, while what-ever is still anchored in truth is despised and marginalized as the enemy of progress.

Our great nation was on built on literary prowess (always the mark of a wise and understanding people). It was not founded on imagery such as our beautiful scenery, or on nature worship, nor on carved images of man and beast. And certainly, it was not built upon the kind of men, who appear tall in the limelight, but whose only offerings con-sist of short sound bites. Rather it was hammered out upon unified ground achieved through the exchange of great ideas and principles in the context of a historical, biblical connectedness.

If you could do perfect wax images of the founding fathers, and arrange them around a common table, would this *show you* the principles and motivations these men fol-lowed? Absolutely not. This would be like being locked in a library without the ability to read, or trying to determine the temperature by drawing a picture of a thermometer. There is one way to know what went into the founding of the gov-ernment. It is strictly by literary means, by reading historical writings and studying the legal documents.

So dust off those history books. Open them up. Read. The same thinking that motivated the writers, is now verbally available to the mind of the reader. You may approve or disapprove what you discover. But you are no longer a stranger to what happened. The ideas conveyed have been impressed upon his your own thinking. It is ideas, not images, that ought to move, and motivate, and correct the course of individuals and nations.

This grasp of national history is important. But even this does not hold a candle to the most important history of all, the history of the interaction of God with man since the foundation of the world. This is foundational to all human wisdom. If we don't get this one right, we don't get anything else right. This "rightness" is not found in today's crass materialism, nor in the idolatry of the past. It is found in the Bible, the Word of God to man. So open up *that* history book. Read away the ignorance and apathy that is choking us.

In contrast, the image-based culture is given over to sensuality (the Bible calls it the lust of the flesh). Doing the right thing gets shunted into a corner, in favor of doing what we want to do. So great becomes the determined pull of self expression, that even the courts will formulate brand new rights through some alchemy process on the diamonds of the constitution. (What they have really done is turn those uncommon diamond principles back into common carbon).

There is also a vital lesson in this second commandment for the scientist. He may do an autopsy on a man. He may determine what caused the death. However, he is destined to hopeless confusion if he expects the cadaver to yield the answer as to what caused the life in the first place. The same applies to all history of the universe. For example, even if NASA could sift the whole of Mars through a sieve, it would not yield the answer to that planet's origin. It is strange that brilliant scientists seem not to understand this.

The answer to this dilemma is easy. Go not to the material universe or to that which is made to unlock its origins. Go rather to the mind that made it. If you will but give room to the Word of the Creator (Genesis 1), you need not waste your time looking for answers where there are none. Neither will you be shamed into repeatedly discarding high sounding, yet hopelessly outdated theories, about how it all happened.

Unfortunately, our society has grievously turned away from literacy. Many are mere gazers. Looking is the basic medium of advertizing. In advertizing, the appeal is to the vanity of the looker. So what does looking accomplish? Looking incites desire. Desire craves satisfaction. Are you satisfied merely looking and smelling that T Bone steak?

Gazing is also the basic medium of the entertainment industry. In entertainment, looking provokes lust, and lust provokes emulation. The gazer moves toward that which quickens his pulse. He reaches for the prize, not through the intellect, not by the communication of the mind, but through the sensuousness of the body. What is gazed upon becomes a need, even an obsession. And when engaged, it becomes a habit. Even while the entertainment industry denies it, the advertising conglomerate knows that it is true. What works for them works as surely for Hollywood. The same appeal to sight that used to prompt one to "walk a mile for a Camel" did sell cigarettes aplenty. It still sells cars and Hawaiian vacations, but it will as readily sell marriage into divorce, teens into vice, or children into violence.

It is small comfort knowing that many gazers will not buy the harmful product, either because they cannot afford it, or because even in their impaired state, they see through the shallowness of the appeal. Nor is it any comfort that most lookers are satisfied short of raping or killing. They know they cannot "afford" the consequences. However, in lust itself, the damage is done. Character is drained. The commandment of God is violated. The idol, though not fashioned in wood or stone, is engraved upon the heart.

Christian principles fair no better when the quest for religion is turned from verbal revelation (the Scriptures), unto graven images. Statues of "saints," or of Jesus Himself, do nothing for the preservation of truth. The heaven of heavens (I. Kings 8:29), cannot contain God.

God did accommodate earthly temples in the Old Testament covenant, but even that is no longer the case. He pays no homage to architectural splendors of brick or stone, giving preference instead, by His Spirit, to the hearts of the humble. He never did, nor ever will inhabit any figure or supposed likeness of himself. An image of Jesus on the cross does nothing for deliverance from sin. It serves not even as a watered down version. It is too low to offer any possibility of reaching him. We need not be surprised then, that he even forbids the attempt.

So what shall we learn from this? Everyone of us desperately needs the mind of God over us and over our doings. This is not through image, but through language. When we, in all sincerity, read and meditate upon the Scriptures, that single greatest Mind of all the universe is revealed to us. The whole spectrum, from our lostness without God, to the way of salvation through Christ, is opened to us. Faith in Christ comes not with clever emotional stirring as with clanging instrumentation, nor with image-based churchly entertainment, not with sacred appeal of "religious" surroundings, but in hearing again the Word of God.

THE THIRD COMMANDMENT
EXODUS 20:7

THOU SHALT NOT TAKE THE NAME OF THE LORD THY GOD IN VAIN

The key to keeping this command is a personal grasp of the greatness and power of the Almighty, in contrast to the weakness and frailty of man. So great is this contrast, that it is difficult to come up with illustrations to define this difference. No one would dare to take the name of God as a swear word, or to invoke his name hypocritically unless he falls far short of the most elementary reverence for God. In fact the misuse or abuse of the name of God puts one on the same level as the fool who says in his heart that there is no God. *The Lord will not hold him guiltless, who takes his name in vain.*

Court room decorum could perhaps serve as a feeble illustration. The judge doesn't come in early, take a seat, and then wait for the accused to show up. Rather all is in readiness, the prosecuting attorney is there, the defense attorneys are there, along with the accused, the clerk of courts, the court reporter, the audience. All is in readiness. The moment arrives with every eye on that opening door. The judge makes his entry. His robe signifies his authority over the court. Now all arise to their feet, until directed by the judge to be seated. It is expected to be a moment of awe. There is vested power with that judge. The case proceeds. The attorneys may raise various objections. However, the judge decides. There are numerous possibilities in relation to evidence, but again, the judge decides what is admissible.

The judge is always addressed as "Your Honor." To disobey the judge, or to show open disrespect, is known as "contempt of court." This could lead to removal from court, fines, or even criminal charges. To lie to the judge or to try to knowingly mislead the court, is known as perjury, and is likewise subject to punishment. The whole point of courtroom decorum, is to provide the best of human effort to carry out justice, which calls for enough reverence to keep false testimony and dishonesty away from the bench. The judge, after all, cannot see the heart of man.

Now this is mere shadow illustration, and the power of the judge is mere vested power, granted him for a season. On the sidewalk, his robe and his gavel are worse than useless. In court, he can sentence a man to die. On the street, he can't even make an arrest. If he boards a bus, his fellow passengers do not arise in his honor. In the grocery checkout he is not addressed as "Your Honor." He awaits his turn at the checkout, like any other man.

But with God it is not so. His power is not vested, but intrinsic. His judgeship is essential to whom he is. Further, if for violating earthly court decorum, one can be cited for contempt, how much more when one addresses contemptuous speech toward the very judge of the universe. God wields all power, and every earthly power is given of God, but for a season. The decorum prescribed for the court of God, (this third commandment), is not to protect God from possible wrong conclusions. It is to strike enough fear into man, lest for lack of reverence, he falls under the wrath of God. Thus the man who would dare to blaspheme, or to take the name of God in vain, is essentially challenging what dare not be challenged, the authority of the God of the universe. He is behaving as though his own word were higher than God's word. On occasion, a fugitive escapes the jurisdiction of an earthly judge, but there is no escape, from the judge of the universe. *"For every idle word that men shall speak, they shall give account thereof to God."*

Under consideration is more than a personal avoidance of condemnation, but also the means by which believers are to challenge every abominable form of speech. As Christians, we are responsible not only for what we say, but also for the speech we make peace with. Would you live peaceably as a witness to murder, to adultery, or to thievery? This would make you an accomplice to the act. So let's consider one more. Have you made peace with the sound of words of blasphemy against the God of heaven ringing in your ears?

For too many, the answer is yes. Do you think you can name the name of Christ as your Savior, even while piping all manner of blasphemy and depravity right into your living room via TV, Internet and other media? In so doing, you have blunted the authority of God over your own life. Small wonder that you are at least tempted with minced oaths, and vile words coming out of your own mouth. This is sure evidence that the fountain within needs cleansing with the water of the Word of God.

Finally, there is our relationship with other people. There are neighbors and friends, and also the workplace environment to consider. Many think that Christian witness is limited to the positive note of the gospel of Christ. Not so. It may well mean being a reprover of cursing. Well spoken, even-tempered reproof is often the beginning of God-consciousness in the life of the unbeliever. You may be the key and representative of the commandments of God. You will not be a partaker of evil deeds. This will strengthen you to glorify God in your own heart, and to short-circuit the personal temptation to vile language.

And no, this is not just my personal ideal being presented. It is direct biblical instruction. *"And have no fellowship with the unfruitful works of darkness, but rather reprove them . . . all things that are reproved are made manifest by the light, and whatsoever doth make manifest is light"* (Ephesians 5:11-13).

Those who call out the name of God in blasphemy, can find but one means of escape, that is, to repent, and to call upon that name once despised, in order to be saved.

68

THE FOURTH COMMANDMENT
EXODUS 20:8-11

REMEMBER THE SABBATH DAY
TO KEEP IT HOLY

"Remember the Sabbath day, to keep it holy. Six days shalt thou labour, and do all thy work: But the seventh day is the Sabbath of the LORD thy God: in it thou shalt not do any work, thou, nor thy son, nor thy daughter, thy manservant, nor thy maidservant, nor thy cattle, nor thy stranger that is within thy gates: For in six days the LORD made heaven and earth, the sea, and all that in them is, and rested the seventh day: wherefore the LORD blessed the Sabbath day, and hallowed it" (Exodus 20:8-11).

The very first Sabbath was the example of the Almighty God resting after the creation week. It is not a picture of a weary God, unable to continue the pace of creation, but a day of celebrating the finished creation. The Sabbath was a divine pause after the most productive work week ever.

God rested after there was nothing more to be done, nothing to improve upon. He framed it all by his power. Ever since that creation week, he continues to uphold all things, by the same Word of his power. God has never opted out of his creation, or even put it on automatic pilot. The makeup of the atom is a scientific mystery. It doesn't appear to have a mechanism to hold it together. It appears as though it should fly apart. But as with many things, the believer is given a scientific edge. God has ways of upholding what he has made.

The Sabbath is a divinely ordered reminder, a time to cement the principle that "this God is our God forever and ever," and that we are his people, "the sheep of his pasture." Since we are firmly in his hands anyway, we pay an awful price when we forget. Thus the reminder of our accountability to God. We also look at the Sabbath principle as a divinely ordered halt, an opportunity to match our stride with to our Creator. Further, the Sabbath is a dress rehearsal for the redeemed. It is a remembrance of the ultimate rest of the soul, prepared for us in Jesus Christ

Because of widespread neglect and misunderstanding, this commandment rates a close look. So let's rehearse the commandment with its practical implications.

The term "Sabbath" or "sabbatical," as given in the Old Testament, may give the impression of a day of ease, or in the case of a sabbatical, a prolonged time of dodging routine responsibilities. However, the practical result was quite contrary to that. The word Sabbath literally means to intercept or to interrupt. It is intense, implying a complete cessation, a complete shutdown. It was the mark of followers of God, quite independent of their convenience. Keeping Sabbath required that all production was halted, that machinery fell silent, and that buying and selling ceased. People who operate their businesses seven days would face a major adjustment. But that was only the regular weekly happening. An even bigger test came every seventh year. That was the time when all farming operations and all production ceased for the entire year. Talk about impeding one's personal economy! But, there was to be yet another test. The fiftieth year was designated as the year of Jubilee. It followed the forty-ninth year, which was the regular sabbatical year. This entailed two years with neither planting nor harvest, slaves being given their freedom, and land that had been sold because of debt, reverting to the former owners. (The Bible doesn't record whether Israel ever kept the Jubilee). Oh yes, we didn't mention that through all of this, they were to pay a tithe (10%), of all their income.

Knowing human nature, we are hardly surprised that they wanted out of this financial straitjacket. I can also imagine that there was some trepidation when they first disobeyed and planted crops on the seventh year. The good harvests in those "*verboten*" years were probably very reassuring (since the pragmatist is always looking for what works). But even while they were counting and trusting in the extra cash, God was doing a different form of an accounting. He was keeping a record of their disobedience. In due time, God exacted their Sabbath breaking with seventy years of captivity, one year for every sabbatical year violated.

Was God simply trying to make them poor? Not at all. Following the ways of God was a guarantee that they always would have enough. God required them to limit their ways of gain to his will, that they might trust his supply, and his generosity. If they would not, then he would deal with them in judgment, as he had done with the heathen before them.

They were also prone to violate the Sabbath, even as they followed the letter of the law, shutting down the machinery, and refraining from buying and selling. How? They took this sacred day, not for physical rest and remembrance, but as self-centered celebration. Call it "Funday" (Isaiah 58:13. They substituted the genuine delight in God, and turned it into a search for personal pleasure. But in these issues of disobedience, they did the one thing that godly people dare not do - that is, they forgot that the God who created them, always controls the security, the economy and the blessed-ness of the people. Their ill-gotten gains blinded their eyes to the utter futility of laying up treasures on earth against the troubles to come. The stash they accumulated meant nothing against the invading Babylonian army, and accom-plished nothing against the siege, the suffering, the starva-tion, the slaughter, and the seventy-year captivity to come.

I'm not aware of any New Testament call to Christians to literally keep sabbatical years. However, the love of money, the accumulation of wealth, and the invention of ways to prevent personal losses spell trouble with God. *For that which is highly esteemed among men is abomination to God* (Luke 16:15). *They that will be rich fall into temptation, and a snare, and into many foolish and hurtful lusts that drown men in destruction and perdition . . . But thou, O man of God, flee these things.* (I. Timothy 6:9-11).

CONSIDERING THE CREATION

Do you consider belief in a literal 6-day creation simplistic? If you do, it is because you accept more farfetched ideas than this. In fact, a literal seven day creation week fits the world of nature, in a wonderful way. Let me explain. (By the way, civilized people have reckoned time in seven day weeks ever since).

Life is always dependent on the following: First is the genetic code. Nothing is random about the development that takes place in a fertilized egg. Randomness would cause it to collapse upon itself in disorder. All the input for its development is already in place. Without the established code, nothing could develop at all. Science has recently made major breakthroughs in mapping out the code. But it all goes to show that true science leaves evolutionary theories with no credibility. Intelligent life always follows intelligent design.

Second, living things cannot survive without being complete. (Half-developed hearts, lungs, wings, legs, *ad infinitum,* cannot survive on their own). Living things in development stage, must find every need supplied in a suitable of host. (The butterfly host is the cocoon. The developing chick is protected and nourished by the egg. The unborn human has the womb of the mother). From this foundational truth, we then face that age-old question, "Which came first, the chicken or the egg?" God could have programmed an egg with the genetic code, and found a way to incubate that egg. But He chose rather to make roosters and hens. From there, all was in place, to produce great flocks of chickens. In like manner, God made a man and a woman, not an unborn baby. The man, God called Adam. The woman, Adam called Eve ("mother of all living"), for she was to be the mother and the original incubator of the whole human race.

A third necessity for life is the supporting environment. Interference in the quality of air and water can quickly turn deadly. We have only minutes to live in a room deprived of oxygen. We also must find quick protection from any number of lethal gases. Marine life cannot live without water. Animal life cannot survive underwater. Barren wasteland, sulfuric atmosphere, and boiling cauldrons accomplish nothing toward creation of life, except to fill biology textbooks with strange ideas.

The above imperatives point to a short order of creation. Many, many things, exactly formulated, had to happen both quickly and completely (not over millions of years). God created light, water, atmosphere, and vegetation, followed by marine life, birds, and animal life. This surpasses everything big bang, natural selection, or neo-Darwinism could ever hope to accomplish in millions or billions of years. In review, life, to be viable, had to come forth fully formed, and fully functional. It had to be supplied with a genetic code, else the chicken lays eggs in vain, and the first squiggle of life would have also been the last. But this life had to be greeted in the immediate context of a user-friendly environment because respiratory systems and digestive systems take no vacations.

This is why evolutionary theories keep getting punctured by reality. The eons of time, so jealously guarded by Darwinists as the dynamic for evolution, should actually have brought total extinction long ago.

Now for the simplicity and effectiveness of the Sabbath commandment. For failure to truly honor God with the weekly reminder of the divine order, we accept bad science. We forget where we came from. We don't know where we are going. We lose meaning. We cannot get our bearings, morally or spiritually.

Before you go out to work or otherwise violate the Sabbath, which in the New Testament is called the Lord's Day, stop and ask yourself the following questions:

- Am I one of those church people that cannot be depended on, because sleeping in or the lure of the lake has the greater appeal? Am I part of the possible majority of Americans, who has forgotten that I came from God, and that my life is a gift from God? Will I acknowledge him by observing the day of rest he has designated? Have I made the sad mistake of accepting evolutionary falsehood, thus missing completely the answers to life's questions? Why am I here? Where am I going?

- Have I forgotten my maker? Do I live under the illusion that I face no accountability and that my moral and ethical choices are not God's business? Having missed the day of rest, have I also missed that greater rest of soul - the peace that is found only in Jesus Christ.
- God was productive on the six days of creation. His rest came after all was complete. Do I expend my energies as a healthy and able-bodied person, in useful, productive pursuits?
- If I ignore God's plan of weekly rest and reflection, am I also blinding myself to the approach of the end of the world and the coming judgment of God?
- Finally, if I fail to keep alive the Sabbath reminders, how am I to keep alive the greater implications of our salvation, that of entering into the Sabbath rest of the soul? (Hebrews 4:10,11)

If any of the above fits, then we miss the intended blessings of the Sabbath commandment.

WHICH DAY?

A few people, on discovering that we are doing a series on the commandments, put in an early bid, that we would make a case for a Saturday Sabbath. There are groups today, to whom seventh day keeping is a cardinal doctrine of faith. According to a current publication, *Behold, He Cometh*, from Cornerstone Publishing, Graham WA, they believe that Congress will enact and enforce Sunday - keeping laws, the violation of which will eventually lead to the death penalty. (This seems counterintuitive, seeing that we have put aside Sunday "Blue Laws.") This publication claims that enforced Sunday-keeping is the biblical Mark of the Beast.

74

No less surprising is the contention that all the world will be divided into just two classes, Sabbath Keepers and Sunday Keepers. We conclude from these teachings, that these people mean to be justified before God by day-keeping.

Now the Bible does teach only two divisions; but not over the misinterpretation of the Sabbath. The final judgment divides between the *righteous* and the *wicked,* otherwise called sheep and goats, Matthew 25:31-46.

But let's look at the case for Sunday keeping, translated "first day of the week," in the New Testament.

We already know the history of the seventh day Sabbath. It began with God, not with man. It was made for man, not man for the Sabbath. Man was to enter into this rest, lest he forgets his Creator. However, New Testament teaching makes it clear that the Sabbath also foreshadowed greater aspects of rest. In Hebrews 3:16-19, the missing "rest" of the unbelievers in the wilderness was not the weekly seventh day, but a reference to inheriting the "rest" of the promised land of Canaan. Yet Hebrews chapter four shows us that even that promised land of Canaan, never could be the ultimate rest for the people of God. For after Joshua, (mistakenly translated Jesus), had brought the people into Canaan, it was necessary to speak of the ultimate rest as "another" day (Heb. 4:8). Thus the seventh day was adequate to remember the Creator, and as a foreshadowing of the literal promised land of Canaan. Yet one could enter seventh day rest, and even set his feet in the promised rest of Canaan, without realizing the only sufficient rest. That greatest rest is the liberation of the soul, finally and only accomplished in the finished work of Christ on the cross. It is not entered by keeping certain aspects of the law, but only by living faith in Christ.

The seventh day rest was one that was "earned" by working the prior six days. However, the rest entered through the grace of Jesus is freely received through repentance and faith, and is not preceded by merit of works. This brings us to understand the principle of *"another* day." It shows that salvation is not entered by the principle of the seventh day, but rather by the principle of the first day (another day).

This is foreshadowed in certain Old Testament feasts. (The following references are all from Leviticus 23.) The feast of Harvest engaged "the morrow after the Sabbath," (10-11). Other references are 23:16 "the morrow after the seventh Sabbath"; (23:36) "on the eighth day shall be a holy convocation"; and (23:39) "on the eighth day shall be a Sabbath." These special days fell on Sunday by rotation of calender days, and showed that the principle of "the first day" was engaged even then, by introducing a development greater than the seventh day.

This takes on special significance as we see the unfolding of the historical events of the resurrection of Christ. Matthew 28:1, records the women headed to the tomb, *after* the Sabbath, as it began to dawn toward the first day. While they were en route, there was a great earthquake, and the angel descended, rolling the stone away. Mark 16:9 states that Jesus arose on this *first day*. Jesus showed himself to the disciples on the evening of that *first day,* John 20:19. The next eighth *day* (Sunday), when they were together again, Jesus again appeared unto them (John 20: 26).

The question then arises whether the apostles gatherings continued on the first day, or whether Sunday keeping was some later perversion, as the seventh day advocates claim.

Again, we find the answer in the Scriptures. Acts 20:7 is a reference to an obviously common practice of gathering of believers on the "first day." Then in I Cor. 16:2, a command goes out, specifically designating the first day, as the day to contribute their financial offerings for the week. This is hardly a functional command apart from a common practice of the church getting together on that day.

There is one more point about Sunday keeping that is both fascinating and compelling. The Greek to English translation is always *first day of the week.* That is the correct designation of order. However, this rendering hides another aspect of the day. A literal translation from Greek is actually *first Sabbath*. That is right. The word that is translated "day of the week" is the same word that is commonly translated "Sabbath," the same as when translated for the seventh day.

We conclude then, that the first day Sabbath is the one that rightly accommodates the resurrection of Jesus Christ, and the redemption freely given through him. The Lord's Day is the "high" Sabbath or "first" Sabbath, even because Jesus is set apart as the "first fruits" of them that slept (I. Corinthians 15:20).

Now the question may arise whether it is wrong to keep a seventh day Sabbath, rather than the first day Sabbath. We are prepared to leave that to the believer and his God. However to insist on a seventh day keeping as a cardinal doctrine of justification is indeed a serious error. Anyone who would be justified through Old Testament law is obligated to keep everything written in the law (Galatins 3:10), which is impossible. Any throwback to salvation through keeping Old Testament laws is a perversion of the gospel. The Bible says that *no man is justified by the deeds of the law* . . . (Galatins 3:11). *Whosoever of you are justified by the law; ye are fallen from grace* (Galations 5:4).

THE FIFTH COMMANDMENT
EXODUS 20:12

HONOR THEY FATHER AND THY MOTHER

"Honor thy father and thy mother: that thy days may be long upon the land which the LORD thy God giveth thee" (Exodus 20:12). *Children, obey your parents in the Lord: for this is right* (Ephesians 6:1).

Honor thy father and thy mother is the entry level commandment. It is foundational to every other commandment relating to God, and to other people. In other words, the honor of father and mother is key to making or breaking all the rest. But also, in a very real sense, it is the pattern and groundwork for a relationship with God. The bonding of the child to the parents happens in immaturity, before the child understands the logical connections of the relationship. Yet the honoring child becomes an extension and a credit to the good characteristics of his home. In maturing, he becomes a positive representative of his family. His honor is his bond to those who are responsible to establish his goings. This is the same pattern of honor of everyone who is in a genuine relationship to God. As the life yielded to the parents in growing up, the life yielded to God will serve as a credit to the kingdom of God, even to the point of the believer being a representative of God on earth.

On the other hand, Scripture has many dire warnings for those who are disobedient and rebellious. Apparently, one who despises the rightful authority of his parents is an easy target for the powers of darkness. Such rebellion actually carried the death penalty in the Old Testament, (Deuteronomy 21:18-21).

Human logic might declare that this commandment is misplaced. Shouldn't the priority go with parental responsibility to the child? Or, should not at least one of the ten commandments charge the parents with loving their children?

But God's ways are higher than our ways as the heavens are higher than the earth.

If God had enjoined parental faithfulness first, in the Ten Commandments (which he does numerous times elsewhere in Scripture), and not addressed the honor of children to parents, then parental sins and failure would quickly become the catchall for children to fail. This would in turn set up every succeeding generation for failure.

As it is, God knows the imperfections and challenges of every home, which also follows through as the children are engaged in other spheres of authority, in schools, in employment, in government, in churches, and then eventually in their own homes. As it stands, every individual is commanded to develop relationships of honor and respect with those in authority, beginning with their own parents. So God has charted a way where the parents may indeed have eaten the sour grape, and yet the children's teeth are not set on edge.

Let's be clear here at the outset, that this writing is not about excusing parental sin. The awful deeds today, where children are verbally berated, or physically or sexually abused, are beyond excusable. The adults who do these things may well be the cause whereby a *little one* (a biblical description), *is caused to fall*. To paraphrase Scripture, a millstone about the neck and drowning in the sea, would be a preferable to the actual judgment of God, against such deeds.

On the other hand, God is Master at bringing beauty out of ashes, at bringing joy and triumph out of defeat, and of taking the evil intention of one, and turning it into good for the intended victim. That is exactly why it is so vital, to live right, and to live honorably toward authority, even when the authority is so wrong. In this, the individual honors God, and will in turn, be honored of God.

God has a unique plan in a fallen world to mold people into the character and image of his Son Jesus Christ. He doesn't merely do this despite the falleness of the world, and the shortcomings of authority. He uses those failures as actual tools for success.

He demonstrated this in the sterling character of Joseph, onetime outcast of his father's house, then sometime ruler of the land of Egypt. Joseph's father Jacob, despite the love he had for his son, set the stage both for sibling rivalry, and the hatred of half brothers, through Jacob's practice of polygamy. But it wasn't enough that Joseph should be sold into Egypt. His career in Egypt had a way of multiplying trials, false accusation, and prison on Joseph's head. But unlike the common response of many, Joseph never kept score against others for their injustices against him. Keeping score could have come quite naturally. We know how it works. It comes easy to keep a mental list of the failures of parents, or employers, of the church, or church leaders. When the level of bad reaches a certain point, isn't bailing out justified? They surely had it coming, didn't they? That's how Christian young people turn on their parents, and why many turn their backs on the church. And the bitterness feels so right, so justified.

So why didn't Joseph join the blame game? Because Egypt needed a man wise, and of magnanimous character, who can keep skinny cows from devouring fat cows (the famine dream). And Israel (formerly known as Jacob) needed a son who can nourish him and keep him alive when everywhere all the signs point to starvation. But neither will happen without Joseph earning a Master's Degree in Honor.

And yes, there is a Son even greater than Joseph. Now the Eternal God, the Father of Jesus Christ is the perfect authority. But into the earthly scene, God sent his Son, where sin was devouring righteousness, and the skinny cows of sin were still as mean and skinny as ever, and where all men were doomed to spiritual death through the famine of their sin. It wasn't a safe mission, nor even a just one. Christ did not receive the honor due him as the Son of God. This world didn't even know him. His own people didn't receive him.

And into this scene God the Father delivered his beloved Son over to evil men, to be mocked, and scourged, and slain on a cross. And so Jesus' honor to his Father, brought him into obedience unto death. Why did Jesus do it? Because he loved to do the will of his Father, who so loved us. Why did God do it? In giving the Son a sacrifice, he rolled back the condemnation of sin, brought back life from the dead, and established the greatest exaltation of his Son.

The grace of Jesus Christ is powerfully portrayed, in the son or daughter who is respectfully subject to father and mother, even though father and mother appear heartless toward the child. The same is true of the loving and faithful wife living with a cruel and hateful husband. If the grace of God does not move these hard and faithless ones, at least he has surrounded them with examples of the love of God himself. He is also making rare jewels in the spirit and character of the meek ones who so love the erring.

There is a single theme that ties this all together. Reverence. Reverence toward God. The chain of command is God's design whereby human relations are carried on divine circuit boards. We are not designed for independence, nor to find our way apart from the authority structure assigned us by the loving God. Every child of God may rest assured that parentage and circumstances are all arranged and controlled by the divine hand.

Most of us have ample cause to honor of father and mother, because of the labor and the sacrifices they went through, and for all the good they did for us. To be ungrateful to them would be utterly shameful. However, the command is given for a more personal reason. *That it may be well with thee.* Ultimately, the respect we pay (it is actually an investment in our own future), results in blessings on our own head. The honor to parents, and our love to our neighbor, is the channel of the grace of God, given to an obedient heart. The love of God within the heart banishes the need for dishonor, for bitterness, for retaliation, and for evil speaking, against those over us.

If we begin to weigh the worthiness of those we are called to honor, we will be doomed to judge wrongly. In fact, we will develop the negative traits we resent in others. In other words, bitterness moves one to become the embodiment of their own accusations against authority.

OBSERVATIONS

Willful disobedience is the too-tall, too-proud opinion of self. It is the inflated sense of personal worth with an egotistical notion of infallibility. It is the notion that all that matters is *me*. The greatest irony of all may rest in the lonely discovery that when no one else matters, *me is* also rendered meaningless. As the rock singers, The Rolling Stones, put it during their immoral, unrestrained, self-indulgent career: "*I ain't got no satisfaction.*" That explains why the rebellious generation becomes the self-destructive generation.

Disobedience is mankind's oldest snare revisited. Our first parents, Adam and Eve, failed the test. Too late, they found their own reasoning and inspection of the forbidden fruit totally misleading. When a man is persuaded that he doesn't need the command of God and the counsel of others, he is buying into the ruin of his own soul.

Honor and obedience, on the other hand, form the true but humble sense that personal worth is tied into the need for others. It comes from an understanding that not all the pieces of the puzzle of my own life are delivered in my own box. God has distributed them to parents and to other authority figures in my life. They are not given as my exclusive possession. They were not given me at birth to put together on my own. Rather, they come to us little by little, as we learn obedience to parents and other authorities. As we honor and obey, those pieces become our own. But if we reject authority, those pieces will turn out missing, when we most need them. Adam and Eve might have had their quest for wisdom fulfilled in following the command of God. Instead, they saw it destroyed in partaking of the forbidden fruit.

Here again we face a paradox. Obedience is a life lived in true wisdom. It is a child living out wisdom far beyond its years. Through obeying parental command, the child portrays the experience and understanding of his parents. (It is borrowed wisdom because full understanding is still beyond him). Someday he will understand. The spoiled child, however, obviously doesn't borrow wisdom from his parents. Because he has none of his own, he puts himself, and his parents, in a bad light.

The same principles apply to children of God. The Christian who obeys only if he understands, halts his own spiritual growth. He doesn't need to understand all the reasons for the biblical commands. If you want to boggle your mind, just try to understand the reasons for all the dietary commands and rituals Moses gave to Israel in the Old Testament. But God did not demand their understanding. He merely asked them to obey. The result? They, too, would be living on borrowed wisdom - the wisdom of God Himself. If they were faithful to God's commands, they were known by their neighbors as a wise and understanding people, and by their enemies, as people to be feared. Their obedience rendered them special to God. It was God who exalted them and caused other nations to fear them. When they disobeyed, however, he used enemy nations to bring judgment upon them.

If we would be salt and light in a troubled society, we dare not copy the independent spirit and the sinful practices of those who do not know God. To know him is to obey him. It is obedience that goes out as a powerful testimony to all the world (Romans 16:19).

Biblical honor reaches out in recognizing the worth and the dignity of all people (*honor all men*). This honor is regulated by God's commands. Children and young people are to honor parents above peers. We are to honor the wisdom of age and experience, above the attraction and vitality of youth.

We are to honor the positions of governors and kings, in recognition that all powers are of God (Romans 13:1). Honoring God also sets limits on obedience to human authorities. There is a long history of honorable people who could not, in good conscience, bow to the wrong commandments of men, because the honor of God was at stake. As with the apostles (Acts5: 29), they ran out of options: *'We ought to obey God rather than men."* This is not the cheap disobedience of self-will, but rather for the honor of God.

WE'VE LOST OUR WAY

Parenting comes with a challenging job description. A generation ago many of us knew that father and mother were not be trifled with. Our parents meant what they said. As youngsters, we were not consulted about chores to be done, or what was appropriate bedtime for a 10-year old. After evening prayers, we were off to our rooms. Now if we wanted to lie there and stare at a dark ceiling in sleepless self-pity, we could probably do that. They probably wouldn't know the difference anyway.

But we really didn't stop to analyze our own rights. We didn't try to make sure their ideas were only the best. We did not ask ourselves whether they were sufficiently loving in their commands. We didn't question whether they were older and wiser. We didn't have to. We knew where the lines were. Or I should say, we disobeyed just often enough to affirm that the rules had not changed.

It also seemed that our parents had a conspiracy going. They had a way of being together on everything, at least concerning us. It was impossible to run from one to the other to get our own way. Or perhaps they were merely being biblical. They made sure both mother *and* father received the same respect by being on the same page. Both were to be feared (Leviticus 19:3).

Let me say though, that those occasional corporal consequences of disobedience, were only momentarily painful. What they really did was set our little world at right again.

Security was restored. This was restoration back to the secure path of obedience, punctual and complete. Mom and Dad were in charge, as they were ordained of God to be. Our parents had a big job to do, but only the limited scope of our childhood years to accomplish it. They were serious about getting it done. The reverence we learned led toward a singular goal, respectable, responsible adulthood. There were enough killers and rapists, liars and rogues on the loose then already. They were not about to add their offspring to that number.

We will set the record straight for those readers who are steeped in modernity. What I am describing is not child abuse. We did not get kicked in the pants. We were not rapped alongside the head. We didn't get our eyes blackened or our ears boxed. We were not thrown into fire or water. We were not subjected to parental tantrums. We were not yelled at, belittled, or treated as numbskulls. Back then parents had the godly sense to know the difference between inflicting pain (which was sometimes necessary), or inflicting physical and psychological injury (which is abuse.)

You see, the failure to correct a little stealing, a little lying, a little curious sexual experimentation, does beget thieves, liars and perverts. These shame the father's heart, and bring grief to her that bare him. They also overload the courts and the prison system. Honor thy Father and Thy Mother does not lead to death row, for it infuses honor and respect toward the God of heaven, and toward all of God's earth.

There is probably truth in the maxim, that the child's view of God is defined in his view of his parents, especially of the father. This being the case, good parental discipline becomes a proper introduction to God who knows all about us, and loves us too much to leave our sins unpunished. His goal is not so much our ease or pleasure, but our integrity and our maturity. But this holds the possibility for error in either direction. We want to avoid projecting an image of an uncaring and unfeeling God, intent only on awful correction on the erring. Yet there is nothing gained at all in a concept of God, loving in permissive way, robbed of moral superiority, unable or unwilling to impose divine standards upon human behavior. Such a view leaves a sense of no-one-in-charge in the universe.

Don't feel sorry for the chastened child. Just punishment meted out, afterwards yields the fruit of righteousness. Such a child is set on a path of maturity. He maintains the innocence of one who has nothing to hide. His boundaries are well defined. He is secure in the care and nurture of the ones who brought him into this world. He's the one with creativity. He has behind him the grace and discipline to do well in the challenges that come his way. Through obedience he borrows from the hard-earned experiences of his parents.

We complain today that our children do not do as they are told. That, in fact, is rarely the case. How can they obey when we sow confusion by stopping short of telling them what to do, or change the orders every day? Typically, we have reneged on control. We may plead, cajole and bargain. We try to persuade them to our point of view. We make suggestions, hoping they will agree. We tell them lies, by threatening consequences that never happen. But we stop short of parental order. Yet, short of command, we are merely matching wit and will. We find ourselves both outwitted and out willed. We get weary of the battle. We yield to their wishes only to be repelled with their ingratitude. We would love their respect, and get petulance and snobbishness instead. But, we get just what we deserve when we bring the contest down to their level of childish immaturity. But they are not getting what they deserve. These are spoiled children, cheated out of the experience of just punishment.

What peace and refreshment will be restored, if we will have the courage to retake the high moral ground of parenthood. We would recognize that authority is no mere human invention, but a divine order. We would also learn that God has an order of authority between husbands and wives. They are of equal importance without having equal roles (husbands love and lead, wives submit). It is in from this biblical mandate that parents function in solid harmony before their children. This is God's way to turn illiterate little savages into models of civility, integrity, and responsibility. What liberty to find that in place of lock and key to every cabinet, and senseless attempts at persuasion on things they don't want to understand, the lock and key are on their own hearts, and restraint is rooted in respect and honor.

We will also find it as the Bible says, "*the first commandment with promise.*"

THE SIXTH COMMANDMENT
EXODUS 20:13

THOU SHALT NOT KILL

Whoso sheddeth man's blood, by man shall his blood be shed. Genesis 9:6

Thou shalt not kill. This commandment of God is at the heart of respect for human life, vibrantly created in the image of the Creator God. Thus the violation of it is especially grievous. It intrudes into realms that belong to the Creator, that is, to divine control of life and death. It is also a sin against the image of God in man, and with death, establishes with finality the destiny of one will rise from the dead, either unto life, or unto eternal judgment.

But this commandment cannot be sustained when divorced from the God who gave it. It has been banned from public schools for its "religious" connections. Yet it is only in its religious context that it effectively engages its true authority. That is the dilemma of the modern day. We don't want schools to be killing fields, but we don't want God telling us what to do either. Without God, killing becomes a viable option to be used against certain segments of society for the convenience of the rest. The unborn and the elderly are usually targeted first, as deemed the least worthy of living. Ultimately, law and order breaks down and all human life is cheapened.

Surely the commandment is a direct hit on violence, murder, and terrorism. But it is also a mandate to recognize and to act upon the seriousness of murder. It is the responsibility of civil authorities (whose kingdom is of this world), to bring justice upon those who take human life into their own hands. In biblical teaching, the murderer forfeits his own right to live. The government, according to Romans 13:4, *is the minister of God, a revenger to execute wrath on him that doeth evil.* Justice is to be carried out without regard for wealth or fame or social status. When presumptuous killers can buy their way out of a court of justice, or when laws are perverted to protect the guilty, the land is polluted with the blood of the murdered.

We had originally written on the sixth command, *Thou shalt not kill,* Exodus 20:13, in the immediate aftermath of 9/11, and the horrific loss of an estimated 4500 or more lives to terrorism. All this from nineteen men armed with little more than determination and destructive ingenuity.

Since 9/11, some are asking why God didn't stop this. The idea is, that if God is good he would not allow things like this to happen. But if this is your position, then I would pose a more personal question. When is the last time God stopped you from doing wrong? Has he ever manhandled you to keep you from lying, or stealing, or committing adultery? Should He zap you, or your TV, if you choose X-rated, or violent programing?

Not so. God deals with us as intelligent, free moral and free choice agents. If someone crashes a barricade with "BRIDGE OUT" warnings, was it the highway department's failure to stop that car? If God is responsible to stop the killings, what point is there in the commandments? If we will but hear and fear the command of God, then he has indeed us stopped us - on the most effective level - that of mind and heart. No further restraints would be needed.

In fact, God's way of preventing murder and terrorism doesn't engage at the act of killing. It deals with the underlying motivation, the anger and hatred of the human heart. The New Testament makes this plain. One who *hates* his brother is a murderer, Even one who calls another a fool is in danger of hell fire.

Nations have particular sets of laws. To abide by those laws is to live in all the security and protection available. But lawbreakers challenge the authority and security of the state, and are deemed a threat; even as enemies of the state. The lawbreaker has forfeited his basic freedoms. This is the case until justice has been satisfied.

The same principles apply with God - in the ultimate sense. His laws are absolute. He governs with standards of righteousness. He will not have us be selective against evil. His law is the standard against which all nations are measured. He has set up the rulers and kingdoms of this world. He can as surely bring them low.

We Americans have a high estimation of our place and importance on the world scene. We think ourselves the only superpower. We defend our interests, worldwide. We claim the high road of democracy and human rights.

But pride is bound to lead to deception on its way to a fall. We have been bold to deny biblical truth, turning rather to ban the God of Christianity from the classroom and from the public square. We thought godless systems could support the same peace and prosperity that we have enjoyed for generations

But we were wrong. The wrong view of God has not sustained our claimed basic right to life. Selective respect for life cannot sustain justice. We thought great wealth and vast resources could replace absolute morality as a basis for security and safety. That may explain why the giant was sleeping while terrorist plans were put in place.

So we came under attack, vicious, deadly, and brutal. And as suddenly, we start wanting at least certain atrocities and certain kinds of killing, to be evil.

But we have also been brainwashed with violence as the medium of our entertainment. Violent scenes and the killer mentality of the screen have spilled over into real life. Even the toy departments in our stores reflect this cult of violence. We have followed a formula of producing heartless criminals at tender ages.

No, I don't believe New Yorkers are sinners above other Americans. Yet in 1943, New York had forty-four homicides. Less than fifty years later, in 1990, and despite a decrease in population, the number was 2245. At that rate, two years of homicides, would approximate the body count of the 9/11 terrorist attacks.(At this revision, homicides have dropped sharply from the high record. About two million people behind bars in the nation should make a difference).

Abortion is arguably the greatest atrocity committed against Americans, yet it is by Americans. The numbers from 9/11, don't rate as a blip on the radar by comparison. Since the Supreme Court ruling of 1973, men can legally have their pleasure at the price of blood. They send their wives/girlfriends to abortion clinics. Thus, when they march to war, it is with the blood of innocent civilians already on their hands.

MORE ON LIFE AND DEATH ISSUES

And the Lord God breathed into his nostrils, the breath of life, and man became a living soul. (Genesis 2: 7).

All of life belongs to God. Every aspect of life is God's business. Human wisdom is hard pressed even to define it. Webster's dictionary says life is "the quality that distinguishes a vital and functional being from a dead one."

In today's world of a high tech and high pressure organ donation program, this could mean that the body is alive (vital and functional), while the person is "brain dead." Unfortunately, the nature of donor injuries, and the extreme resilience of the human body, does make the donor program something less than 100% exact science. I cannot answer for you, but I would not want organs from someone who might have had the slightest possibility of survival.

Webster's definition of life is very adequate to describe what happens in the abortion industry. Those millions of unborn babies who were very much "alive and functional," are killed and discarded. Burial is deemed unnecessary. These unwanted babies are reduced to material for garbage bins.

Another raging issue is stem cell research, using human embryos. Those who oppose such research are accused of blocking effective treatment for thousands of people suffering from a variety of major illnesses and diseases. But this accusation is based on the "right" of science to pursue every option apart from any moral considerations. It is also premature, because research and experimental treatment with stem cells on patients with Parkinson disease has been done apart from government funding. But it is my impression that the results, though obvious, were actually from mildly to cruelly negative. Keep in mind also that with conventional medicine, dosages can be changed if needed, or medications discontinued. But not so with living implanted cells. They become part of the body system. Treatment is irreversible.

The other front of life and death issues is legally assisted suicide. Administered by physicians, the program has been up and running in Oregon. Vermont is poised (or already is), second. If these pioneer programs seem to be "successful," it is only a matter of time until the morality of euthanasia is no longer to be challenged. What is portrayed as an act of mercy can be turned into a mandate to eliminate those who are no longer considered useful.

There is some confusion in defining euthanasia. (Perhaps the attempt to confuse is deliberate). The administration of lethal drugs or withholding food to cause death, comes under, *thou shalt not kill.* Letting nature run its course, such as refusing bypass surgery, dialysis, or chemotherapy does not violate the command. I think believers could do well to personally ponder how much they would invest to expand the normal complications of the aging process, and the deterioration of health. Is it for the best?

I am in no way suggesting that this should be a government or a doctor's decision. Doctors today are expected to be less than devoted to healing, something decidedly more sinister. Their job description should not include decisions on who lives - or dies.

If this all sounds like a dance upon hot coals between life and death issues, it certainly is. If this is the lofty height of progress and civilization, then I fear for the crash ahead.

The needed moral directives to principles of life and death fail in the rejection of God. The scientific mind in a well-equipped lab may produce an effective vaccine to save thousands of lives - or a deadly high grade anthrax powder. Again the skilled fingers of a surgeon can surgically save the life of a fetus - or end it with an abortion. In neither case does the skill level have any bearing on the morality of the accomplishment.

The Readers Digest ran a joke not long ago of a scientist naively declaring that he would match the creative powers of God. God accepted the challenge. But as the scientist eagerly scooped up mud with which to fashion his man, he was stopped cold with a simple declaration from God. "Not so fast. You must get your own mud."

This bit of humor underscores the point well. The scientist without God's material would have nothing to work with. So maybe he should temper the arrogance of playing god, with things that belong to God. The china shop of morals should get respect. Raging science unattuned to the Creator, will only bring destruction to principles that we cannot afford to live without.

This means the human mind, can never be trusted apart from a divine infusion of truth. This vagrancy of mind has exactly correlated with the door that has opened to abortion and euthanasia. If your mind can approve these, then you could also be sold Nazism, racism, and terrorism. The latter would be just as "right."

I say this to point out two great absolutes. The first one is this. However far we have strayed from biblical truth, just so far are we lost in a directionless wasteland. We want the right to move the moral fences to suit our pleasure. Yet we crave the security of a standard of right and wrong. We condone violence on TV, but we hate the reality of it in the streets, and in our homeland. When hit with 9/11, we want terrorism to be morally wrong. Suddenly, it's comforting to be a nation under God.

The second point is the one that needs to stir the heart and conscience. God is the answer to moral questions (as with the Ten Commandments), and ultimately enforces those answers (as on judgment day). This God is a permanent fixture. He is not here today and gone tomorrow.

It is indeed high time to return to the author of life and the authority over death. The verdict on murder is crystal clear. Those who kill bring innocent blood on the land, and the sentence of death on themselves. The looming question in the stem cell debate is this: Shall we tamper in the laboratory with life designed for the womb? Shall we rival the role of God? Shall we enter the realm of the questionable on the promise of health benefits?

To those who assent to assisted suicide we say this. Compared to what lies beyond a godless life, the worst sufferings and pain of this life would seem like paradise. Why end one misery, only to be subjected to far worse? America, prepare to meet thy God.

THOU SHALT NOT KILL II
WHICH KINGDOM?

In the Old Testament era, being God's chosen people established them as an earthly kingdom, the literal nation of Israel. It is obvious that God called his people into warfare, using them to carry out judgment against nations and kingdoms, whose iniquity was full. Killing was justified where God himself marked people for death and destruction. (This included the death penalty for various transgressions among themselves, that the Bible specifically names). His people served as the instruments for God to accomplish this purpose. This yields quite a bloody picture of Old Testament saints.

But what of the New Testament era? This writing brings us to the most difficult and controversial issues of modern Christianity. This is so, not because the conclusions are hard to come by, but because most churches view combat duty as a Christian obligation of citizenship. In our nation especially, we have long lived with a God and country mix of faith. This view suspends the tenets of Christian faith that are at odds with war, opting for loyalty to a perishing kingdom. But this is at the expense of the call of Jesus to follow the principles of the eternal kingdom. It also abandons the prevailing position of the New Testament Church for roughly the first three centuries of church history.

Charles Colson says that Christians may suffer for their faith, but they may never build prisons for those of other faiths. Taken to its only logical conclusion, Christians could die for their faith, but could not go to war, and kill for their faith. (I doubt that Colson would allow such a conclusion.). This is the kind of dual world that western Christian evangelicals live in. As civilians they want the peace of Jesus. They ask what Jesus would do. But as soldiers and politicians, they will not do what Jesus did. Those who seek to defend Christian participation in warfare would replace the cross on which Jesus died, with a sword in his hand.

Colson also claims that the right to freely speak of one's faith (in the context of religious freedom), is the essence of human dignity. But the essence of human dignity is not revealed when there is no price attached. It goes far deeper than being permitted to freely speak and to live one's faith without fear. Human dignity is best portrayed in one who suffers persecution or even death in the practice of his faith. But taking the life of another, even on the battlefield, is the antithesis of Colson's theme. The enemy is fair game for slaughter, because he is on the "wrong" side in the battle.

Human dignity is inseparable from the Creator of human life. It is the result of the stamp of the divine, of being made in the image of God. As the Bible says, all nations are of one blood, therefore there are no racial value differences. The enemy in combat is your close kin. There is but one place to go with this. Your enemy must be regarded with godly awe and respect. Like you, he travels this way but once. Therefore, let his end be in God's hands. After that, he goes to the eternal destiny assigned him by his Maker.

Not for a moment, are we suggesting that people will naturally act in a dignified manner. The professor who drills evolutionary theory into his youthful class is but expressing his personal bankruptcy of value while undermining the dignity of his students. The soldier who takes deadly aim and squeezes the trigger, is denying the image of God in the enemy soldier, and desecrating his own.

Yet neither is the essence of human dignity expressed in religious freedom, (as Colson assumes), where people express divergent faith views without fear. There is no particular glory nor dignity in taking a position that costs nothing.

Ironically, Christian faith may be most effectively expressed in a context of intolerance and persecution. (That is, on the receiving end). The best measure of human dignity comes where it costs dearly to believe and to do what is right. Its essence shines clearest when neither threat nor favor can lure it from the truth of God.

And where was human dignity displayed on the day Jesus died on the cross? Not in the Roman governor who passed the death sentence. Not in the Jewish crowds who willed it so. No, the supreme dignity of the day resided on the center cross. It was in Jesus. He could have called twelve legions of angels (one angel alone could have done the job of deliverance). He didn't. He could have come down from the cross. He didn't. That's how we know he didn't come to destroy mens lives, but to save them. Saving them meant that he must not save himself.

Some of you will surely say, "but we must defend our freedoms." But what freedoms are we seeking to defend? Is it the privilege to be the world's mega-consumers, languishing in lives of ease, and practically unparalleled luxuries? Is it 24/7 access to media entertainment, much of which is unfit for the human mind? Is it the freedom to turn from the biblical truth once delivered to us? Is it the freedom to spend our moral capital into oblivion? At this stage, it is hardly to protect the right to engage the culture with biblical truth. The point here is not to lightly esteem our country, or citizenship in this country. Rather, it is to expose the blindness of equating our country, or any country, with special favor with God, and to claim our defense as a "Christian" duty.

In fact, the kingdom of God, is not especially hampered, for lack of religious liberty. Had Rome granted Jesus religious freedom, the Savior would not have died.

The triumph of Jesus over death is likened to seed sown in the ground. Out of the "death" of the seed planted, there springs first new life, followed by bountiful harvest.

The disciples had been so sure that Jesus had come to forcefully deliver Israel from Roman rule. It is not surprising then, that Peter moved forcefully, with a willingness to shed blood, in a valiant effort to keep Jesus from being captured. During the trial and crucifixion, none of the disciples were comprehending the power of God soon to be unleashed before their eyes. The mutilated dead body of Jesus on the cross, after a few days in the tomb, would soon be vibrantly alive - forevermore. The kingdom that Jesus came to establish was not one of real estate, nor of national boundaries. It would be a kingdom within kingdoms. It would outlast the rise and fall of every earthly nation. An armed Christian could only be counter productive: the kingdom of Jesus Christ is not established, nor defended, with the sword.

With the resurrection of Christ, the rest is history. From the band of the few, who totally abandoned former political and nationalistic ambitions, the gospel of truth took wings through the known world in a matter of decades, A.D. And where the gospel went, people were transformed. Thieves quit stealing. Adulterers left off their sin. Killers repented. Enemies were reconciled. Churches were born. Churches grew. Not without great cost. Christians were hated and persecuted from one kingdom to the next. Often, they had no certain dwelling place. Yet they refused to stoop to the level of an eye for an eye. When deprived of homes, family, and country they did not form a moral majority to bring reformation through politics. Nor did they regroup to take back by force what was rightfully theirs. Their deprivation of earthy benefits bespoke a much greater citizenship in heaven, a citizenship available to all races and all peoples of all time.

But alas, even Christians covet a place of security and power in this world. By the 4th century AD. the church was losing its vision, and mostly succumbed to a marriage of church and state. Under the Emperor Constantine, Christianity became the official religion of Rome. Ere long the sword, that inferior weapon which the disciples had put away, became the mainstay of the faith. From fugitives and vagabonds even in their own countries, the "Christians" gained the political pinnacle. In the early church, the cross of Christ was a personal instrument that spelled the end to sin and self. New believers received baptism at the threat of persecution and death. But under Constantine, the cross was perverted into a symbol of earthly conquering. The coercion and forced "conversions"of poor peasants, brought them nothing of the love and mercy of God. Consider the Crusades, and the blood shed of Muslims back then, for the purpose of reclaiming the "holy" city. Could it be perhaps "Christian" force, and bloodshed by "Christians" back then, that paved the way for the Islamic militancy of today? (Does what goes around, come around?)

The appeal of political and military might, was so compelling, that even Martin Luther, and Ulrich Zwingli (of Reformation fame). would not proceed without the protection of the political and military powers of civil government.

Today, the battle front is twofold. There are, and will continue to be, wars and rumors of wars. Nations and kingdoms will fight. Loyal soldiers will always be in demand. For all of this there never will be a war that ends wars (until God intervenes). Nor will warfare "make the world safe for democracy."

The second warfare is on the eternal scale. Its focus is not on overpowering the enemy with bombs and bullets. It is not in vain negotiations of peace. *(Peace, peace, when there is no peace)*. Rather, it lies in the power of the gospel, especially where men endowed with Christlike spirit, will lay down their lives for the truth. They have both their Master, Jesus Christ, and the early church, and even modern day martyrs, for their examples.

For you fellow Christian, which will it be? Would you take the life of another at the risk of your soul? Or would you surrender your life that another might be saved?

THE SEVENTH COMMANDMENT
EXODUS 20:1

THOU SHALT NOT COMMIT ADULTERY

"He that committeth adultery lacketh understanding; a wound and dishonor shall he get, and his reproach shall not be wiped away. He that committeth adultery sinneth against his own body."

There are two commandments that are especially close to the heart of God. Both involve human life. Both involve the authority of God over human life.

The one is the Sixth Commandment, and concerns the end of life: *Thou shalt not kill.* This is taking the life of another person. But God reserves this right as his own. God says, *"I kill, and I make alive."* If God were capable of killing someone by mistake, no problem; he could bring him back to life again.

The commandment before us, *thou shalt not commit adultery,* safeguards the conception of life. Peter defines this unique empowerment to reproduce human life by the male and the female in marriage. They are *"heirs together of the grace of life"*(I. Peter 3:7). God created this empowerment, and strictly regulated it through marriage. Conception, birth, and parental care; all come under divine regulation. Marriage is the "cocoon," in which the next generation is both conceived and nourished. *"Marriage is honorable in all, but whoremongers and adulterers, God will judge"*.

Why then is sexual immorality the focus of the entertainment industry? Why is "unfaithfulness" splashed around as though it were a positive term? Why is a "safe" sexual relationship couched in terms of *protection* against deadly disease, or preventing *unwanted* pregnancies? Married sexuality is both safe and disease free. Yes, it is subject to pregnancies; which merely goes to show that reproduction is working according to the divine plan. (The protection needed is not against disease and the blessing of having children, but against illicit sex).

We see then, why our society is paying such a horrible price in terms of broken homes, abused and neglected children, and battered girl friends, all for a form of love that is supposedly free. If unfaithful love is free, why is there more mistrust and jealousy of sexual partners, more pain, more neglect, more aloneness and loneliness, and more uncertainly? Why are there more jilted lovers, more restraining orders, more shelters, more homicides, more suicides. and yes, more unhappy and guilty people than ever before?

But let's define *love that is truly, morally free.* We didn't invent it. We don't have the liberty to reinvent it. Its plan came directly from God, from the very day He created man. Left alone with the animal world, Adam had the privilege of naming the animals. However, none had any semblance to marriageable material. Not one of them could return Adam's intelligent gaze.

The only answer to Adam's aloneness would come by special creation. "She" was taken *from the man* during a God-induced anesthesia. Whereas Adam and Eve were both products of special creation, ever after, the man with his wife were entrusted with the reproduction of the human race. So it was that one of the greatest delights of marriage (the sexual union), and the greatest responsibility (the conception and bringing up of children), came packaged together, reserved for marriage.

When Adam awoke, and saw Eve for the first time, no introductions were needed. However, God did give them (with us), instructions. Yes they did belong to each other. Exclusively. Permanently. They had sole rights to the other's body, but to *no other,* as long as both would live. God decreed the terms of marriage *from the beginning,* and designed the sexual relationship to bond the marriage. This takes out premarital and extramarital relations, divorce and remarriage, polygamy and homosexuality in one fell swoop.

Marriage is the only context where love is free, because biblical marriage is indeed honorable. It is free from sin, free from fear, free from the raging jealousies of jilted lovers. (Even jealousy bears witness that sex was to be reserved for the one and only). No protection is needed from a marriage partner that is permanently and exclusively your own. Sexual purity until marriage and fidelity in marriage do not carry the risk of sexually transmitted disease.

Neither is protection needed against conception. The permanent home, blessed with children under responsible parenting, is the greatest prize and the greatest asset of any society. If single people would refuse the defilement of fornication, thus of unwed parenting, there would be ample room on the planet for children conceived *in* marriage.

The free-love culture does not love babies. Casual sex does not have procreation as its object. Even so, fully a third of the children born in America, are now born to single mothers. Most illegitimate children are supported by welfare. Many are now reared by grandparents. But, so called free love is shaping up into a society that is no longer free. There comes a point where such an arrangement is no longer self sustaining. The cheating that goes on is dead weight on those who live by the rules of marriage.

Now I know that some readers will vehemently disagree. They are sure that they are acting as responsibly as many married couples they know. They are financially independent and intellectually capable of single parenting. And what if this were arguably true? It is still a false premise of human sexuality. (It is also true that some counterfeiters do an excellent job of printing money).

The common focus of avoiding diseases and preventing unwanted pregnancies is simply misguided. The worst tragedy is the illicit sex relation itself. To give your body to someone in a context other than marriage is the gravest mistake. Those who do so are selling out too cheap, and selling their souls in the process. There is no place in the kingdom of God for the fornicator and the adulterer. Bargain counter sex is life on something lower than the animal level of gratification. I say lower than animals, because so much of it is driven by pornography and the entertainment media. It destroys the very capacity for the intimacy and security for which it seeks. It trades the high ground of what is good and noble in marriage, for cheap and sordid betrayal, and guilt before God.

No, this writing is not a match of wits, or a matter of personal opinion. We did not design human sexuality. God did. We did not decide how children would be conceived. God did. A sexual relationship apart from marriage is an affront to God, a sin against the sexual partner, a sin against one's own body, and a sin against an unplanned, unwanted generation of babies.

THE WAY BACK

Unfortunately, the road back will be difficult. Sexual sin has not only gone unchecked; it has been wildly promoted. Even in the churches, immorality and divorce run about as rampant as with the unchurched. Illicit sex has become the greatest American addiction. We don't have the fortitude to resist it so long as we allow ourselves to be entertained by it, right in our own homes We've even lost the community decency to keep pornography out of the convenience stores. "Respectable" women wear apparel once surely reserved for harlots. We are accustomed to these things as though they were normal. We end up loving what God hates, and despising what God loves. We have much rubbish to clear away, before we can even rebuild.

First, we must agree with God. Sex is for the private and permanent bond of marriage, and for the reproduction of the race. "Sexy," is not for public show. It is not to sell product. It is not for public entertainment. We must not only accept this as true, but embrace it as though our lives depended on it. They often do. We must commit our bodies to purity until marriage and to fidelity within marriage.

Finally we pastors and teachers must recommit to seeing the battle through. We may not prevail over the sins of the world. But we are responsible to be salt and light to our communities. We must be true to our marriage vows. We must teach youths to flee sexual impurity. We need to reinstate clear standards for modest (concealing instead of revealing), clothing on both men and women. We must regain reserve and restraint in male/female relationships.

Many believers (probably includes you), really mean to say "yes" to God. That surely means saying "no" to the corruption around us.

THOU SHALT NOT COMMIT ADULTERY II.

Subtitle: **Thou shalt be in bodily appearance and conduct as is becoming to holiness, to preserve thine own, and thy neighbors' marriage.**

Were they ashamed when they had committed abomination? Nay they were not at all ashamed, neither could they blush (Jeremiah 6:18). These words by the prophet highlight the peril of our day. The private and sacred is flaunted like fake jewelry in a flea market.

While I waited for a recent eye exam, I couldn't help but hear the casual conversation between staff members. One comment by the receptionist to other staff ended with . . . *since I moved in with my boyfriend.* After the doctor got off the phone, the question raised was whether the caller was his wife, his girlfriend, or his mistress. This "normal" conversation in a professional work environment is but a small indicator of the shamelessness and the lost reserve between the sexes.

In the last installment we stated that illicit sex is America's worst addiction. This time we will examine one of the major reasons this is so.

With exception to the time before sin came into the world, the Bible always portrays nakedness in an unfavorable light. The first act of Adam and Eve, after sin, was to hide, and to clothe themselves with fig leaves. God, however, clothed them with coats of skin.

God's provision of clothing was not an act of judgment, but an act of mercy. God took from them the garments that could not hide their sin, and covered them, as an act of redemption. This act of God illustrates both the vulnerability of inadequate clothing and the protection of being fully clothed. Nakedness, as defined biblically, according to W.E. Vine, ranges from torn clothing, scanty apparel, undergarments only, to no clothing at all.

So the difference between being naked and being clothed is not between no clothing and scanty clothing. It is the difference between insufficient clothing and being properly clothed. So we have a jolt for "Christian" men who strut bare chests and bare legs in public. They are not clothed, but naked; to their own shame. In a truly decent society, such men would run for cover.

In this lack of understanding, the acceptance of indecency, though alarming, is not surprising. It is the conclusion to our inherent loss of reserve and decency as a society. The poor souls who end up on some nudist beach differ from the rest of their "beached" peers, only in degree Sun and sand have become mere excuses to flout shamelessness, and to overload sexual appetites. This is hardly less true on sidewalks and in shopping malls. This predominant acceptance of indecent appearance is the catalyst of the moral breakdown.

Deliberate carelessness in covering the body, is a quarrel with God. May we suggest two reasons why this is so.

The first is of a spiritual order. Had God not intervened, Adam and Eve would have remained in a semi-clothed state of separation from God. The covering of their shame, however, allowed them to set both their faces and their hope back on God.

Even in the Old Testament, covering for sin required the total sacrifice of the substitute animal. It also required "full coverage" of the priest who performed the service. They were not to go up steps to an altar, lest their garment fail to adequately cover them. Likewise the total sacrifice of Christ on the cross provided the full and complete salvation from sin.

I would remind you Christian readers that skimpy clothing runs counter to the principle of your salvation. In the Bible (II. Corinthians 5:14), mortality is likened to nakedness, and clothing is synonymous with life. Scripture also describes believers, as being clothed in white robes. In Revelation 3:18, complacent believers are warned of being exposed in the shame *of their nakedness*. What then would be God's message be to those who do not know the shamefulness of nakedness?

The second reason centers around the commandment of God; THOU SHALT NOT COMMIT ADULTERY. Modest clothing is one of God's protections from sexual sin. For reasons not fully known to us, the coming of sin into the world has greatly distorted the mind in relation to nakedness. When it comes to the revealed anatomy of an attractive woman, the fallen nature of any man comes to full alert. Unless there is deliberate avoiding or turning from such temptation, this inverts beauty into lust; a wrong desire for what he has seen. If this is a private encounter with his wife, then the relationship can be honorable and the bed undefiled (Hebrew 13:4). Only in the exclusiveness and permanence of marriage, do male and female belong to each other, in this way.

The runaway sin of our society is caused by revealing to the public eye that which ought to be private and sacred. The defilement and the devastation of this sin are everywhere. In such a context many youths discover the degrading counterfeit of love, even before finishing high school. In so doing they trifle with the love and security of a lasting, happy marriage. Couples who ought to get married, don't get married, choosing rather the pleasures of sin for a season. Couples who should stay married get divorced, while chasing the mirage of greater fulfillment with yet another partner. In any case, widely advertised used goods, is bound to face the disappointment of being desired only as an object of lust.

We are saying then, that the pearl of virginity is too often bartered away in a process that pleases the eye while it compromises the soul. Weep for the precious young ladies who were never taught from childhood, that the appealing sexual aspects of the body must be guarded from the lustful public, as carefully as the most precious of jewels. Purity, once stolen, cannot be reclaimed. Pity the young man who falls before the seductive powers of a scantily-clothed woman. According to the Scriptures, their lives will never be the same. A lack of full dress with its attendant lack of reserve, has been key in the ruin of many. Even Christians who stay too close to the fire, will get burned.

Would you escape the ravages of sexual sin? Would you preserve the institution of marriage? Would you avoid compromising your relationship with God in conduct and appearance? Prove it by getting your dress standards from God through the Scriptures, refusing to pattern after the appearance of those who fall because they have forgotten how to blush.

It is time that pastors get serious again about hemlines, and necklines, and any other shameless invasions of fashion, for either men or women. Without biblical teaching and a biblical model, total corruption is the sure result. Our ladies must also be taught to exercise their "right to privacy." This has everything to do with protection from roving eyes and lustful advances. It has everything to do with keeping themselves pure. It has *nothing to do* with giving away body and soul, and then "choosing" to end "unplanned" pregnancies.

THE EIGHTH COMMANDMENT
EXODUS 20:15

THOU SHALT NOT STEAL

THE NINTH COMMANDMENT
EXODUS 20:16

THOU SHALT NOT BEAR FALSE WITNESS

These two commandments are so closely related, that we will consider them together. Both grow out of a common root. Stealing deprives the other of material goods. A false witness seeks to deprive another of respect and good reputation. *(The hypocrite with his mouth destroys his neighbor)*. And what is a hypocrite? In the case of stealing and false witness it is a double standard. It is a willingness to do to another as you would not want done to you. If any thought is given to the victim, it can only be by further degrading him in such a way as to justify what you are doing.

There is another reason for addressing these commands in tandem. It is this. We tend to relegate stealing to non Christians. Outright theft is beneath those who claim to be Christians. But when it comes to false witness . . . So perhaps in this marriage of stealing and false witness, we will better understand the seriousness of sending or receiving unverified reports. Our churches are not harmed with a proliferation of stealing candy bars out of convenience stores. The same cannot be said for the latest gossip. And we have before us a further challenge: When someone else has done the stealing, you will surely want to avoid trading in stolen goods. You don't want to be an accomplice to theft. But this should be equally true of false information. Those who act on such information are indeed partakers of the evil deed. If we are serious, there are ways of avoiding such condemnation.

"Bearing" false witness is an astounding concept. This is not the only time the Bible speaks of bearing or "carrying" our speech (as though *on* or *in* our person). Think concealed weapons. So long as the weapon is carried, even unseen, the individual is armed. The weapon is part of who he is at heart, before he draws and fires. A slip of the tongue isn't really that. It can be fired only because it is carried. So is the false witness. One who carries good words is armed with blessings. But the false witness is both armed and dangerous.

There are numerous biblical safeguards in place to keep us from being partakers of the false witness. The liar's words can destroy only where people choose to ignore the biblical analysis of truth.

- One problem is simple gullibility. *The simple believeth every word, but the righteous looketh well into his going.* It is wrong to pass on conclusions before compelling evidence is in. There is no excuse in instantly accepting the latest report blowing through town. Several years ago, the first report of a tornado hitting a neighboring town, stated that the place was "totally destroyed." While I wasn't tempted to repeat this analysis of the damage, (wait and see is good enough), it would have been embarrassing to run a correction later.

Taking personal responsibility and correcting any inaccuracies we may have passed along will go a long way to temper our zeal to be "first" with the "latest."

- There is a very limited range where repeating verified negative information about another is actually in order. This is typically those who are either part of the problem, or part of the solution. There are things that do become common knowledge; foreclosure action on a property, a couple getting a divorce, etc. Again, there is no rush, and whoever dispenses such information is responsible for accuracy. Otherwise, he is both a false witness, and a liar.

- Scripture is clear that reports not verified by two or three witnesses, must not be used against an individual. It seems that God would rather occasionally have a guilty person go free, than to have an innocent person condemned.

- The guilty party should be the first to know. Matthew 18: 15-17, outlines the approach. First comes private confrontation; tell him his fault between you and him alone. If this does not resolve the matter, then take with you one or two more, that at the mouth of two or three witnesses, every word may be established. If this still doesn't bring resolution, then finally the matter is brought to a head before the church.

- Remember that these are not trifling matters. They are honesty and integrity issues.

Some years ago, the editor of a well-known news magazine wrote to the effect that in order for a nation to survive, something like 80% of the people must be honest 80% of the time. His numbers may have been a bit higher. This would translate into the point that thieves and liars are not only a threat to themselves, but also to the whole culture. So much for the modern notion that the private life of leaders has no bearing on public service. These commandments, then, are non optional elements to personal and social integrity. God's test of character for men is first personal and private. The private issue establishes one's standing with God. The public issue that follows is whether one can serve his neighbor as himself. This fits the New Testament summary of God's law, called the Second great commandment; ***Thou shalt love thy neighbor as thyself.***

I'm not into sports. So don't be surprised if my terminology is a bit lacking here. But did you hear about the baseball player who is so valuable, that his team's owner is going to allow him to make up his own rules as he goes? This means he can override any call from the umpire. Also, when he is up to bat, and the hit looks like a home run, he has the option of calling it a home run, without running the bases. He is instructed though, to break the rules gradually over time, so as not to offend the sensibilities of baseball diehards (those who are impossibly slow to accept anything new).

You're right. It won't happen. It would be the doom of baseball. Baseball is a game. But even games don't survive without rules.

But on second thought, it has happened already. Life is too serious to be called a game, yet the rules are being altered over time. The biblical "umpire of certainty" is defied. The home run is declared without running the bases. The opposing players don't get a chance at stopping the ball, and of tagging the batter "out". (This game even gets played in church).

So today, integrity is in short supply. Students cheat on exams. Executives cheat on golf scores. Employees take more merchandise out the back door than shoplifters take out the front. Some call in sick to spend a day on the lake, or to do whatever. Recently, the postal system reported being short an incredible $60 million worth of mail baskets, most of which had reportedly found their way into private offices and businesses (handy for storage). A power company falsifies maintenance records, and hides the condition of aging equipment. Movie makers rewrite history, forever altering the perception of what happened in the past. Even school history texts are rewritten to fit today's version of "politically correct." (Example: The first Thanksgiving was celebrated so that the white settlers could show their gratitude to their Indian friends). In the process of rewriting history, the heroes of yesterday may be counted for villains today.

Integrity is an unimpaired quality of soundness, of honesty, and sincerity. Integrity cannot knowingly or willfully alter facts. It cannot operate on greed. Issuing a false report at the expense of someone's character, or accepting such reports without verification, grows on the same branch of the same tree as tax cheating or robbing a bank. They all point to the same impairment. In math, the integer is the whole number (complete, not divided). Likewise, in the character of people there must reside an integral factor that constitutes wholeness of the person's character. (*Thou desirest truth in the inward parts,* Psalm 51:6) The life of integrity is not compartmentalized into honesty *and* cheating, or lies *and* truthfulness. This is the irony of even 98% honesty. It is not 2% impaired, but 100%.

Integrity does not depend on the value of the damage done. One news item reported the deed of a city employee. She embezzled a very small amount of money from the city. The city had spent $14,000 on prosecuting her, an amount far exceeding what she had stolen. That might appear ridiculous compared to the theft. But what if she had embezzled $14M? In fact, that lady's problem was the same as that of the one who cheats big-time. Missing money, unless it is an honest mistake, is really a matter of missing integrity.

Need I remind you that at the top of huge business conglomerates that have recently imploded (we could name several), are powerful men who are integrally impaired? Do they always lie? Probably not. Did they start lying only when millions or billions of dollars were involved? Probably not. A more plausible start would be as a child stealing from the candy counter, or as a student in school exams, or the young business man on golf scores. Yet in the end, the impairment of a few powerful people threatens to bring down the greatest economy on the planet.

Fact is, the commandments that we refuse to live by - we cannot live without. God did not give us commandments to make life difficult. Practically every woe in this world can be traced directly or indirectly to the breaking of the commandments of God. (Even sickness, and death had their beginning with the introduction of sin into this world.)

I expect that the most avowed secularists and atheists want some sort of value system in place to stabilize society. But we must insist that valid moral principles have their source only in God, and that they *never* change.

Years ago, in my school days, there were times when the teacher would leave the classroom unattended. What amazes me is how quickly we could be transformed by the illusion that no one was in charge. But we were wrong. The teacher always came back . . .

Is not the fickleness of youngsters being replayed on a much larger and more dangerous scale? We have whole generations being taught that there never was a "teacher" (God), or if there ever was, he is totally irrelevant to modern man and the modern world, and that he is never coming back.

Until he comes, the Ten Commandments are the Teacher's monitors, showing us the manner and the justice of God's judgments. However, the commandments by themselves do not contain the dynamic to deliver us from sin. It is heart change that is needed.

The commandments are teachers to lead us to repentance. We all find ourselves in the classroom of those who have *sinned and come short of the glory of God.* I'll grant you that some cleanup might happen through our best resolve not to steal, nor to bear false witness, and to challenge others in the same. But know this, that the sins we have already committed both stain the soul, and offend against a holy God. But if we will heed the message of God, we will find ourselves falling at the feet of the Christ who died to deliver us.

If we don't heed God's call to repentance, we Americans will be doubly guilty, because we once knew these things. We used to teach it in the public forum, including our schools. Now we live in denial as though the divine document, etched in stone, were irrelevant to our times.

PRACTICAL CHECKPOINTS OF INTEGRITY
THOU SHALT NOT STEAL:
- Petty Theft. Stealing so-called small items from employers, out of stores, etc.
- Armed robbery. Stealing with force, and with threat of bodily harm.
- Under reporting income. This amounts to paying less in taxes than is owed.

- Wasting company time.
- Misrepresenting items for sale to get a better price.
- Violating copy- rite laws.
- Giving your word, then changing the terms or conditions of the agreement.

THOU SHALT NOT BEAR FALSE WITNESS
- Deliberate lies about another person
- Reaching or receiving unfounded conclusions, and then repeating them as facts, or using them to establish a course of action.
- Embellishing the negatives of others, first in imagination, then in words.
- Failing to follow the biblical mandate of verification through two or more witnesses.

THE TENTH COMMANDMENT
EXODUS 20:17

THOU SHALT NOT COVET

Thou shalt not covet thy neighbor's house, thou shalt not covet thy neighbor's wife, nor his manservant, nor his maidservant, nor his animals, nor anything that is thy neighbor's. (Exodus 20:17).

When the neighbor appears to have it made, owning the that best of everything, and his life appears like a modal of success, and you find yourself drawn to model the same, that is covetousness. If you live your life with the goal of happiness in accumulating wealth, and material things, that too, is covetousness. If you would sue another at law for to collect what you legally have coming, that too, is covetousness. If you cannot bear the thought of losing what you own, well, that too, is covetousness.

Covetousness displaces the love for God as the giver of every good gift, into the love of things that pass away. It removes the shield of trust and contentment. It is the mirage of happiness, fulfillment, or security apart from the God who created it all. It turns a jealous eye toward the possessions of another. In fact, the Bible condemns the covetous man as an idol worshiper. Covetousness then, is a deadly exercise, a sin that separates the soul from his God.

This commandment against covetousness cuts across the grain of some of the most cherished American ideas. Where would this country be without the protectionism of insurances and retirement plans? "Uninsured" is equated with probable intolerable losses, and with being irresponsible. It is essentially an industry driven on anxiety, and fear of loss. Never mind that insurances never prevent a single fire, accident, illness, or death. They merely reassign the responsibility of paying for the losses.

The protectionism view is so entrenched that with many it would rate as *Economic Essentials 101.* It has become a tide we're not expected to buck. Practically all (even people of faith) are persuaded that one's own assets will sooner or later be found wanting. Thus security is pursued in buying into larger holdings; insurances, stocks, land holdings, and housing bubbles. However, *Economic Essentials 101,* failed to disclose the lesson that really shouts today; that indeed there are no banks or securities that are too big to fail, and that a housing bubble easily becomes a housing bust. Millions today are paying dearly for blind trust in these much lauded "securities."

On the other end of the spectrum, anti gambling laws, representing at least token support for honest work ethics, have fallen like dominoes. Today, state-run lotteries, Power ball Jackpots, and casino gambling have turned respectable across main street U.S.A. But — we have again silenced a great moral principle — the fact that greed is always perilous, and that it ought to a crime to remove moral principles out of financial dealings. The Bible calls it covetousness.

Is this not irony? We are expected not to risk our means to theft, fire, illness, accident, or act of God. (The risks are relatively low. That's why they are insurable). Yet the gambling industry (and even the government), encourages otherwise sane people to risk hard-earned cash at race tracks and slot machines, or trade it for millions of absolutely worthless government-issue lottery tickets. Losses to individual gamblers can reach hundreds of thousands of dollars. One Minnesota man lost $800,000.00 over the last few years in illegal bets. Meanwhile a very few, (who have a higher probability of getting struck by lightning), strike it rich. But this totally ignores the most important questions on gambling. Is God pleased? Do multimillions in any way improve character and quality of life? Can money buy happiness and peace of mind? Can you claim your millions and build your castle on slave labor? (That is, fellow slaves to gambling). The casinos now dotting the nation are not temples of economic stability, but of ruthless greed. But no, casino revenues are not helping state budgets. Gambling takes more than it puts in, possibly about three times as much.

Meanwhile, everybody pays for covetousness. A greed-driven economy must factor in the cost of gambling derelicts, of frivolous lawsuits, of exorbitant court settlements, of medical malpractice and drug company liability, and of fraudulent insurance claims. The price of greed is on everything, from cigarettes, to automobile repairs to the infamous skyrocketing cost of medicine and of hospitalization.

In many cultures of old, men fashioned their own gods, out of wood, stone, or precious metals. To these idols, men fell down and worshiped.

Idolatry has come a long way. Today's idolater wouldn't spare a glance at some graven image, except perhaps in pity for the "ignorant" pagans who worship it. Today's idolater may drive a Lexus, and own the biggest house in the suburb. He may have millions invested as retirement security. He doesn't know it, but he, like his pagan counterpart, is also trusting in gods that cannot save. And his kind too, has been around for a long time. Jesus described him two thousand years ago in Luke 12: 16-21.

The ground of a certain rich man brought forth bountifully: And he thought within himself saying, What shall I do, for I have no room where to bestow all my fruits? And he said, This will I do: I will pull down my barns, and build greater; and there will I bestow all my fruits and my goods. And I will say to my soul, Soul, thou hast much goods laid up for many years; take thine ease, eat, drink, and be merry. But God said unto him, Thou fool, this night shall thy soul be required of thee: then whose shall these things be, which thou hast provided? So is he that layeth up treasure for himself, and is not rich toward God.

Perhaps the more we have, the less we understand.

A man's life does not consist of the abundance of things that he possesses. Behind the most expensive facade that money can buy, lives a soul that money cannot touch. The essential needs of that soul can be met only in the God who made it. Neither do material goods add security to those who pursue them. The wealth that is worshiped, is always left behind. *We brought nothing into this world, and it is certain that we will carry nothing out.*

Perhaps the more we have the less we understand - that security and contentment are gifts God bestows upon the faithful. More, is not the answer. *He that loveth silver shall not be satisfied with silver, nor he that loveth abundance with increase.*

We started feeding hummingbirds, years ago, on a single station feeder. Since there were so many, we decided to go to a four-station model. Alas, initially our purchase brought great distress to the hummingbird kingdom. The idea of sitting together enjoying our offering of sugar water was a concept they could not handle. The birds could not see beyond the quantity in the feeder into the boundless supply of water and sugar from our kitchen. Likewise, we easily shortchange God, by fretting over things at hand, forgetting that with him is boundless supply. Without Him we are nothing and have nothing. He operates a self-serve buffet, far beyond our comprehension. He manages not only the needs of all humanity across the world, but also sees to the needs of the animal kingdom, the birds of the heavens and the fishes of the seas.

Perhaps the more we have, the less we understand. Jesus was once met by a young man of great possessions who asked how he could have eternal life. When Jesus told him that by selling all and following him, he could be assured of treasures in heaven, the young man turned sadly away. His heart would not allow him to give up what he could not keep, in order to gain what he could not lose.

If our greatest values are things we can insure, padlock, or keep in a safe, we are paupers indeed. How can things we must protect, be protection and security to us?.

Far better to learn contentment (*godliness with contentment is great gain*), and to exercise generosity toward one's neighbor. The Bible bids us sell, and to give, not just what is left over, but from the first of our income. This is laying up treasures in heaven, rather than creating an illusion of happiness in the things belonging to our neighbor, or security in wealth, in insurances, or in gambling.

HOW SHOULD WE
THEN LIVE?

WHATEVER HAPPENED TO HUMAN DIGNITY?

Morally confused people minimize the difference between people and animals. Are you one of them? There is an increased emphasis on pets as an extension, or even a replacement of the human family. In 2005, the London Zoo had an exhibit of human males and females, next to an exhibit of their "primate cousins." At that point, the differences probably didn't seem very great. There are **a lot of similarities** between humans and apes. Also, these young men and women seemed blinded to moral responsibility, as they reportedly copied the behavior of their "cousins."

This lack of understanding is as if a man has lost his fortune, and practically everything he owns. Any day now, he will be put out of his house. In a last yard sale fund raiser, he sells a few personal possessions, hoping for enough to pay for a few nights at a boarding house. He considers a $50 offer for a piece of art that had been passed down through the family for several generations. The successful buyer suppresses his excitement, then drives away in triumph with the purchase. There are, after all, **a lot of similarities** between a framed print worth $50, and the rare original by a famous painter. But it is the difference that counts. That difference is destined to net the buyer $1.5 M at Christie's Auction House in New York. The seller was a rich man . . . until he sold out in ignorance.

A far greater loss applies when we lose sight of **the difference that counts** between people and animals. Animals hold their course through history not by weight of decision, but by instinct. No worry about rising crime, drug abuse, family breakdowns, debt loads, or effective response to Katrina-type natural disasters.

People on the other hand, map out their destiny with choices in relation to morality, ethics and integrity. To trade off these choices for animal passions is to compromise the very essence of civilization.

But this is not suggesting that the even the best of human ideas and reasons are sufficient. In fact, fifty years of social experiments mapped out by the best brains have resulted to the widespread abandonment of any standard of right and wrong. The result is such a drain of character and depletion of moral capital that many people become a menace to themselves and a danger to others. This is not the rebirth of freedom. It is the undoing of it.

The most serious business we have is to effectively teach the generation that follows, how to navigate the slippery slope of human experience and passion. Way too soon, we abandoned the case for moral absolutes, having disclaimed the notion of the Creator God who holds us to actual commandments of right and wrong.

Thus have we lightly surrendered the badge of honor and human dignity. We have forgotten that people are on a path of immortality, destined to live again forever after death. To be created in the image of God sets people forever apart from pets, and dictates that we dare not live like apes. To know God, to find the will of God, and the power to do right is in keeping with the value of the rare original. This alone fulfills the call to true human dignity.

REDISCOVERING THE FORGOTTEN TREATY

I have shared the following anti adultery material with a number of people who have lived in direct violation to the teaching. It has been interesting to note the agreement, and thoughtful comments that follow. It is as though a light has gone on for the first time. So far, there has not been a single case of contradiction, even though the exposure had to be painful. So why the agreement?

The answer goes back to the first moral failure. I'll keep the story brief. Adam and Eve, after being made in the image of God, were warned of God not to eat of one particular tree in the garden of Eden. They ate the forbidden fruit anyway. Immediately afterward, they tried to hide the shame of their nakedness with fig leaves, and they tried to hide from God. Why?

The Bible says *they knew that they had sinned.* In a single stroke, they had turned from a comfortable peace with God and each other, to the persuasion that what they had done was horribly wrong, Then as always, transgression brought condemnation. Then as always, confusion and consequences followed in hot pursuit. (Did you know that transgression of God's law is the direct cause of death for us all?)

The high sounding claims that so many people erect against moral standards and moral accountability do not satisfy. The human conscience and spirit react like a faithful judge, demanding justice. I have seen murderers put on a brazen front in the courtroom, only to find them in private with a conscience in howling reproach. This is not because society has demanded too much from them, but because the conscience has a treaty with God. The Bible says that *God has given light to every man that is in the world.* God has programed the human conscience with a core knowledge of right and wrong.

Unfortunately, tampering with this treaty comes easy. A very common method is to make excuses. We can blame our sins on parents, friends, enemies, poverty, abuse, discrimination, or even somebody cutting us off at the freeway exit. Isn't blame just an underhanded way of salving our own conscience?

I meet a lot of folks who believe that they are good people, or at least better than most others. Apparently the conscience is lulled as they approve what is right, though they don't always do what is right. So the shoplifter will justify her theft, because in her mind, robbing a bank is far worse. Another is convinced of his own honesty, because he lies only in a pinch.

Perhaps your personal treaty with God has been gathering dust for a long time. When was the last time you asked yourself why you expect to get by with using God's name as a curse word, or lying, or stealing, or hating someone, or disobeying your parents, or engaging in sex outside of marriage? The day is coming when the treaty between God and your conscience will be honored on God's terms. *Every mouth will be stopped and all the worlds will be guilty before God.* It won't help to claim you didn't know better, because really, you do.

WHAT SEXUAL REVOLUTION?

"NO HUSBAND NO PROBLEM." So claimed a headline of the January 16, 2007 *St. Paul Pioneer Press.* Fifty-one percent of women in America are now living without husbands. According to Professor Stephanie Coontz, "there is no going back to a world where we can assume that marriage is the main institution that organizes peoples' lives." Nothing is offered on what will organize peoples' lives. Neither is there any clue on how the children (and the men) are faring. In fact, you wouldn't guess from this article that women even continue to have babies.

If you will follow for a few moments, we will share how this anti marriage mentality destroys us. So let's bring in some much needed perspective.

Even the "No Husband No Problem" ladies aren't doing so sumptuously. According to *US News,* March 12, 2007, one in four females ages fourteen to fifty-nine is infected with a sexually transmitted virus. Of these, 7.5 million are fourteen to twenty-four years of age. (It is *not* good to raise the risk of sterility and cervical cancer in this way.)

Another recent news item equates high alcohol consumption with females who eschew long-term commitment in favor of "hooking up." The alcohol eases the anxiety and the underlying aversion to being used as a sexual commodity.

So how is the rest of the population faring? From *USA TODAY,* February 14, 2007. *Overflowing Prisons to Cost States $27.5B.* Present prison population in the nation is 1.53 million. Expect an increase of 13% in the next five years. The $27.5 billion is to build *additional* facilities and to meet the expense of housing the *additional* prisoners.

Following are some personal observations from years of volunteer jail ministry:

- Most of the men had not married or were not presently married even into their late 20s and their 30s.
- Many of these men are fathers, frequently having children by more than one woman.
- Female inmates are typically single mothers. To a high degree, their lives revolve around their children.
- A goodly number of inmates are suicidal. A few carry the scars of their intents.
- Inmates rarely have any practical knowledge of what makes for a good marriage and family.

The moral foundations that made America strong are being destroyed (if not already gone). Our justice system is overwhelmed with no relief in sight. The people we are locking up are not the elderly and infirm, but those whose brain power and strength are at their peak. What a positive force for good they might have been! Yet we are so dysfunctional that we fail to convey even the minimum standards by which these people may live free.

Our whole culture is tired. Tired of endless rounds of fraud, deception, and greed permeating businesses, political offices, and even churches. Tired of sound bites and silly answers to serious problems. Tired of the bad behavior of the celebrities who entertain us, and of highly paid sports heros who expose a rotten core. Tired of gang activity, domestic abuse, child abuse, and murder that squeeze into every community.

So let's define our problem for what it really is. First, animal-like behavior doesn't work for humans. Our most pressing social problems are moral and spiritual, (problems between us and God). Second, the longer the time and the further the retreat from God, the greater the damage.

And the third? Morals stand or fail together. This means that selective morality doesn't work. We would like to borrow from the ancient commandments, *thou shalt not steal,* and *thou shalt not kill,* to fix the rotten floor of crime and domestic violence. But our efforts are vain, so long as we ignore the leak in the roof. We teach this problem by unveiling another of the Ten Commandments, *Thou shalt not commit adultery.* (This includes every form of illicit sex).

Sexual sin is rampant; worldwide. Yet any thinking person should know that an intimacy as involved as sexual relationships is bound to have major repercussions. If this were not so, illicit sex wouldn't need to be artificially repackaged for pregnancy prevention and disease control (having accomplished neither). Violators would not live in fear of serial sexual partners. "Safe sex" would not be the deadliest myth on the planet, promoted by people who are blind to the consequences lurking in the very shadow of this pleasure.

We somehow twisted a wonderful gift from God, designed specifically for permanent marriage and procreation. We tried to reinvent it as an evolutionary toy, given to us from primate ancestry, destined for an adult Hollywood version of Mc Donald's Play land. Far from it. Rather, it is a gift from God. It merits obedience to God's instructions. It doesn't carry an "adult only" rating, but a far sterner one; "for marriage only." It *makes of twain one flesh.* It was designed to conceive babies. The man and woman who heed those instructions, reserve their bodies for marriage, and write their vows in permanent ink. They do indeed effectively organize peoples' lives. Their babies are wanted. They train their children in integrity, loyalty, and duty. The result is order, security, and freedom.

The man in this marriage will be rewarded. He will be a faithful and consistent provider for his wife and children. He has a powerful incentive to maintain a good work ethic, to pay off the mortgage, and to keep a well-maintained home. He exercises a healthy reserve with females other than his spouse. He knows a precious intimacy with his wife, a treasure that he cannot afford to lose. Bar hopping and criminal activity would come at a price he cannot afford. He sets the example on which the next generation can build. In the culture, he is a giver, not a taker. He models the biblical teaching, *"he that loveth his wife loveth himself."* He exalts the righteousness, that in turn, *exalteth a nation.*

In contrast, sexual immorality is a badly botched counterfeit. It bonds sexual partners shoddily and ends up straining and tearing at the very fabric of the relationship. Because *there is no fear of God before their eyes,* the sexually immoral can readily exercise the option of cheating in any other realm.

We see then, that there is no such thing as a standalone sexual revolution. It becomes a total cultural revolution. It has generated landfills of media garbage in the guise of entertainment. It has produced hordes of sexual addicts. It has left in its wake millions of ruined marriages, and millions more have dashed the potential of a good marriage. It has produced the gaping financial hole known as "welfare," which would more aptly be termed "poorfare." It has lined the pockets of pornographers, drug dealers, and pimps. It has made prisons a fast growth industry. It has desensitized people to murder, with the killing of more than 40 million of the tiniest U.S. citizens. It is the loathsome nesting ground for the dark deeds of sexual predators. It issues free tickets for AIDS and STD's.

That is why locking the door on sexual gratification outside of marriage (*thou shalt not commit adultery*), would be priceless. Would men be less happy and less fulfilled if they opened themselves to God's command? Not likely. If men were compelled to choose celibacy over marriage, family, and responsibility, would they? Not for long. But in the present culture of no moral judgments, men opt to steal their gratification. (So long as groceries are free, why buy the store?)

What these men don't understand is that a good marriage could save them from death, and is worth the "purchase price" many times over. The difference between **having women** versus **having a wife** is the difference between the endless lies of pretense, and the real treasure of a mate exclusively your own. It is also the difference between guilt and fulfillment.

The natural tendency of women seems to be focused more toward serving others, especially their own offspring. As a result, single mothers may be able to instill the same attitude in their daughters. Did you ever wonder why mothers and grandmothers raise the children, rather than fathers and grandfathers? Even so, in the absence of the responsible husband/father figure, the young women are easy prey to vile and abusive men, (as were their mothers before them).

The male children tend to run in packs. Unfortunately the young men are initiated into adulthood through the back alley, alongside their peers. They fall for the bait of "getting what I want for myself." But the man who grabs the pleasure without the price, will find that the pleasure came at the price of his own manhood. He may pay dearly in child support, but is left with no role in this tangle of relationships. The sad result is confused, angry, and often violent men, at odds with an ordered society, severed from real life challenges and responsibilities. Their sons in turn, grow up without their fathers, repeating the cycle.

There are compelling reasons why the groceries shouldn't be free. If a girl could be taught that she is well worth the price of waiting for marriage:

1. She will be spared being handled as cheap merchandise, with its trail of tears, fears and anxieties. She would not need to resort to alcohol and drugs.
2. Her focus on reaching adulthood could first be to serve her husband. She would then have a clear focus in mothering *their* children. This instead of the long, lonely, insecure road of "doing for *her* babies."
3. Children would be supported by their fathers instead of by the state (or left to fend for themselves).
4. The girls could avoid the "house of straw" syndrome. The hungry uncommited wolf thinks little of using,

abusing, and abandoning the easy prey, to move on to the next conquest. But some day, in a perverted sense of jealousy, he may double back for the kill. He can't stand the thought that she might be with another wolf.

It is true that in today's culture neither sex has been taught to wait. But I also believe that if "free groceries," (not only sex, but also welfare) were cut out, many men would resort to learning how to be decent husbands and fathers. Boys could again learn to become men by following their fathers' footsteps. This would start reversing the engines of negative social trends.

Just another thought. In today's shameless moral climate, many females look way too available. If we would reverse course, ladies will need to be decently clothed.

MY PEOPLE PERISH FOR LACK OF UNDERSTANDING

Across the land, we build some of the most spacious housing developments ever. They are built solidly, from the foundation up. Symbolically, such housing fits an ideal. But what kind of an ideal? Mafia headquarters? Animal shelters? Housing for pimps and prostitutes? Crack houses? Gay couples with adopted children? Divorcees, running boarding houses? Live-in pairs, on high alert against former lovers? No, a thousand times, no.

The outward show of such housing suggests the inward presence of a happily married couple. The spaciousness suggests that they will not be alone, that this house will be occupied with a growing family, and with the activities that effectively bring children into responsible adulthood.

But exit the fear of God and absolute morality. Bury these homes in trash culture by way of 24/7 media garbage. Bring on the booze, drugs, and illicit sex. The same housing developments spell great human tragedy, as they disintegrate into dens of iniquity.

Without God, understanding is lost. Human dignity is nothing. Nothing should matter. We shouldn't matter. What we do shouldn't matter. What people do to us shouldn't matter. Love and hatred, and truth and lies shouldn't be definable, let alone make any difference. We may have tried to live that way, but it doesn't work.

Ultimately, the most adamant atheist must create for himself a dual world; a fictional one where nothing should matter, and a real world where practically everything does matter. Search out the cross of Jesus Christ, the Son of God. We find there a love so great that people otherwise destined for eternal torment can find forgiveness, and cleansing from their sins. But in that cross, we also face a shuddering reality; that sin is unspeakably insulting to the character of God, and that apart from the cross of Jesus Christ, no one can be saved.

Have we awakened your conscience? You can further find your way with faith that comes from hearing the truth of the Bible.

Ye shall seek me and find me, when ye shall search for me with all your heart (Jeremiah 29:13).

The wages of sin is death, but the gift of God is eternal life through Jesus Christ our Lord (Romans 6:23).

LET MY PEOPLE THINK

People in our nation are sharply divided on moral issues.

Multitudes are dismayed, unsettled, even fearful of the social changes that sweep our nation. Others are bent on creating a moral free zone where nothing is sacred and nothing is censored.

The removal of the Ten Commandments and other religious reminders from the public square are hailed as truly liberating by some. Others view it as the last gasp of a dying culture.

Practices like abortion and gay issues, once considered sinful or at least punishable by law, are now protected by law. Is this because of genuine concern for a legitimate separation of church and state? Or is this the replacement of the Christian world view and traditional morality, with an atheistic world view and relativism? What do you think?

Is all this merely a needless clash of wills and opinions?

I think not. I propose that there are only two options in these disagreements.

The First Possibility. There never have been true moral absolutes (things truly neither right nor wrong). Things like smoking pot, drunkenness, gambling, lying, premarital sex, adultery, divorce, abortion, and homosexuality, never did matter. American consensus and American law was simply misguided for 200 years. *(To be consistent we must say misguided, for how could it have been wrong, where nothing is wrong?) In this view, religious reminders need to be removed, and past social taboos should be forgotten. Let's call this *subjective truth,* changeable according to personal or cultural preference.

The Second Possibility. The old morality of God consciousness, of truthfulness, of honest labor, of respect for authority, of wholesome entertainment, of sexual restraint, of permanent marriage, of modest clothing (clothing that actually covers), of sanctity of life (abortion would rightly be tagged murder), and of love of family and children came with the territory (like an instruction manual), as an inherent part of being human.

This second option would mean that moral standards are not for us to pick and choose, and that they are over us, because they are not human inventions at all. This is called *objective* or *absolute truth,* an unmoving basic standard of right and wrong, for all people, for all time.

Is there evidence for objective (absolute) truth?

Let's be sure we understand the terms. If we talk about subjective truth, we are into personal preferences; as in strawberry versus vanilla ice cream, or Ford versus Chevy trucks, or an Arizona winter versus a Florida winter, or which toppings make for the best pizza. Fine; take your pick.

However, there are many areas where preference doesn't work. We are stuck in absolute mode every day in our natural world. We can set the alarm according to preference, but we have no power to change the sunrise. We can ski down the slope in cooperation with gravity, but the return is by ski lift. If we desire tomatoes from the garden, we don't get them by planting turnip seeds. (We reap what we sow.)

You can design your house according to your subjective preferences, but the building codes will specify absolute minimum requirements for your foundations and materials. (There will be inspectors, to make sure you comply). And even your preferences must take on absolute form. Until you decide on specific dimensions, layout, and the specific construction materials, your construction project will go nowhere.

Likewise, you are truth bound on the highway system. If you merely preferred that the light were green, or preferred that the truck was not coming across your lane through the busy intersection, your preferences could cost your life. Your preferences will not change the outcome.

In fact, nature is one huge sky high case for objective truth. The unseen laws of nature command an unwavering consistency into the whole life support system of this planet we call earth. This simply means that the things of nature, that we do see, are bounded and controlled by laws of nature that we cannot see. We should then, admit that there could exist a parallel set of God-given moral laws that would govern the deeds of all people. I propose that this not only *could* be, but that it really *should* be the case. There could hardly be a better plan, than that divine order should govern the affairs of men. The very order and well-being of people cultures depend on it. Keep in mind; it is not only in our gardens, that we reap what we sow.

The basis for subjective morality

The best possible case for subjective morality is the theory of evolution. It is a theory that is totally worthless and therefore ignored in the advancement of science, discovery, and invention. It is, in fact, contrary to scientific advancement. If nature were in flux as would be consistent with an ongoing roll of evolutionary dice, there would be no "laws" of nature.

The sole attraction of the theory is the fact that it presents the opportunity to deny divine authority. It dismisses out of hand any accountability to any being higher than we. It is the highly prized excuse to dismantle all traditional morality. This is so because it is impossible to assign permanent morality to anything, based on an evolutionary beginning. As has been observed, "without God anything is permissible."

It is noteworthy the even a theory claiming evolution could not itself evolve. It took the intelligent mind of Darwin to postulate ideas of how his own intellect came from no intelligence at all. Generally, those who believe in evolution, think that somewhere there are brilliant scientists (perhaps intently scrutinizing test tubes in musty labs), who have the inside track of vital evidence in support of the theory. In fact, nobody does. If you know someone who does, *please let me know.*

In light of advanced scientific understanding, even atheists like Anthony Flew, over awed by the known complexity and symmetry of nature, are in danger of backsliding from their denial of the Creator.

What we see is not the result of a cosmic roll of dice. Consider that millions of necessary factors are "just right" for life on this planet. It has been pointed out that if the universe had a control room, and we could observe it, every dial in the how-many-miles-long, control panel, would be found in just the optimum setting for life to flourish on planet earth. So highly ordered and so complex is the makeup of even a single living thing, and its support system, that scientifically speaking, the proposed, nothing + time + chance theory of evolution earns but a single adjective — *impossible*.

Perhaps the idea of God frightens you.

Someone has said that there either is a God — or there isn't. Either prospect is frightening. But seriously, what we can know about God as introduced in nature, and made known in the Bible is indeed worthy of fear. Factor together what is known of the universe; the intrinsic power, the sheer magnitude, the genius of design, the abundance of living things, the resplendent beauty, the telescopic vastness, the microscopic minuteness, and all its glory, then what must its Designer and Maker be like? What will it be like, when we personally stand before this God?

So high is the probability (if you can even call it that), that the God of nature is also God of the Bible, that there is no excuse for any thinking person, not to believe in the commonality of both. Suddenly, it is neither judgmental, bigoted, nor presumptuous to believe that the Creator God *does* reign supreme. Shall we who are made of dust by the divine hand and made alive by the breath of God, presume to choose our religion as though it were just another flavor of ice cream? Is it really too much to expect that this God has a special purpose (as he claims), for people in his world? Is it too much to claim that human dignity has no parallel in an ape swinging through the trees, or in a kennel with the dogs, or in a bug that has just spattered your windshield?

Is it not beneath the intelligence and grace of human dignity to live as though by animal instinct, to surrender to lust and passion, and to live as liars, thieves, rapists, murderers, and sodomites? Is there even such a thing as satisfaction without restraint, or love without commitment? Shall we live in a God-ordered universe as though there were no God?

Is it farfetched to believe that we have lost our way in social order, in politics, in ethics, in marriage (as in one male and one female), as in all moral standards, without the revelation of God? Is it possible that without the order of the Holy Scriptures, we are caught in violation and consequences of spiritual laws as sure and as unyielding as the law of gravity? Shall we not believe that God is angry with our pseudo intellectual arrogance, and that sin and rebellion against this God shall be punished with everlasting fire in a place the Bible calls hell?

Can we even survive without the Ten Commandments of God to show us our need, or without His Son Jesus Christ to redeem us from that need?

Are these questions important enough for you to find the answers? If so, read on as we pursue further evidence.

*I don't understand why subjective moralists get so upset with those who believe in moral absolutes. The worst that could be said about the absolute moralist, is that he has inferior tastes, for example, that he really should prefer chocolate ice cream.

THE HUMAN CONSCIENCE

One of my greatest delights is in presenting the case for Christian faith to those who do not believe. The reason for this is really quite simple. I happen to know that I already have an ally inside that individual. We call that ally "conscience." (The conscience once and for all sets people apart from dogs, crocodiles, chickens headed for the barbecue, hummingbirds, tigers, mosquitos, green grass, and zebras.)

The fact of conscience is easily proved. True, the conscience can be misinformed, dulled, or even seared (a biblical term). However, the conscience is an ally to moral absolutes. The noisiest advocates against traditional morality still insist on retaining at least a few absolutes, if only to use against other people. People who steal still insist that it is wrong for others to steal from them. Liars have convictions against being lied to. All but the most vocal advocates of free love still know that love is by its very nature, exclusive. They know that sexual promiscuity is merely taking advantage of another, the exact opposite of love. That is why committing adultery puts intolerable stress on a marriage. It is also the reason why committing fornication or adultery is one of the most hazardous occupations on earth. Sexual cheats end up getting abused, beaten, or killed.

We are saying then, that even while people do wrong, they still retain a standard of righteousness within.

Conscience is hardly something we would invent. It keeps giving feelings of guilt and unsolicited advice. It may insist that I've been unkind to my wife, when I don't appreciate that bit of information. The conscience makes the embezzler nervous, and causes the thief to watch his back even when none pursue. Even at its lowest ebb, it still acts like a smoke detector, sniffing out and condemning (or suing), the wrongs of others. Isn't that where jealousy and anger come from? Isn't it because someone has violated the perceived moral space of another?

Indeed, in a world teeming with all kinds of animal life, we human beings face a unique dilemma. Recently in our area, wolves attacked and killed an old work horse. Do you suppose that those wolves are now conscience stricken with their attack on an innocent horse? Will the larger wolf community bring these renegades to justice? Do you suppose those killer wolves will be sentenced to ten years as vegetarians (or five for good behavior), by the wolf judge? Our minds may deny certain moral absolutes, but the conscience refuses to comply. We keep on living as though there really *is* a standard of right and wrong. We maintain court systems. We crave justice. We want to see evildoers punished. Why? It is because of the way we were made. Our Creator God has that orientation for justice — perfectly.

WHAT IS SIN?

As a woodworker, I well know about the beautiful piece of cherry wood that looks so useable, until the perfect standard (my tape measure), proves it to be an inch short for the intended purpose.

So it is with morals. I look so "right," at least in a world where many do things much worse than anything I have ever done. I would never lie or cheat — not on the grand scale that so many do. I may seem far removed from murder and adultery - but what about hatred and lust?

We have a conscience that still approves good; we do good deeds for others all the time, and we leave the really bad stuff to others.

That makes us pretty good people, right? Wrong. May I suggest that we move beyond the comparison of small or great sins into the glare of the perfect standard.

Adam was created perfect in a perfect world, by the perfect God. But there was a day when Adam and Eve parted company with perfection. They ate the forbidden fruit. This was the day sin entered into the world, and death because of sin. Sin is the transgression of God's law. Every death is confirmation that sin is at work in every one of us.

We all have the same problem: There is none righteous, no not one. All have sinned and come short of the glory of God. The analogy of the cherry board and sin breaks down in this respect. The board was good. Sooner or later it will serve in another project. Not so with sin. Sin is an inward problem, making sinners unfit for the kingdom of God.

Are you ready for the test? The law is God's perfect standard. We don't go to the Ten Commandments to discover how good we are. Rather we find there that we need forgiveness and salvation.

I. Thou shalt have no other Gods before me.
II. Thou shalt not make unto thee any graven image.
III. Thou shalt not take the name of the Lord thy God in vain.
IV. Remember the Sabbath day to keep it holy.
V. Thou shalt honor thy Father and thy mother.
VI. Thou shalt not kill.
VII. Thou shalt not steal.
VIII. Thou shalt not commit adultery.
IX. Thou shalt not bear false witness.
X. Thou shalt not covet.

You may deny that there is a God in the heaven, and claim that these laws don't matter. But the fact that many people have faith that God doesn't exist will change nothing. With all the evidence of objective truth in nature, is it not foolish to deny the authority of these moral absolutes?

On the other hand, any sober reflection on the above commandments is bound to bring two conclusions:

First, obedience to these laws would make for very good cultural practices. Talk about secure, clean living neighborhoods! If people could obey these laws, we would be forced to turn prisons into factories.

Secondly, when we are tried on a personal level, on every count we would hear; "guilty, guilty, guilty." We realize that we have probably have broken *every* commandment, especially when we understand that God's holiness equates hatred with murder, and lust with adultery. We must conclude that it is humanly impossible to keep these commandments, and that therefore we all come under condemnation and judgment as sinners.

THERE IS ONLY ONE ANSWER

The wages of sin is death, but the gift of God is eternal life through Jesus Christ our Lord. Once we agree with God on the hopelessness of our condition, the answer is nearby. God has, in Christ, provided for us to be saved from our sins. This is what the Bible says:

- Repent, and be baptized every one of you for the remission of sins and ye shall receive the remission of sin. (God calls all men everywhere to repent.)
- Believe on the Lord Jesus Christ and thou shalt be saved.
- That if thou shalt confess with thy mouth the Lord Jesus, and shalt believe in thine heart that God hath raised him from the dead, thou shalt be saved.
- If ye continue in my word, then are ye my disciples indeed. And ye shall know the truth and the truth shall make you free.

SUGGESTED BIBLE READINGS

Genesis 1-3; Exodus 20; John 1-3; Acts 1-2; Romans 5-8; Matthew 2This Christian message brought to you, is specifically designed for a cross-cultural exposure to the essence of the Christian faith. Its purpose is to build faith in the God of heaven and earth. We are persuaded that He is eternally and vibrantly alive.

We further believe that only in Jesus Christ can we know God, and the reality of eternal life.

We do understand if you first find this material to be disturbing and upsetting. It is indeed unsettling to consider that we are here by design, and not by chance, and that our lives are wrong before the holy God. We would like to comfort you with the fact that the people sharing this with you have been in that same place of condemnation over the very same problem, which the Bible calls sin.

Be assured that once we have reached that place of condemnation, and the cry of the heart is for deliverance, then God's mercy is truly at hand.

For God so loved the world, that he gave his only begotten Son, that whosoever believeth on him, should not perish, but have everlasting life (John 3:16).

THINK ON THESE THINGS

From a news letter just received, I learned that an airline captain from Atlanta had found a sticker in the front of a Gideon Bible placed in his Salt Lake City hotel room, carrying the disclaimer in the box:

This book contains religious stories regarding the origin of living things. The stories are theories, not facts. They are unproven, unprovable, and in some cases totally impossible. This material should be approached with an open mind, and a critical eye towards logic and believability.

Obviously, if the Bible cannot be trusted on the origin of living things, then the moral authority of the Bible is itself in question. Now one would expect that when biblical morality is rejected, people would no longer believe strongly about anything. In fact, they have no reason to. Those who hold that there is no absolute moral authority, should have no problem with anything that anyone would choose to believe.

For some unreasonable reason, it doesn't work that way. Instead of believing in nothing, people will believe in anything. Take a look at what is deemed most important in our own community. Is it godliness, faithfulness and integrity in marriage, family, children, and business, or is it shopping, dining, drinking and illicit sex (while relationships designed to last, are falling apart)? What does happen is that we become people who major on minors. We mistake pleasure for satisfaction, and think that indulgence will bring peace. We reject the notion of moral authority from God, and then whip up religious zeal over secondary causes. We drift to the opposite of what we were created to be.

I'm not suggesting that current local issues, like power lines, forest management, and preservation of historical sites are unimportant. What I am saying is that we lose our way in the lesser issues, because we have rejected the Christian moral compass in the greater causes. Too often our zeal and devotion are spent on environmental issues and our tears fall for old trees or old buildings. Are we then the same people who are cold and unmoved by the breakup of marriage and family, the termination of the lives of the unborn, and the many lives scarred in tender years with sexual and physical abuse, because of irresponsible parenting?

Consider the the wisdom and insight of some from the black community. A black woman stepped forward to give her counsel on the same - sex parenting debate. She said that they had tried it already in the black community for a few generations (mother and grandmother), and that it doesn't work. She should know. Nothing makes this plainer than the sad results of a 70% illegitimacy rate.

A black man who has done well as an educator, interviewed for a magazine, said this; *If you have a good family with a mother and a father, as I did - and most of the people in the community where I grew up did - you didn't need these (government) programs.* Is not the opposite equally true?

When we substitute, *Thou shalt kill*, with *thou shalt not cut down trees*, or, *Thou shalt not commit adultery,* with, *thou shalt not tear down old buildings*, or when we equate dog life with human life, we will indeed merely go in big circles, lost forever in the woods of bad logic.

The substitutes for the logic and believability of the Bible are not working. The energies that should fortify marriage, family, church, and community, must be expended instead in adding jail cells, running treatment and abuse centers, and managing and paying for the welfare system. And the cost in human failure, misery, and lost potential, are beyond the power of calculation.

We are trading the freedom, prosperity, and peace of being God-fearing, for the "security" of bars and locks to save the culture from corporate thieves, burglars, rapists, and murderers.

You can choose for now to claim that the Bible is outdated and unbelievable - and wander in the woods. Or - you can assume that the creation account of Genesis introduces us to the God with whom nothing is impossible. I have pon-

DEFINING GOD DOWNWARD

A late, notable U.S. senator once addressed the negative social changes sweeping the nation as "defining deviancy downward." Such a statement is at once both intriguing and alarming. The implications are twofold. First, it suggests that standards of decency are folding, even as the social taboos of the past gain acceptance. But even more seriously, it implies a foundational shifting of moral/ethical standards. Unfortunately, such a foundational shift knows no stopping place. No anchor remains to preserve a commonality of decency.

Another former senator has written under the title, *A Nation Adrift.* He suggests that the drift is the result of leaving the Christian heritage, especially the hope of salvation in Christ, for "salvation through technology, or science, or material affluence, or the welfare state." I believe recent developments confirm such a shift. Where Christian faith was once the mainstay of American, constituting what the Supreme Court called a "Christian" nation, the focus shifted, and we tried to anchor ourselves in education, material affluence, and pleasure. However, these things are insufficient keepers of morals and ethics, and we became easy prey for lower standards. Personally, I believe that Elvis Presley, and then the Beatles, were the apostles of the rebellion and immorality gospel.

I would submit that the downward shift in decency has its parallel in an even more serious shift, that of defining God downward. Perhaps for many, deviancy was acceptable because God had been left undefined. But in a nation where possibly 80% would identify as "Christian," there has to be a tremendous void in understanding between what God is like, versus the perception we have of God. It works like this. The way we live, and the things we do, correlate exactly with what we truly believe about God.

This has been the trade off - the stocks of prosperity are being inflated upward, while stock in God was defined downward, finally to be relegated out of social and political relevance. God may be acknowledged in the Sunday worship hour, only to be totally ignored in our ways, our doings, and our relationships through the rest of the week. That is where we miss it. We may not mock God. Without God, we accumulate knowledge, but lose the key to wisdom. Catering to the lusts of our bodies has robbed us of virtue. A greedy pursuit of wealth has robbed us of ethics and integrity. The anchor for a yacht cannot anchor the spirit of the man. The most glamorous cruises will never dock at the shores of heaven. The greatest fillet mignon will but mock the hunger pangs of the soul. This is the spiritual vacuum that so many Americans have been drawn into. It cycles ever lower, through booze, drugs, pornography, violence, and illicit sex. Yet, much of this actually goes on under the "Christian" label.

Let's imagine for a moment, a "Christian" bank robber. He could rob a bank based on the following:
1. He doesn't believe God will recognize him behind his face mask.
2. He thinks that a loving God would not punish him, because he "accepted Christ" when he was ten years old.
3. He thinks God will be pleased if he gives a generous portion to the church.

Absurd? Absolutely, but please don't laugh. Just replace "bank robber," with a hundred other sins Christians are caught in, and the reasons are the same:
1. God doesn't see.
2. God forgives because I am a Christian.
3. I can always make amends by doing something good.

The outlook is bleak. How will a ship without chart, compass, or anchor, ride out the gale? How can it enter a safe harbor?

What we have described is clearly a case of what the Bible calls perilous times. Perhaps you thought the devious course of the past few generations has been thoughtfully and carefully charted out in the light of superior knowledge gained through technological advances and scientific method. Nothing could be further from the truth. We are rather riding out the results of defining God downward.

The fact is, any culture that shuns the knowledge of God will but ride its own lies and cheap substitutes down into oblivion. This phenomenon is clearly described in the Bible (Romans 1:8-32), of which we take space to quote snatches. It well describes every horror we face in western civilization.

Because that, when they knew God, they glorified him not as God, neither were thankful; but became vain in their imaginations and their foolish heart was darkened. Professing themselves to be wise, they became fools, and changed the glory of the incorruptible God into an image made like corruptible man, and to birds, and four-footed beasts, and creeping things. Wherefore God also gave them up to uncleanness . . . and even as they did not like to retain God in their knowledge, God gave them over to a reprobate mind . . . Being filled with all unrighteousness . . . Who knowing the judgment of God, that they which commit such things are worthy of death, not only do the same, but have pleasure in them that do them.

We may define God downward in our minds, but we cannot ever change him. He is, and eternally will be, the only true God. The whole of creation is his. We are personally in his hands. He cannot be impeached, or removed from office. He is best and biblically described as the "Holy God." In him is no moral or ethical wavering. He is Truth personified. His commandments come to us based in his character. God will not change and he cannot lose. In forgetting, we are the losers.

This brings us to our present lostness. In departing from God, we take the liberty to define our wishes as to what God should be like. He allows us to misinterpret him, or even to explain him out of existence. He does not interfere with our ingratitude as we foolishly misinterpret his creative powers as chance processes of evolution in our biology texts. He allows us to value whales, eagles, and spotted owls over our own babies. He permits the cheap substitute of lust for love, popularity for character, money and material things for the peace and security of living in his will.

We have, (even in the churches), come a long way in substituting the good and certain ways of God for the false destructive ways of godlessness. The challenge is whether it is still possible to call a nation to repentance, beginning with "the house of God" (Christians).

Will we stir ourselves to lay hold on God?

God is patient. He is merciful. Yet ultimately, he is indeed the God of justice. His judgment will prove his intolerance of both sin and sinners. Judgment will show that bringing God low was only in our imagination. He will be exalted – eternally.

THREE VIEWS OF THE CHURCH

This article is not about shades of variation within various church denominations. (For example, within Protestantism, infant baptism is practiced by some. Others baptize only on a personal profession of faith. Some baptize by sprinkling or pouring, while others baptize with immersion). Rather, I am describing three distinct views of the church itself, and how these ideas relate to the concept of personal salvation. These are the Catholic, the Protestant, and the Anabaptist views.

I write with candor, as the best possible front for the exchange of ideas. But I also write with a certain trepidation, knowing that generalizations will not do justice to every reader. And while I try to be objective, I also come from the personal framework of my own understanding as an Anabaptist. But more importantly, I write with a goal. May you the reader, identify your own place in church life in light of the Scriptures. As this sparks your interest, may the light of truth be your guide. In other words, the goal is to accommodate our own ways to biblical truth.

Finally, this is also written within the time frame of hundreds of years into history. It is easier to capture beliefs as they emerged, rather than trying to sift through all the core beliefs today.

I am not ascribing to the modern readers, all the core doctrines of their own denominational history. Some of those beliefs have changed over the centuries. For example, many Catholics make more of personal faith than the church may have required in times past. And unlike Reformation times, practically all Protestants believe in voluntary church membership (these would abhor the idea of persecuting those who disagree). To a large degree, most Protestants and Catholics also believe in a clear separation of church and state.

The Anabaptists (where I find my identity as a Mennonite), had quite a checkered history. In the context of its beginning, any "Christian" who was not Catholic or Protestant, would come under the label of "Anabaptist." Anabaptism did indeed have some unsavory fringe elements, which at times distorted the overall view of Anabaptist identity.

THE FIRST VIEW   CATHOLICISM

The Catholic system dominated Christianity from the time of the early 4th century, when the Roman Emperor, Constantine embraced Christianity, and made it the official state religion (hence *Roman* Catholic Church). It continued as the prevailing religious body, until the challenge of the Reformation in the early 16th century.

Catholicism is what is known as a sacramental system. This means that the salvation of the individual is accomplished and sustained by various rites through the church. It is centered on the authority of the church bestowing salvation and forgiveness of sin on the individual. The sacraments are natural elements such as water for baptism, and wafers and wine for the mass, with the priesthood as the go-between for God and the individual. As applied and blessed by the priest, these elements are to convey spiritual, even supernatural powers of grace to the recipient.

The first sacrament is the baptism of infants. The infant is saved into the church by this sacrament. Without this, he is counted lost. The essential element for adults is the mass. The bread and the wine are believed to literally change into the body and the blood of Jesus Christ (called transubstantiation) – thus imparting the life of Christ to the recipient. Catholics are expected to faithfully adhere to the doctrines of the church, for example, the celibacy of the priesthood, and the renouncing of birth control and abortion. They are also expected to go to confession, and to do penance when they fail.

The term Catholic means universal. Through its millennian as a world power, Catholicism was to be embraced by the entire population under its domain.

In summery, Catholic salvation is facilitated through the church.

THE SECOND VIEW   PROTESTANTISM

Protestantism came in with a hammer – Martin Luther, the priest, nailing a list of 95 Catholic excesses, to the church door at Wittenburg, Germany in 1517. At almost the same time, Ulrich Zwingli, a powerful pastor, started the Reformed church movement in Zurich, Switzerland.

The intent of these men was not so much to leave Catholicism, as to protest and correct its excesses, with the hope of change. And change did indeed happen, on a scale that they didn't anticipate.

Actually, change was already in the air. The Renaissance created an atmosphere of enlightenment, and of learning, of openness to change, and revealing what had been hidden. To a large degree, people started to assert their own ideas of truth and justice. Due to a long decline of morals and integrity, Catholicism was in trouble from within. With this background, plus popular support, Luther and Zwingi soon faced a break with Rome, followed by the Protestant Reformation.

The strength of Protestantism was in preaching. The Bible had been hidden from the masses for a millennium. Now it read and expounded – from the pulpit. Salvation took on a personal dimension. The church did not have the power to save. Every individual needed to be personally saved through faith in Jesus Christ. The sacraments were valid only as every person had his own faith. The reformers basically accomplished what they had set out to do – to clean up the excesses that had crept into Catholicism – but now under their own umbrella.

Yet major flaws remained. Protestantism still embraced the power of government to gain its ends. Despite the emphasis of justification by faith, the reformers were adamant on working to gain their ends through sympathetic city counsels and civil rulers, and to coerce people into believing. Thus personal justification by faith, was not so personal after all. Entire populations were simply swept into the Protestant fold as Catholic authority was forced into retreat. The rising tide of Protestantism failed to lift the individual boats – the gains in genuine conversion and moral uplift were minimal. In summary, Protestant emphasis goes to faithful preaching and individual justification by faith.

THE THIRD VIEW   ANABAPTISM

In Switzerland, certain scholars; followers of Zwingli, moved from loyalty to disenchantment. Their champion obviously knew that the Zurich city counsel should not dictate the practices of the church. They knew, for instance, that Zwingli did not believe in infant baptism. They were disappointed in the fact that when the council would not be moved by Zwingli's preaching, the reformer backed away from his earlier Biblical positions.

These students had envisioned in Zwingli, the man who would free the church from the state. They would not embrace a partial reformation. They had a vision to see the church restored to New Testament status. When Zwingli failed to work this change, they debated him. When he entrenched himself in favor of union with the government, and against these former friends, the break was inevitable.

Restoration to the New Testament concept of the church was not impossible. But it came at an awful cost. In January, 1525, a small band of men, including Conrad Greble, Felix Manz, and George Blaurock, held their own service and baptized each other. Thus the Anabaptist church was born. These adult baptisms signaled two things; a personal profession of faith in Jesus Christ for the remission of sin, and voluntary entry into discipleship and Christian brotherhood.

From this meager beginning, these men went on to preach the gospel, and baptizing those who responded. These Anabaptists, rejected infant baptism because it had nothing in common with repentance and faith. They also rejected the sword, and any political alliances, as contrary to Christian discipleship. The depth of commitment and the sincerity of the Christian lifestyle made them very effective missionaries. But the powers of Europe responded with persecution and bloodbath against these defenseless people. Anabaptist "chasers," roamed the countryside. Many were captured, tortured and imprisoned. Thousands died for their faith.

Anabaptism? They called themselves brethren. (They were labeled Anabaptists for their because of their "rebaptism" as adults). They joined no political front. They sought no earthly kingdom. They stood for personal holiness and purity of life. They gave themselves to communion and correction from within the church, among believers, and by believers. They embraced brotherhood, the concept that Christians are members one of another. Under challenge and opposition, Anabaptism tends to refine itself. Let it condone wrongdoing among its members, it taints itself, and destroys its effectiveness. If armed with a political agenda, and a sword of steel, it would destroy itself.

In summary, the Anabaptist emphasis is on personal conversion, and life in the context of brotherhood. It promotes the two kingdom concept, of which the practical results are defenselessness, nonconformity, and separation from worldliness (living in the world, without being of the world).

PAVING THE WAY TO PERVERSION

And even as they did not like to retain God in their knowledge, God gave them over to a reprobate mind to do those things that are not convenient. Romans 1:28.

Human dignity has been degraded, yet again, in recent court rulings (2004), in both the U.S. and Canada. In the recent legalization of homosexual marriage, a Canadian court has ruled against the 1999 Canadian government affirmation that marriage is the union of one man and one woman. It is a decision not likely to be appealed.

In the meantime, the U. S. Supreme Court has struck down state anti sodomy laws. In so doing, they have severed current law from the moral code which was recognized and incorporated by state legislatures, from the founding days of the nation. These laws were a last stopgap reminder of a human moral obligation to do what is right, over doing as we please. This is the only way to the right outcome. (To illustrate, what would happen if the courts would not only legalize bank robbery, but would even sponsor training programs for robbers, starting, for example, in first grade.) Yet the courts have been striking down laws, and then protecting the very things that had been criminal acts, giving us license to degrade ourselves even further in the nether regions of moral perversion, and thus to destroy ourselves.

We may find ways to change the laws, and legally walk away from transgressions in our respective countries. However, this is mere self-deception, for it changes nothing at all in the court of God.

But let's take this opportunity to see how we got to this point. We have, in fact, been handing the courts this power by embracing the so-called sexual revolution. This revolution spawned a total social revolution. "Free love" comes to demand sexual intimacy without consideration of marriage, reproduction, or sexually transmitted diseases.

That is how we became a birth-control culture. Margaret Sanger was a fierce proponent of sex education and birth-control (think Planned Parenthood). She actually fled the country for a time, because her promotions were illegal. But this subculture soon came to dominate our increasingly hedonistic value system.

But this is also how we became a divorce culture. Who wants to be stuck with making the first marriage work when you meet so many other attractive possibilities along the way? The courts complied. Anyone who wants a divorce can surely get one, with no grounds and no stigma attached.

But, we still had problems by the millions. It's called unwanted pregnancies. Birth control wasn't doing the job. The failure rate has a way of overtaking those who are so free to exercise their passions. This is what led to *abortion on demand.* This moral free - fall society needed abortion as the failsafe of the anti-child, anti-procreation mentality. Again, winning this development was dependant on the courts. In *Roe* versus *Wade*, the courts legalized a huge chunk of homicide, which has by now decimated the city of the unborn by forty to fifty *million* people.

We do have a host of other negative consequences for which there are no easy fixes. Legal decisions can't fix rampant sexually transmitted disease, physically and sexually abused children, battered or murdered sexual partners, monstrous welfare expenditures, and soaring crime rates. These are all price and parcel of the sexual revolution.

So now we see how the courts have come to take on issues that don't belong to them. Rather than focusing on how to justly apply established moral laws and freedoms under God, the moral principles themselves are put on trial. But beyond that, it has also made shambles of our moral code. In this departure from absolute standards, all moral principles can, and likely will be, challenged. The few social taboos that are left, such as child pornography and pedophilia are merely lacking politically-correct timing and support. Pleasure and convenience have taken precedence over responsibility, and unbridled hormones have won over dignity and self control.

Thus the legalization of sodomite relations and same sex marriage needed merely to await acceptance and timing in this new world order of non reproductive sex.

In fact, redefinition of marriage is mere pretense. There is no essential difference in gay marriages, versus group marriage, man-boy marriage, or incestuous marriage. If there is no overriding standard for marriage, then what is the basis for any restrictions?

In fact, the rules of marriage could be changed only in relation to their origin, that is, if God was mistaken, and if it was our responsibility to correct course. But the biological interdependence of male and female for reproductive capacity, and what happens to those offspring, are in themselves a decisive clue that the rules and institution of marriage are not to be tampered with.

Claiming legitimacy, for same-sex unions is discriminatory. It flaunts what is against nature, as though it were natural. It boldly claims that the value of that relationship is no different from that of the traditional marriage. It stakes this claim on the wrong-headed notion that all desires have the same claim to gratification. It assumes the "right" to sexual fulfillment with none of the inherent responsibility of children, family, and future generations. It claims sexual orientation as a civil rights issue, on par with race or gender. And apparently, it even claims that what one desires sexually, trumps biology itself - the gender one was born with.

Same sex marriage is a contradiction of terms. It is on par with Christian atheist, flat earth scientist, or living fossil. It demands the legitimacy of marriage, and the benefits of marriage, all without fulfilling the obligations of marriage. At best, it could be compared to counterfeit money. The counterfeit does not negate the value of the genuine, but it is dead weight on the economy. Now you could claim that your counterfeit money should have some value because of the time and investment you put into producing it. But don't take that claim to court, it will probably get you prison time.

In parallel, so long as we truly respected the divine origin and order for the human family, there was no way western civilization could descend to the present state. We couldn't equate the marriage of male and female, with same sex relationships on any level. We couldn't pretend the differences of the male with his female, could equate to the sameness, and the deadness of the male and his male partner, or the female and her female partner.

The biblical record, supported by the well-defined trail of civilized history, is that life and marriage, came from the same source and the same time. In the Genesis record, it is God who formed the male, closely followed by making the female. Within this process of creation, he fashioned them for reproduction. God presented Eve to Adam, being exclusively his own, and charged this pair – *"be fruitful, and multiply, and replenish the earth."* Furthermore, he was not to put her away (Matthew 19:3-6). This is the introduction to marriage and the human family. This is one man, married to one woman, who together bring up their children. This is called family. It is also called civilization. Its opposite is called barbarism. To those who can't appreciate the pattern, traditional marriages and families are the sole carriers of civilization (remember, counterfeits are a drag on civilization), and the sole reason why the human race has survived to this day. The populating of the whole world depended on that first couple, and from following the God-given directive to this day. Every baby born into the world (even those born out of wedlock), is confirmation of the moral and the social necessity of the traditional, permanent marriage union.

This is heart and soul of any nation. Have we in the churches so cheapened and disgraced marriage with adulteries and divorces, and despised the gift of children, that we are now subjected even to changing the definition of marriage? We might have been so blessed, and might have been a light to the nation, in fully embracing the moral laws of God. *"For ye know what commandments we gave you by the Lord Jesus. For this is the will of God, even your sanctification, that ye should abstain from fornication: That everyone of you should know how to possess his vessel in sanctification and honor; not in the lust of concupiscence, even as the Gentiles which know not God"* (I. Thessalonians 4:2-4).

The black and white of the moral code, given of God, is not a burden, but a favor. It is a gift from God. It is the sure foundation for all of history, including all generations of Americans. Even those who wish it were otherwise are blessed by those who are truly married. They have no idea how dark and confusing the world becomes when we exalt our opinions against the unchanging law of God, and then reap the dire consequences.

So let's quit pretending that bad is good, and good is bad. Our social ills only multiply as the last barriers against perverted forms of sexual expression are attacked.

One might suppose that in all this, we have, or are in the process of destroying the institution of marriage.

Not so. Alas, we only destroy ourselves. The rock of marriage is God's institution, and as such, is indestructible. Till the end of time, there will be people who believe, and who will do the will of God in marriage. And they will be blessed.

HOW WILL THIS HOUSE STAND?
(A PARABLE)

Back in 1776, a new "house" was built. The foundational principles on which this "house" was planned was very different from any other known houses of the day.

The architects of this house envisioned a safe haven for the oppressed, the downtrodden, and the persecuted peoples, from various nations and kingdoms across the world.

In the older European "houses" of that day, individuals were not permitted to serve God according to the dictates of their own conscience. Those European houses operated under one dominant religion. The house of your birth was the house of your religion as it was with your parents before you. Your baptism within days of your birth had nothing to do with personal choice or personal faith. It did have everything to do with powers of those who ruled over the combined Church/State scheme of things. In those days the church free from the constraints of the state, and the state free from religious powers was unknown.

In contrast, those who designed this new "house" had a vision that transcended that narrowness of constraint and coercion in church affiliation. They believed that people of varying religious persuasions should and could still get along in the community and in the marketplace. When Sunday came along, the people of this new house could go different directions to the church of their choice. They did not believe that a person should be persecuted or put to death for being a Lutheran (for example), in one "house," or for being Catholic in another. (Persecutions and executions were very common occurrences in the Europe of Reformation and post-Reformation times.) "Christians" were killing Christians, if you can figure that out.

This does not mean that the architects of our "house" were anti religion, or anti Christian. Far from it. They didn't tell you *where* to go to church on Sunday. (They did close the doors, to going shopping on Sundays). They knew that freedom is not borne nor maintained in a vacuum. Freedom in the household, they said, was an endowment of the *Supreme Builder of Houses* (to paraphrase the Declaration of Independence). They also knew that freedom could never be maintained on a self-indulgent philosophy. The household they envisioned could succeed and prosper only on a high level of personal integrity, and absolute moral principles.

That is why, as the house was built, moral absolutes were laid like steel reenforcement throughout the structure. Many notable government buildings reflect this concept, with engravings of the Ten Commandments and other biblical passages.

Furthermore the *Rules Committee* of the house, continued to affirm, at least through 1931, that the reenforcements in the house were decidedly Christian, and that the Bible is a part of the common law of the house. (Their particular definition of "Christian" is a debatable point with this writer, but it was the documented official position of the house, as defined by the *Rules Committee.)*

And the house did prosper. Since the days of Solomon, it is not likely that any house was so blessed, so exalted, and so sought after. From all over the world, people came for the security and the freedoms of the new house. The great majority respected the *Ten Rules of Conduct* as had the founders before them. Divorce was rare. Abortion, homosexuality, and blasphemy against God, were prosecuted as criminal acts. Through responsibility and order, the people had indeed found a haven of freedom. For the most part, they could sleep with windows open and doors unlocked.

However, this house is no longer the same. After 1931 the *Rules Committee* seemed reluctant to call the people of the house "a Christian people." Perhaps in deference to occupants of non Christian religions, and perhaps for the sensitivities of atheist boarders, the historical positions were muted. By this writing the official position of the *Rules Committee* has turned far from the position that former rules committees held for generations. Today, whatever is not considered to have redeeming **secular** value does not to stand the test of being legal, at least not for long.

Now it is true that when the *Board of Elders* of the house gather, (not to be confused with the *Rules Committee*), they begin with prayer to the God of the Bible, just as they always did. (Only in our day would anyone question whether other gods should have equal status).

Meanwhile, in another part of the house, where the children gather in the *Rooms of Learning*, it is no longer legal for them to hear what the Elders pray across the hall. Nor is it permitted to teach them the difference between right and wrong. As for the *Ten Rules of Conduct,* they were banished from the *Rooms of Learning* a few decades ago. Strangely, in these days of freedom from right and wrong, and though more and more money is spent to help the children learn their lessons, many of them actually seem to have problems learning much of anything. Far too many of them are cheating their way through their lessons. They seem to be disoriented through TV, Face book, and other electronic marvels. Some are killing themselves slowly with alcohol, sexual diseases, and drugs. Others take the fast way with suicide and murder. When these youths get in trouble, they are taken into the *Room of Just Sentences.* Here the Judge tells them that stealing and killing and bending the mind with drugs, is wrong after all.

From the *Room of Just Sentences,* these are again transported to some of the priciest rooms of the house; the *Rooms with Bars.* (Apparently, these rooms with iron bars now take the place of the steel reenforcement that once held the house together.) In any case, these rooms are designed to keep them out of the rest of the house. Here the young who did not learn the difference between good and evil are confined with those who have made a career out of expressing freedom by trying to destroy the house. Building *Rooms with Bars* is a fast growth industry, because today, rooms like this are needed for close to two million people. Isn't it ironic that once the children are out of the *Rooms of*

Learning, where Christian ministers are not allowed, they can then be taken to the *Rooms with Bars,* where Christian chaplains are paid out of the house allowance? On the other hand, if they stay out of trouble, they may get elected to the *Board of Elders.* Here they can also have their paid preachers inside the hallowed walls where to Elders meet.

What then is the moral of this story? My concern is not the survival of Christianity. Genuine Christian faith can survive anything, even as it did the rise and fall of the great *Soviet House of Atheism.* True Christianity is the only belief system that can afford to give recognition to individual choice. This is borrowed from the **Father of the Heavenly House**. He is so good, so merciful, so magnanimous that he continues to send sunshine and rain on both just and unjust. He is so far above being threatened that he didn't need to make people as robots. Like their Father, true Christians can reach out in mercy and even pity to their own adversaries. This is the acid test for those of you who claim to be Christians. Right does not need to prevail in our country, our careers, or even in our lifetime. Where it prevails in the heart, it is inseparable from the One whose House will ultimately prevail.

Friends, the sober question concerns the future of the house of 1776. Christianity can indeed survive the fall of this house. But, pray tell, how can this house expect to survive the rejection of Christian principles?

WILL YOUR OWN HOUSE STAND?

You have probably recognized that the house whereof we spoke is this United States of America. There can be little doubt, that the nation on its present course is forfeiting its place in the world as a bulwark of integrity, freedom and prosperity. How long and in what condition it survives at all, is in the hands of the Almighty. However, instead of focusing overmuch on the bartering away of right for wrong on a national level, we should consider the makeup of houses that indeed will stand.

"Success," it has been said, "is having the final advantage." That is why Jesus shows us two major principles of ultimate success in the building of your personal spiritual house.

The first is in the planning stage. In Luke 14: 28-29, Jesus addresses the problem of trying to build with insufficient funds, (*who builds a tower when the price is more than he is able to pay?*) Even the Bible gives illustrations of people who desired the peace of God, and the offer of life eternal in Jesus Christ and expect heaven when they die, yet offer mere lip service to the Christ who would truly set them free from sin. For personal ambition, or the love of fleshly lusts which war against the soul, the spiritual house is left unfinished and desolate, never suitable for the glorious habitation of God.

The second, from Matthew 7:21-27 is the very foundation. The house that stands is firmly anchored in the foundation of the Word of God. This means that the Christian, having been saved by faith, now orders his life around what the Bible teaches. He no longer lives in the dictates of the lusts of his sinful body. He loves God and keeps his commandments. Such a house stands firm through wind, water and flood, (as in trials, rejection, and persecutions), for this is not merely his house, it is God's house.

One can build faster and easier apart from the principles of a firm foundation and solid structure. Such a house lacking a firm foundation may look good. However, such a work is all in vain. It will not stand the test of judgment.

For the last number of decades, the emphasis of Christian teaching has shifted away from the holiness of God. Many in our churches never hear the terrifying declaration of wrath and judgment upon sin and sinners. Instead, the emphasis has shifted to "God has a wonderful plan for your life," and that one will find "love, peace and fulfillment" out of a quick, once-for-all "decision" for Jesus Christ

This shifting emphasis produces multitudes of people who do not understand the condemnation of their sin, and thus have never known true repentance and reverence before the holy God. These are the ones, who either fill the churches with false converts, or become embittered and disillusioned in a Christianity that seemingly has failed them.

TOO MUCH LIKE THE WORLD

The original article was written in response to a reader request to Reaching Out on the above subject. This article describes why all people, including Christians, are drawn toward the world, like moths drawn to the flame (with equally devastating results).

THE NATURE OF THE WORLD AND WORLDLINESS

Obviously, the biblical teachings and warnings about the world gain little comprehension or concern, even among "Christians" today. The idea of "worldliness" seems a bit too quaint and old fashioned to be suitable material for the modern pulpit. We seem to have outgrown the notion of biblical righteousness that God would require of his people, and that would actually bring about a visible, practical difference between Christian and non-Christian. We would rather enjoy the pleasures of this world, and model after those who do not profess Christianity. We prefer to be "Not Perfect; Only Forgiven." We are not prepared to see an inherent sinfulness in the world order, nor to see this world, as ripe for the judgment of God. Fruit once forbidden is now to be enjoyed.

But if the above analysis is correct, then a line has been crossed that results in enmity against God. *Whosoever will be a friend of the world is the enemy of God. Love not the world, neither the things that are in the world. If any man love the world, the love of the Father is not in him.* As we will see, the inner life of the individual is a battleground where worldliness would love to hold sway. The life that is unattuned to the mind of God, is easily motivated by what fits the biblical descriptions of worldliness.

But first, we need some background. We will see what the Bible says about the world and then proceed to the practical applications.

The biblical "world," used many times in Scripture is the Greek word *Kosmos;* meaning primarily an arrangement, or an ordered system. Before sin came into the world, there was nothing inherently wrong or dangerous about the world, or being in the world. But ever since the fall, the world system gravitates away from God, and is marked for destruction *(the whole world lieth in the wicked one)*. The word Kosmos pertains at least to the following three things:

1. The planet earth on which we live. This natural world was created by God, and was perfect in its origin. Because it is life sustaining, it is also by default the support system for whatever transpires on its face. Before sin came into the world, this was no problem. But because of sin, the earth has become the stage for every kind of evil and atrocity imaginable. Even by Noah's day, practically every commodity, and every activity (including feasting and getting married), was pleasure oriented, and devoted to wrong doing. The Creator God was left out of the world and the activities of the people that he had made. As with the coming of Jesus, a few thousand years later, the world of Noah's day, knew not God. That brings us to one of the clear definitions of worldliness - enjoying the world, while willfully ignoring the claims of her maker. God was so grieved that he regretted having made man (Genesis 6:6). In that great worldwide flood, God destroyed every living thing outside of Noah's ark. Everything man had devised and accomplished was destroyed, and the earth itself received a new make over (the world that then was, being overflowed with water, perished). II. Peter 3:6.

2. The People that inhabit the earth. When the Bible says that *God so loved the world that he gave his only begotten Son* (John 3:16), the reference is not to the planet earth. God was not sending his Son to save the earth. God was reaching out in love and mercy to the people he had created in his own image. Though Noah and his family were righteous, surviving the flood did nothing to change or eradicate the sinful nature. The tendency to sin continued right on through Noah and his descendants, and on through our day. Thus the love of God in the sacrifice of Christ was *to save his people from their sins.* It was God's prescription for the regeneration of people through the death and resurrection of Jesus Christ.

3. The third aspect of "world" is the one that really connects to all of us. Though sins are committed in all kinds of circumstances, and all kinds of places, sin would be powerless except for inherent pull of worldliness within us. The most sobering description of worldliness is found in I. John 2:17. *For all that is in the world, the lust of the flesh, the lust of the eyes, and the pride of life, is not of the Father, but of the world.* It is noteworthy that the three points mentioned are all inward motivations that have led us all into sin. The basis for worldliness is responding to lusts within, which if unchecked leads to sin and sin unto death.

This biblical description of "world" fits exactly what transpired when sin first came into the world.

God commanded Adam not to eat of the one tree of forbidden fruit, The Bible calls it the tree of the knowledge of good **and evil** (emphasis mine). But Eve carefully analyzed what that fruit was like. This is what she found:

- It looked like it was good to eat **(lust of the flesh)**.
- It had a pleasing appearance **(lust of the eyes)**.
- It showed promise of making her wise, an idea planted by the tempter, **(pride of life).**

In that moment, using the best "science" of the day, Eve had developed a reasonable case for eating the forbidden fruit. And so she ate, and gave to her husband, and he did eat.

This observation comes as a lesson for all time. Sin is packaged as being perfectly reasonable. This also explains why worldliness is so appealing. It evokes a sense of well-being based on what seems to be the best intelligence available. For example, here is the way a popular gospel singer excused her infidelity. Her reasoning? *"You can't help who you fall in love with.* " Thus sin appeals to the flesh, and finds comfort in the intellect.

On the other hand, the wisdom of God was offered through a simple command. *Don't eat of that tree.* Was that unreasonable? Only if God had not created the tree and the people. The command was given because God understood the consequences. However, the command of God incites no appeal to the lust of the flesh, or the lust of the eyes, nor any whatsoever to the pride of intellect. Obedience to the command would have accomplished peace and perfect security, as the mind of God was embraced in the hearts of his people. This is wisdom.

Now fast forward to 1989. This is the year when fossil hunters in South Dakota discovered the skeletal remains of the biggest T Rex dinosaur ever found (now on display at the Chicago Field Museum). Following are the conclusions of brilliant scientists using the best "science" available for the study of dinosaurs:

- That there are totally naturalistic explanations (evolution), for both the existence and extinction of dinosaurs.
- That this dinosaur (named Sue), must have descended from birds because it had structurally supported hollow bones as birds do.
- That Sue ("her" skull alone weighed six hundred pounds), died sixty-five million years ago.

Now can you imagine some meek individual who believes the Genesis record of creation, stepping into this circle of prideful scientists to suggest that this great T Rex lived about fifty-five hundred years ago, and could possibly have been contemporary with Job of Old Testament fame?

On the best reasoning of the day, both Eve and the scientists missed the wisdom that would have rendered their conclusions utterly wrong.

The mighty T Rex, Sue, on a normal day at
home, at the Chicago Field Museum.
She is introduced here, by my wife, Katie.

For the past 150 years the church has cowered, as science (so called), has advanced claims concerning the age of the earth and the evolution of life on this planet. As a result, even many denominational leaders have distanced themselves from the Genesis account of creation.

However, the Bible stands as a unit. To go with the tide of evolutionary opinion at the expense of the Genesis record, is a disclaimer of the historical authority of the Bible. (Jesus endorsed this historical authority). However, the moral authority of Scripture is totally intertwined with its historical authority of the Genesis account of creation. When the historical truth of the Bible is compromised, the moral authority of Scripture cannot be trusted or maintained either. As a result, many Christians, and even many Christian denominations have compromised both their faith in the integrity of the God of history, and their morality by surrendering biblical revelation to the prevailing logic of the day. There is finally no keeping power against the gravest sins of the day. That is at least a major reason why there is very little difference left today in the ways of the church and the ways of the world.

Can we explain everything about creation and the age of the earth? We cannot. However, we do behold the accuracy of Scripture as they attest to truth in many scientific fields. This faith continues to be confirmed as old scientific speculation falls to the modern advancements and discoveries of science. (In the meantime, scientists who see the insufficiency of evolutionary ideas, have good reason to be cautious with their doubts. Their credibility and career, are on the line. The scientific elite, don't suffer "fools", as in creationist ideas, gladly). We conclude then that the ways of God are often beyond human comprehension, and that unbelief will but yield intellectual folly.

But having tasted and savored godless answers to origins (and overlooked the embarrassing inconsistences of Darwinist ideas), many Christians today are as clueless as their unbelieving counterparts. Talk to the average church crowd about the taboos of yesteryears, dancing, smoking and drinking, premarital sex, divorce and remarriage, or shameless exposure of the body, women dressing like men, or women cutting their hair. They will think that you are from another planet. Yet, turn back the clock one hundred years or so. You would find that most, if not all denominations, would have considered the above named things as issues of sinfulness and of worldliness if not of outright damnation. Not anymore. Thus the church and the world become an indistinguishable one.

Were there actual compelling reasons for the church to compromise with Darwinism? It may have appeared like it at the time. Yet all the promised scientific evidence that the Bible (starting with Genesis) is wrong, if it ever did arrive, was merely dead on arrival. This included fake ape-men, doctored embryonic charts, and fossils arranged from simple to complex, but only on paper.

What was it that Eve and the scientists missed? They looked in the wrong place for answers. In her moment of analytical pride, Eve doubted the word of God who had made the tree. The best observation of the fruit could not reveal its dark secrets. And though fossil bones may yield some clues as to how a creature looked and lived, they yield no information as to first cause. The "science" of origins is very like trying to understand what powers a train while denying the presence of the locomotive and dissecting the caboose for answers.

As a scientist may study trees all his life, and never come to the knowledge of where the tree came from, neither can moral values be determined by focusing on forbidden fruit. Right and wrong are not discovered by experimentation, but by command of God.

The only program that can open the understanding in matters all the way from history to morals is divine revelation, (Scripture). This is not anti-science. It is recognition of the limitations of science. The problems of the human race began when Adam and Eve ignored the commandment of the one who had made the tree. Likewise the answers we need today still are found only in the wisdom of God. That revelation of God in the Scriptures still answers every question that is pertinent to us today. The commandments of God will guide us in the right way. I will simply name a few things where Christians could trade worldly folly for heavenly wisdom.

- **Above all, heavenly wisdom pursues the right priorities**, in other words, identifying what is most important. I would carefully and lovingly cite an example. Eve was onto something important as she contemplated eating the forbidden fruit. Her question was not whether she needed food. It was simply whether she could rightly expand her dietary variety.

1. Food is a legitimate thing. But even necessary food, is to be held in check, and enjoyed in temperance. The forbidden fruit, however good the appearance, could be eaten only in disobedience. The appearance and the outcome were polar opposites *(you shall surely die).*
2. The questionable is always off limits, because of the devastating effects on the conscience.
3. All things that are lawful are not expedient. Our spirit is to dominate what we do in our bodies, not the other way around.

So here comes the question. Is it right that the dominant role of sports in the world should have similar prominence in the life of the church? Is this about enough nourishing variety in the diet, or is it empty calories at the expense of needed nourishment? What happens in the sports world, isn't even important tomorrow, let alone next year, or in the day when we stand before God. The only possibility of importance then would be in the negative sense. The bad character of many sports figures, and the multimillion dollar contracts for *hitting or kicking a ball,* do nothing to alleviate my concern. Is the price of the ticket perhaps much higher than the price of the ticket? But you would never guess from the enthusiasm of many, that sports are anything less than the "necessary food" of the church. Could this be the moth, heading for the flame?

- **We would know why human life is special** and sacred above all other life. We would know why pets are not on par with children, and human babies must not be slaughtered like animals.
- **We would reserve sexual relationships for marriage**, and would understand marriage from the commandments of the one who designed marriage for one man and one woman, for as long as they both shall live.

- **We would understand the purpose of clothing**, and why the public show of the body, especially the female form, is one of the most morally damaging things, ever to invade our culture.
- **We would understand that homosexuality is a blight** that comes in under the radar, only *after* a culture has sold out morally, and after the distinct God ordained roles of male and female have been thoroughly confused.
- **We would embrace the call of God** for Christians to take their operating instructions from the Scripture, and pay the price of a practical separation from the world.
- **We would truly repent** of the tragic replacement of the wisdom of God with the degrading and destructive influences of worldliness.

[But] the world passeth away and the lust thereof. [Only] he that doeth the will of God abideth forever (I. John 2:17).

Be not unequally yoked together with unbelievers . . . come out from among them, and be ye separate, and touch not the touch not the unclean thing, and I will receive you, and will be a Father unto you, and ye shall be my sons and daughters, saith the Lord Almighty (II.Corinthians 6:14-18).

THE DILEMMA OF ATHEISM

There are Christian writers and thinkers who claim that no one knows enough facts about nature to rule out the existence of God. The argument goes like this: At best one may know a mere fraction (less than 1%), of everything there is to know of the natural world. We don't know how many grains of sand are on even one beach in Florida. We don't know the sheer volume of oxygen in the air. We don't know how many ground hogs and water snakes are in Wisconsin, etc. So, the argument goes, the atheist would need to know everything about everything in nature, to prove that God does not exist (Presumedly, the evidence for God might be found in what he doesn't know).

Now, for the fallacy of that argument. Everyone (atheists included), believes in builders. Every house is the transformation of various materials into a final completed structure through the intelligence and energy of the builder. However, the builder is not the materials, neither is he the building. The first 1% of the construction, is the same evidence for the builder as the remaining 99%. Once the job is complete, and the builder has packed his tools and left, we do not take core samples of the foundation, nor do we take the house apart, looking for evidence of the builder. Has the evidence of a builder disappeared into thin air? Now that we cannot find tangible evidence, shall we no longer believe in builders?

But that is not the premise for believing in builders. Neither is that the premise for believing in the Creator. Less than 1% knowledge is totally sufficient. We will not find God's footprints in prehistoric rock, or some leftover lunch that God didn't need, nor in forming materials God left behind from pouring the foundations of the earth. We can reach our conclusions without pulverizing the universe looking for evidence of God. We can be assured that 100% knowledge of construction materials will yield the same results as the 1%

already known. No lookout towers need be built nor space flights taken to look for a builder, nor to find God.

Even as builders are not houses, God is not the creation. So the kind of evidence needed to believe in a builder or to believe in God, really is one and the same. The sheer volume of knowledge has nothing to do with it. You may be a complete ignoramus when it comes to construction. Yet this ignorance does not keep you from believing in a builder. However, if you refuse to believe in builders, no amount of evidence will protect you from the foolishness of your wrong conclusions.

We have just let the atheist off the hook on his degree of scientific knowledge. Are we saying then, that there is no folly in atheism? Indeed we are not. The great folly of the atheist is not in the volume of his knowing. It is the refusal to consider the obvious. He lives under a vast canopy that reverberates with beauty, order and harmony, yet defies the possibility of divine cause, insisting instead, that there is no God. He looks in the mirror and sees a complexity of intelligent arrangement beyond comprehension and beyond chance. This evidence points to a Creator par excellence. Yet he attempts the impossible feat of attributing tremendously complex effects to absolutely no cause at all. Finding himself stuck between believing in nothing versus believing in God, well, he chooses nothing. He has just forsaken the sanity of his belief that various building materials never become houses apart from builders. He calmly asserts that he cannot believe in an unseen God, only to leapfrog into insisting that an equally unseen but causeless, unintelligent nothingness is sufficient cause for all that exists. This is not the equivalent of declaring that a new born calf will eventually produce milk. It is like blindly insisting that milk (or more accurately, no milk), given millions of years, must ultimately produce a cow. Science is always tortured and violated in the process of claiming to believe nothing but science.

If a boy of eight doesn't know the difference between a pine tree and an oak, yet knows that God made the tree, he is light years ahead of the brilliant naturalist who studies trees for fifty years, and yet doesn't know where trees come from.

Atheists like to claim that the concept of God only removes the problem of existence by a factor of one. So where did God come from? The answer that is both biblical and rational, is that God didn't come from anywhere.

Now every builder preexists his house. However, he never becomes part of it. True, he finally builds his last house, and rides off into the sunset. Not so with God. In creating the heavens and the earth and all things therein, God also created the time frame in which we exist. We can but move forward at the created time pace toward final destiny. We must expect that God will meet us there. This is not because the Creator shares the time frame of the created (for he is outside of time), but because God is equally present everywhere, whether past, present, or future. Atheists must claim billions of years of time to produce what exists today. If they don't have unlimited time, then they have lost their claim to evolution, and with it, their credibility as atheists. We believers know the difference between billions of years of chance, and the eternal God who has existed, does exist, and will exist forever.

The Bible clearly describes the development of atheism (*Because that when they knew God, they glorified him not as God, but became vain in the imaginations, and their foolish heart was darkened* (Romans 1:21). Since wickedness is contrary to the role for which we were created, it is hardly surprising that wickedness would also discredit the creator by denying his existence.

An atheist may claim to share many of the same values that Christians do. Perhaps this is one area where plagiarism is helpful. There is nothing inherent in atheism that would logically lend itself to any form of good, of morals or ethics. On the other hand the belief in the Creator God, lends itself perfectly to the human need of moral constraints and judgments.

Now for the final dilemma of the atheist. He comes to the end of life. He believes himself unaccountable. He expects to go off into the abyss of nothingness. But - faulty logic changes nothing. Unbelief does not negate the appointment with his Maker (II. Corinthians 4:10).

RELIGION WITHOUT RELATIONSHIP

Do you have it made? Lovely wife and family, smashing success in business, no money worries, capable, friendly, and popular in social life? Do you top off your good life in a respectable church, and with generous giving to your favorite charities?

If so, I can explain to you why Jesus became so unpopular. He was speaking one day to a Jewish multitude. The Bible says these were people who believed on him. So what did he tell them? *If ye continue in my Word, then are ye my disciples indeed. And ye shall know the truth and the truth shall make you free* (John 8:31,32).

They were nonplused. The affront was staggering. Their retort was swift and it was angry. *We are Abraham's children. We were never in bondage to any man.* (We're no slaves).

What Jesus did was no different from calling a respectable, middle-class Mennonite, Baptist, Lutheran, Methodist, or a faithful Catholic a slave. (Lower than welfare and food stamps).

But let's plumb the depth of Jesus' teaching. Obviously, Jesus was not referring to the pre-civil war type of slave trade. Rather, he was describing a bondage that affects every individual regardless of age, gender, race, creed, or social status.

You are quite aware of some of these. You know that not all those in bondage to alcohol are on skid row. Some live in suburbia and attend popular mega-churches. Those who wish they could quit tobacco are not all on a social status beneath you. Not all the adulterers run with the playboy crowd. Some have been respectable folk, from Sunday School teachers to tele-evangelists, and manage to hide their secret lives for years. Then there are those who would never rob a bank. Instead, they respectably find ways to short change the I.R.S.

But even this does not begin to cover the scope of what Jesus was saying. He was not talking about those whose sins brought them to open shame, nor to those whose dark blot was still undercover. Rather, Jesus was addressing the fact that all people either have been, or still are slaves to the sin principle within. The Bible describes it well in Romans 7:18,19. *"For I know that in me (that is in my flesh) dwelleth no good thing: for to will is present with me; but how to perform that which is good I find not. For the good that I would I do not; but the evil that I would not, that I do."*

If you have never identified with such bondage, then perhaps like the Jews of Jesus' day, you have not been close enough to the law of God. It wasn't to their credit to be slaves and not even know it. The truth which sets free must first bring conviction of sin. Again, from Romans 7:7, *"I had not known sin, but by the law, for I had not known lust, except the law had said, Thou shalt not covet."* The struggle gets even worse, *"O wretched man that I am! Who shall deliver me from the body of this death?"* (verse 24).

This is where many churches fail today. People become "good" members, without ever plumbing the depth of their own needs. Like those "good" Jews of Jesus' day, they are turned off at the idea of needing a Savior, one who would atone for their sins. Sure, the Jews knew that the publicans and harlots needed someone to save them. So it is today with people who have never faced up to their own sinfulness, and the impossibility of righteousness apart from Jesus Christ. Apart from repentance, forgiveness, and deliverance from sin through faith in Christ, we merely fill our churches with respectable slaves.

This is why many "Christians" know nothing of mortifying the flesh. They have nothing better to do than to satisfy the old fleshly cravings in acceptable ways (at least in public). In heart, they differ not at all from the godless culture around them. The more we fill our churches with the unregenerate, the more unacceptable the truth becomes. And if the truth is lost on those of us who name the name of Christ, is it any wonder that the whole culture falls into moral chaos? After all, it's been awhile since any culture has flaunted its rejection of the biblical moral code the way we have.

I can't help but believe that for some of you, we have said enough already. You well know that you have sinned by breaking the commandments of God. You know his condemnation of you is just. Your conscience is smitten. Your misery is complete. You have failed more times than you can count. The more you struggle, the tighter the bondage. You are weary of keeping the howling dogs of truth at bay. You know that the respectability of your religion can no longer cover for the sickness of your soul.

How would I know what goes on in the secrets of your heart? It's because we are all made of the same stuff. I have been there. My mind and conscience approved the righteousness of God. But my flesh did not, and the pull of my lower nature made me a slave to sin.

Those sin-shackled Jews of Jesus' day, had the answer right in front of their eyes that day.

Yet they could not see him as the Lamb of God to take away the sin of the world, unless they would open to him in their bondage. So it is with us. Jesus Christ did not come to add an outward facade of fulfillment and respectability over the sin and turmoil within, but to set us free. He offers the law of the Spirit of life that sets free from the law of sin that reigned in our members. Jesus is the difference between covering up for sin, and the removal of it. *If the Son therefore shall make you free, ye shall be free indeed.*

What must one do to be born again? You must believe in him. *"There is no other name under heaven given among men, whereby you may be saved."* You will repent of sin, and receive him as Savior and Lord of your life. You will be baptized in his name. You will confess him with your mouth. Out of such deliverance, you will then continue in his Word to be his follower indeed. There is no other release from the slavery of sin.

A BEAUTIFUL INEQUALITY

But I would have you know, that the head of every man is Christ; and the head of the woman is the man; and the head of Christ is God (I. Corinthians 11:3). In a day when there is much striving for equality between the sexes - actually, an attempt to erase the differences - we would just like to take you for a tour of the other side, the case for inequality.

The Bible passage above, (which other Scriptures affirm), is not giving men permission to stake out and enforce a headship position. It is much more persistent than that. It reads like established law. The law of gravity comes to mind. It just is. But this passage is also larger than the relationship between men and women. It shows that men are likewise in a gravitational pull of authority - to Jesus Christ. It also pulls another surprise. The passage is not just addressed to Christian men and Christian women. It is written as though all men and all women are actually in these power orbits, whether they know it or not. That this authority structure is already in place, can mean but one thing. God put it there. This means then that to respect the power structure is to respect God, and to deny it, is to reject God. I think it is good to know this. It could be a lot less painful, if we knew our limits.

Can it really mean this? Think. You are about to step off a cliff, and you don't believe in gravity . . . In fact, the Bible confirms that unbelief does not let one off the hook. *At the name of Jesus every knee shall bow . . . and every tongue confess that Jesus Christ is Lord, to the glory of God the Father* (Philippians 2:11). It appears then, that embracing the theme of submission to authority really is a matter of damage control in marriage and family relationships. How much available energy can we afford to divert to sparring for control?

But we are still not through with our original passage. This "chain of command" embraces not only the scope of the earthly powers that be. It even ascends to the throne room of God. It claims that there is inequality even there - that God is the head of Christ. You don't need a lot of biblical literacy to know that Jesus himself repeatedly made the same claim while he was on earth. He claimed to be sent of his Father. He claimed to speak the words his Father gave him to speak. He claimed the work he did was assigned of his Father. He clearly stated that he did not come to earth to do his own will, but the will of his Father in heaven.

This will of the Father was the ultimate, treacherous road. It led Jesus through the very humble course of becoming God in human flesh, and of being despised and rejected of men. It led him into and through the agony in the garden. Then in the most extreme perversion of justice, it took him to crucifixion and death on the cross. Even before the cross, Jesus by his submission, portrayed the person of his Father to perfection, *(if you have seen me, you have seen the Father).*

Jesus never refused his Father's bidding, and thus never jeopardized his mission. Consider the end result of his obedience unto death. We received mercy for our injustice, love for our hatred, and redemption for our damnation. He arose from the dead, provided salvation for sinners, and opened the Lamb's Book of Life (so that our names might be written there). The Father, in turn, exalted the name of Jesus above all other. All this was accomplished, not through equality, but through perfect harmony in the will of the Father, attained by the submission of Jesus Christ. Harmony is also created into the differing roles in the human family (*husbands love, wives submit, children obey*), alongside our unequal physical properties. It appears that God was giving us an earthly copy of the order that exists in the trinity (Father, Son, and Holy Spirit).

We see this principle applied throughout the cosmos. Cosmos means order. This order, established at creation, keeps every heavenly body, and every planet in place; a harmonious order of unequals that provides fine - tuned technical support for the earth, and every living being on the face of it.

Remember then, that if you choose to argue against male/female inequality, you are doing so with the gift of breath you receive from this cosmic system of unequals.

As we accept this truth, a glorious light comes on. We are not our own. Neither are we self-sufficient. Inequality allows us to live in the wisdom, strength, and provision of those set in position over us. Jesus was so sustained by his Father. Men are to find the same in Christ, and in turn, pass on this bounty to their wives and families. And that is key to reverence and godly fear in all relationships, (knowing that God is over it all).

Even as I write, I can hear the objections. You don't know my husband. You don't know my employer. You don't know how corrupt our governor is. And you are right. I don't know. However, I do know that the Father allowed evil men, including the Roman governor, the mastery over his beloved son. Jesus made this clear to Pontius Pilate. *You could have no power against me, at all, except it were given thee from above.* God distributed the powers, but do you recognize the powers over you? This writing is certainly not designed to justify the misuse of authority. But I see people, even in our churches, who are embittered toward authority. The ultimate test is not about the worthiness of the authority figure, but about my godly response to that parent, husband, or employer whose motives and integrity may be on the line.

Christian submission is like Christian love. We are commanded to love with a godly love. It does not depend on the worthiness of the recipient. It is applied toward all, whether brother, friend, or mortal enemy. If you have this love, it's because it is generated in your heart by the spirit of God. The same holds with the submission in the authority principle. We don't honor because those whom we honor are always right or always honorable. We do so because we fear God and honor him. In such a response, we become like Jesus. The work of grace in our lives is more than sufficient for every temptation to bitterness. The growth of character is multiplied far above the cost involved.

In summary, the promotion of equality that sounds so good, is but a mythical illusion. It is not true to nature. Unequals are not the exception, but the very rule. The entire natural world forms a wonderful compelling unity, not of sameness, but of differences. The sun is not like the moon, water is not like air, trees are not like soil, acorns are not pumpkins, peacocks are not elephants. What if you ordered roses for your beloved, but the florist sent onions instead (The florist deems onions more useful).

Most of these differences are beyond making the world a wonderfully interesting place to live. They are necessary to our survival. The world literally goes around on unequal forces working in perfect harmony. We can plan our days, weeks and years by the calender, because the earth keeps its location in the exactly right gravitational forces of the sun and other heavenly bodies. Not only is the earth the right distance from the sun for the optimal temperature for life on earth, but it also maintains the tilt on its axis, giving more daylight hours for growing huge vegetables, in far northern climates with short growing seasons. Thus if the earth were "freed" from outside forces, or granted equal status with the sun, or some other planet, such freedom would spell the end of life on earth. Now if you have followed thus far, you see that the harmony of unequals is the only assurance of life on this planet.

Consider the differences in people. We come in a wide variety of body builds, sizes, and skin colors. We have greatly varying differences of life spans, and of talents, personalities, interests, and skills. Yet our interest in people is sparked by these striking differences. Can you imagine shopping, or going to an airport where everyone was an exact copy of you? Can you imagine a universe with five billion clones of yourself? My guess? Such a scenario would drive us insane.

This brings us to the point of tension in this discussion, the most important differences in people. The human race is neatly packaged by gender, male or female.

There are two basic approaches to gender differences. This article is written on the premise of creation, that the male and the female represent divine engineering. This means that men and women are physically different for the purpose of marriage, companionship, and reproduction. This also includes the premise that male/female differences extend into the psychological makeup. This leads us to believe that the biblical premise, calling for different, yet complimentary roles, is truly vital to the human family. We believe that those differences ought to be celebrated, that differing yet complimentary roles are what the human family needs.

The Bible actually includes a token reminder of this teaching. Perhaps you have wondered about the peculiar head-coverings worn by ladies from a few minority churches such as the Mennonites. Is this just a denominational oddity? Not really. It has its origin in I. Corinthians 11:1-16. The covering is worn as a sign and celebration of the blessings and fulfillment in God's order. It is a contractual symbol, that of accepting from God the divine plan for the sexes. Her head is covered in honor and deference to her husband. His head is uncovered and his hair is cut for the honor Christ. As each is committed to his/her head, they form an effective union to nurture yet another generation in the ways of their God.

But the prevailing philosophy claims that female *equals* male - that differences ought to be stamped out, and that all inequality ought to be trashed. It is like insisting that roses really are onions. But there is this huge problem. In this battle of the sexes, there are no winners. The attempt divides, and the outcome is female *versus* male.

The Bible, in ancient times already rejected the modern notion of equality, by listing threes levels of female degradation (Isaiah 47:2).

Taking a job at the millstones. This first one borrows the male job description. It is equality in the job market, and taking on the typical hard labor of males. Asserting qualities of male toughness and competition may seem like the challenge men may need. But this does not elevate a woman. The tough job of a bulldozer operator that she wanted yesterday, is what is expected of her today. Gone is the expectation and delight of a special role and special treatment and respect for the queenly sex.

The second sign is uncovered locks. The removal of her head covering mutes the differing responsibilities and roles assigned by the Creator for men and women, and asserts equal authority. Would you open a business employing fifty people where every position from management, to production, to sweeping floors is left unassigned? If such a business survived at all, it is only on the basis that the fifty people involved would establish an order of authority, and separate themselves into unequal roles.

The third stage of degradation is discarding modest dress (baring the thigh). This step claims sexual liberation, but turns instead into cruel bondage, both for the "liberated" woman, and the men she ensnares. Wanton sexuality becomes the consuming interest, and marks the turning point to destruction in a society.

The negative results from attempted equality are everywhere. There is unprecedented rudeness and disregard of femininity. Far too many women are used, abused, battered, abandoned, or murdered. How long will it take to prove that the battle for equality works contrary to the love, respect, and security she seeks? Liberation and equality renders the woman a fleeting attraction, a rose robbed of her petals. In fact, the problem only gets worse. Instead of returning to the unique treasure of being female, many entrench themselves into the conquest of men, destroying the men who are attracted to them. In biblical language, *many strong men are slain by her.*

Could you now consider that equality of the sexes is not to anyone's best interest? Not for men, who ought to play a vital role as breadwinners, leaders, and protectors of their wives and children. Not the women who are then cast into the role of substitute men. Certainly not the children, brought up in such a confusion of order.

Inequality is not about superiority. God wisely created men and women physically, emotionally, and reproductively different. In God's order, those inherent differences are then bonded together as a greater single unit in marriage. Marriage completes the cycle of human love and human reproduction. *Therefore shall a man leave his father and mother, and shall cleave to his wife: and they twain shall be one flesh* (Genesis 2:24). *And wherefore one? That he might seek a godly seed* (Malachi 2:15).

In the context of marriage, he is the warrior and the leader. But he is not into the battle of the sexes. His "battle" is not against her, but for her. He accepts his responsibilities as divinely ordered (Ephesians 5:22-33). He faithfully fulfills the mandate to be her protector and the provider of her needs. His call is to love her even as himself. He is true to her until death, while the world screams that he may drop her for another . . . and another. Thus he is on guard against the inroads of the attractiveness and the wiles of other women. To fall prey to another would be a self-inflicted bitter end to all he holds dear.

This context makes for two parent households. Here babies are wanted and welcomed. The children are not liabilities. They are the greatest assets. While he provides the safe haven, she pursues her specialty of nourishing, cherishing, and mothering their children. Her submission to her husband is not a heavy burden. It is a weight off her shoulders, for she is then free to accomplish what she does best, investing her talents in the high calling of motherhood. In so doing, she serves to the delight and the pleasure of the whole family circle.

Granted, the rewards of the wife and mother in the home are unequal to the rewards of the typical C.E.O., the state representative, or the county sheriff. But how can the development of another secure, well adjusted generation of young adults, be an inferior or less fulfilling reward?

Thus this short tour into blessed inequality is ended. This God, who has favored us with divine example, and divine illumination, stands ready with grace and the power for us to fulfil our callings as sons and daughters of the Almighty, in the Spirit of Jesus Christ.

THE ENVIRONMENTAL DILEMMA

We recently toured a science museum display that was devoted to the global warming theme. One section vividly portrayed the great devastation of New Orleans from hurricane Katrina. While the posted material did tacitly allow that the connection to global warming isn't conclusive, the effect was geared to such an impression. But there was a more blatant misrepresentation. Sure, the hurricane did bring great devastation. But the worst was still to come *after* the hurricane had moved inland. That was when the levees failed. It is reported (I believe accurately), that the Army Corps of Engineers knew the levees would not withstand a category three hurricane. If that is the case, the greater devastation was the result of human failure, not with air pollution, but in betting that the inevitable wouldn't happen, at least not on the watch of those responsible at the time. A couple billion dollars to upgrade the levees, would seem like a small price to pay against a hundred billion or so in losses. So the greater human failure was disregarded for the greater impact of the global warming theory.

Sound environmental policy is no joking matter. The quality of soil, water, and air especially in relation to sufficient food supply, is the key to quality of life. Wrong conclusions then, whether by neglect or faulty understanding, can become issues of life and death. The subject of the environment is controversial, for it is approached from two widely differing persuasions.

The first view is based on the creation worldview. This view holds that God made the world and every thing in it. It also means that God made people special. They are special because God made our first ancestors after his own image. People also have a special function, because they have the particular gift of being able to cultivate the soil, to manufacture all sorts of needed tools and equipment, to effectively manage natural resources, and to oversee the raising and even the slaughter of animals for food. There is one particular principle on which the whole of this turns. The human population is in a stewardship position in things belonging to God. *Moreover, it is required of stewards, that a man be found faithful*. That which is entrusted to us, will also be required of us. God has no pleasure in foolish, hurtful, or wasteful treatment of his world. We unashamedly stand by this view. Our objective is to give every reader a clear perspective for doing so.

The second view of the environment comes through Darwinist evolutionary lenses. Enlightened people supposedly don't believe that God created the world because the existence of God is beyond the possibility of being verified by science. Yet these same people offer no evidence from the past or present, for the beginning of life, nor for any mechanism in nature to propel evolution upward. (So if evolution had to be verified by science, it wouldn't stand the test either).

In this view, what started from nothing continues to evolve to ever higher levels and becomes ever more utopian. Human beings just "happen" to sit on top of the evolutionary chain. This evolutionary lens can diverge into various different views. For one, man can take advantage of the "survival of the fittest" view. Because man is on top, he can and often does take the natural advantage. The slaughter of entire buffalo herds on the western plains comes to mind, as does the poaching of endangered animals, or cutting timber with no thought of sustainable practice.

On a nearly opposite Darwinist track is a modern form of nature worship. In this view, homo sapiens should denounce their position on top of the evolutionary chain. "Natural" would be totally sufficient as being good - absent human interference. We will see later what happens as this view feeds on itself.

The past rise of science and progress in every field was based on the creation view. We buy, we build, we plant, we invent, we repair, we repaint, we tear down, we bury; all based on the consistency of nature, on the fact that things are *not* evolving. The shift to the second view has produced a new view of science itself. The old science called for test tube accuracy. The new science is subjective and subject to interpretation. This is not so much an accusation of dishonestly, as it is exposing the folly of speculation in order to sustain the view. The new science can take a few bones of doubtful origin, and give us full-blown, full-color humanoid ancestry. It can (and has) turned our climate concerns from fears of a new ice age to global warming in less than twenty years (from the 1970's to the 1990's). It can find "substantial" evidence of life on Mars, long before the returns of careful laboratory analysis refutes the findings. One might hope that environmental policy based on speculative science would be mostly an inconvenience. But it gets worse than that.

Values and priorities get seriously skewed, as the following slogans suggest: "A boy is a dog - is a pig - is a rat." Or this one; "There is no difference between a lamb and a man." Extremism? Certainly. But this sort of extremism is moving mainstream. When a Wisconsin state employee suggested that feral cats could be eliminated, he received threats against his life. Our governor weighed in with, "we don't want to be known as a state that kills cats" (abortions are a different story). Minnesota officers shot a bear that had wedged his head into a bucket. They received threats of the same happening to them. No, these people are not crazy. This is a totally logical conclusion based on the second view. The extremists have simply arrived ahead of the pack.

That long time best seller, *The Celestine Prophecy*, by James Redfield, extols the power of nature and especially the power of mature forests. He expresses the need for a "spiritually maturing" humanity to voluntarily decrease its numbers, so that all nature can live within the energy systems of the planet (whatever that means).

The spotted owl issue is only partially that. Never mind that spotted owls are shown to be very adaptable. But saving the owls also enforces saving the trees. Never mind that forest management gives us both forests and lumber, and actually enhances the beauty and productivity of the forest.

The tree is natural. The tree is sacred. Therefore, we must not cut the tree. The tree deserves a natural death, followed by natural decay (keeping perfectly good timber from being harvested). Those who disagree are the enemy and they are no more important than the tree. The same applies to the threatened thing-a-ma-bug in the swamp. It's not just an extinction of the bug issue. Rather, the bug and the swamp are sacred because they are natural. And they were there before the farmer who is minded to drain the swamp for food production.

This religion is not new. It is as old as Hinduism. Because of the false belief in reincarnation, Hinduism not only refuses to slaughter cattle for meat, but stands by doing nothing, while food supplies are hopelessly pillaged by an uncontrolled rodent population. The rodents are well fed, while the children go hungry. This is not about environmental management. It is not even about the humane treatment of animals. Rather, it is about faith in letting "nature" run its course. But you all know what happens when you let your garden, your flower bed, or the pair of rats in your basement run their courses. You will seek fresh vegetables in vain. You will need to change your mind on what constitutes a beautiful bouquet. Your house will lose both its livability (for humans), and its market value. The above philosophy is wrong - not because it is inconvenient, but because it is patently false. It is not merely false to the Bible but even to nature. That is why it is rife with problems, and can hold not the slightest possibility of a cohesive mandate.

We are not suggesting that starting from creation and the stewardship of man, promises an easy answer to every environmental question. But we are saying that it is the only viable position. There is no other principle that can validate the worthy goal of human and creature comfort, and bounty of forest and field. In the consistency of creation science, (not in evolution), there rests the hope for environmental concerns to translate into wholesome management of life-sustaining natural resources.

DESPISING THE HUMAN DIFFERENCE

Professing themselves to be wise, they became fools . . .
Romans 1:22

A morally confused age seems not to realize that rejecting the place of God leads to mass confusion on a host of other issues. According to *Summit Ministries Journal*, March 2005, Senator Joe Lieberman, got some uninvited attention from *PETA* (People for the Ethical Treatment of Animals). Apparently, the senator has a taste for salmon, which *PETA* thinks ought not to be eaten. Apparently, salmon should be left to die of old age, and then decompose. (I'm not sure how *PETA* would get this lesson across to bald eagles, since they seem to be disinclined to become vegetarians). Now we know that *PETA* is a fringe organization. But it is also true that fringe has a way of going mainstream. Reportedly, *PETA* has gone so far as to compare the barbequing of millions of chickens to the extermination of millions of Jews in World War II.

As we know, Hitler and his henchman eliminated millions of their fellow citizens, men, women, and children, not for crimes they had committed, but merely for being in the way of German ambition. Most of the world abhorred what Hitler did. In world opinion, genocide is wrong. Thus, Hitler was wrong. Even in war, there are supposed humanitarian minimums for treatment of the enemy, according to the Geneva Convention. Civilians are to be spared as much as possible, and prisoners of war are to be humanely treated.

However, I am proposing that Hitler was wrong, not because of world opinion, but in an unchanging, absolute moral sense. In the basic sense of truth versus error, or good versus evil, Adolph Hitler was wrong.

This absolute sense of right and wrong is an example of what the courts in American history used as a common reference point of justice. It crossed all ethnic lines and held all people accountable to certain moral absolutes. It was referred to as "natural law," encompassing a morality commonly understood by the conscience. Attorneys may still file an insanity plea for an individual who commits a heinous crime, but is incompetent to comprehend the wrongness of his deed.

"Natural law," is just another way of saying that morality is not invented by the courts, but that it is an overriding code to which all people are to be anchored. This is like saying that the locomotive is free only when it is bound to ride the tracks. As locomotives are doomed without the tracks, so is civilization without recognition of higher law. (It is in the disregard for higher law, that *PETA* has lost its bearings).

From the biblical standpoint, natural law is readily understood. The "tracks" by which we are to be guided come from the same source that we come from, the Supreme Being, the Creator God. The Bible also shows that the human conscience is indeed agreeable to the law of God (Romans 2:14,15). (Where this is lost, justice is perverted, and there follows a culture of sociopaths.)

Natural law reaches down (I say "down" in the deliberate sense), to a right regard of the animal kingdom. There is an intended insurmountable chasm between the man and the animal by creation. It is God who appointed the man (made in God's image), to have dominion over the animal kingdom (not made in the image of God). Yes, this includes fishing for salmon, and barbecuing chickens for food.

Men may rightly be indicted for cruelty to animals. However, animals cannot be charged with cruelty to men. Moral judgments cannot be applied to animal behavior. Animals can only operate on instinct, including the law of tooth and fang. Thus, a dog cannot be sentenced to prison for mauling a child. However, animals that endanger human life, can rightly be destroyed. This explains why the laws of the land made distinction between killing a man, or killing an animal (a line that is being blurred).

Were it not for the higher, absolute law of God, I would have nothing to say about what Hitler did, or what *PETA* promotes. But neither would anyone else (including *PETA*). A chance arrangement of molecules cannot validate any position on any subject.

Who changed the truth of God into a lie, and worshiped and served the creature more than the Creator . . . Romans 1:25.

Fringe organizations seem blissfully unaware that the "track"is being undermined. One could suspect that some of them would deliberately derail the train. Interesting, organizations that shun the very idea of absolute morality from God, have no qualms about imposing their own ideas as absolute morality. In the meantime, fringe ideas move mainstream. The one-time editor of our local weekly claimed that a "crime" against a dog should carry the same consequences as a crime against a man. (Translation; shooting a dog should get the same prison time as shooting a man) In recent controversy over the propriety of shooting stray cats, our governor made it clear that we don't want to be known as a state that kills cats.

Before you say we should grant the chicken, or the cat equal rights to humans, let me remind you that it's not possible. We can't bring animals to our level. The young men who recently released thousands of mink from Midwestern fur farms don't have a clue. They have merely taken another swipe against true morality. Equating animal life with human life does nothing to improve the lot of animals. It does however degrade people. The London zoo recently proved this degradation by the volunteer caging of nearly naked young men and women next to their "primate cousins"

Actually, the locomotive is derailed already. While we have a fringe insisting on saving chickens (saving from what remains to be seen), true moral standards are falling by the way. Fifty years ago babies could not be aborted, but mangy strays could be shot. With this entrenched legal "right" to kill millions of babies, gay rights and gay marriages are now driving the train. The government of Canada has recently caved in, as has the United Methodist church; a position their president deems "courageous." Are we a civilized nation while shock proofing ourselves on gay issues, and opting for the lives of chickens and stray cats over our own unborn babies? Do we wonder why an ever increasing segment of the younger generation exercises no constraint with immoral and violent behavior?

In any case, before you hug your favorite pet too tight, let me just ask whether the increasingly jealous love of animals is displacing human responsibility to make marriages work, to love and to bring up children, and to conduct ourselves with duty, with integrity, and with responsibility toward God and our fellow men – and afterward properly care for animals – the hallmark of morally upright people. Pets, however dear they may be, exert no moral or character challenge over their owners. In other words, the affection of cat or dog is no measure of your character or morality.

Sadly, today we would remove all memory of natural law. We would rather deface or remove the reminders of moral absolutes engraved on historic monuments and buildings, than to admit that perhaps God would have valid input for the affairs of men. Ironically God doesn't seem to be especially threatened. He himself respects the free will of people. Not so an atheistic, evolutionary culture. In such a context, there is no plausible reason to be arbitrarily dogmatic. One would expect that those who reject moral absolutes would cease to believe in anything. Wrong. These people arbitrarily invent a new set of absolutes, no matter how harmful or illogical.

And even as they did not like to retain God in their knowledge, God gave them over to a reprobate mind . . . Romans 1:28

Whereas "one nation under God" produces order and harmony, one nation without God, fuels strident discord and moral chaos.

THE GRACE OF SALVATION

Martin Luther regained the vision of *justification by faith*, a biblically valid term. However, the late notable apologist, Francis Schaeffer, interpreted this as salvation being received by "faith plus nothing," or as by "empty hands of faith."

The Bible also conveys the truth of *imputed righteousness.* A well-known evangelical leader mistakenly describes this imputed righteousness as the good works that Jesus did, being deposited to the account of the one who believes. (We deal with imputed righteousness later.)

However sincere, these teachings relieve the believer of the responsibility of personal righteous living. But a teaching of salvation apart from repentance, forgiveness, and cleansing from sin is contrary to the biblical demand for holiness of life (*"Be ye holy, for I am holy"*, and *"without holiness, no man shall see the Lord"*). This has led to a false sense of what it means to be a Christian. As a result, Christianity is *claimed,* but all too rarely *lived,* by those who name the name of Christ. We are left with a mere empty shell of salvation.

What shall we say then? Shall we continue in sin that grace may abound? God forbid. How shall we that are dead to sin live any longer therein (Romans 6:1,2). Or in the words of Jeremiah 7:9,10; *will ye steal, murder, and commit adultery, and swear falsely, and burn incense unto Baal, and walk after other gods whom ye know not; And come and stand before me in this house, which is called by my name, and say, We are delivered to do all these abominations?* We are, in fact, not saved by faith only. Rather we are saved *by grace through faith* (Ephesians 2:8). I must insist that this grace of salvation is a gift totally supplied by God. We have no means at our disposal to generate grace, any more than we can sprout wings to fly. If we were to list salvation ingredients (as with packaged foods), according to content, the first and greatest ingredient would not be faith, nor repentance (both necessary), but grace.

Now for an illustration of grace. I've done a little travel to some far regions by air. But I will never own nor pilot a jet aircraft. But what I can't do, I don't need to do. At any time I present a valid ticket for the occasion, I am given a boarding pass. The boarding pass is my right to fly in the plane. I don't have a clue how to navigate the plane. I don't own the plane. I don't even bring my own seat. The boarding pass is my access. The airline takes it from there. I am flying and getting there as though I own the whole thing, even though I own nothing. That is the grace of the airline. And as flying is by aircraft, so is salvation of the Lord.

But what about faith? Is faith the ticket that gets you on the plane? Close, but not quite. Faith is the boarding pass. The boarding pass doesn't give me wings. It doesn't make the plane fly. It doesn't need to. The boarding pass does everything it needs to do, by giving access into the plane. The Bible says, *We have access by faith into this grace wherein we stand* (Romans 5:2). Let's not forget though, that faith must be valid. Faith must connect to an airline that provides planes that are airworthy, and with flight crews that know how to get you to your destination. To believe in a false religion, or to redefine Christian faith, will not get you to the intended destination. It appears that many have faith in faith, rather than true faith in God. But unless they do the will of God, then at the judgment, they will find that Jesus never knew them.

What about the ticket? The ticket has a price tag. Though salvation is free, it is not cheap. Repentance is in many respects like buying the ticket (not with money). He who would gain access by faith into grace must bring forth the fruit of repentance. Repentance comes out of the sense of dread and condemnation for sin. John the Baptist, who prepared the way for Jesus, came preaching repentance. He baptized those who gave evidence of repentance and confessed their sins. Jesus began his ministry by preaching repentance. Peter the apostle, preached repentance as the qualifier for conversion (Acts 3:19). In Revelations 2-3, Jesus Christ called for repentance among the churches in Asia. In repentance, sin is identified and renounced, and restitution is made to those one has sinned against. It is repentance from sin, and faith toward our Lord Jesus Christ that finally aligns the sin-sick heart of men to the saving grace of the holy God. Every true conversion is marked by a revulsion and confession of past sin, and faith cast on salvation in Christ.

There are aspects of salvation that tickets and boarding passes cannot convey. We expect a time lapse from ticket purchase to boarding. When it comes to repentance, faith, and grace, the same need not apply. When the conditions are met, the past sins are forgiven. The salvation is instantaneous.

Salvation incorporates the doctrine of imputed righteousness. God does not count people righteous, based on their track record. Rather, God declares the sinner justified (or reckoned righteous), the direct result of repentance toward God and faith toward the Lord Jesus. Because sin is forgiven, and no longer stands against him, the court of heaven counts the believer righteous without an accumulation of good works. It is based on the heart response and commitment. At the very moment when Abraham believed God (Romans 4:3), it was counted to him for righteousness. This is not a transfer of the good deeds of Jesus to Abraham's account. Rather, it is an accurate assessment of the commitment of the life of Abraham to God, and of the life of faith to follow. Even as the farmer sows his seed and calls it his "wheat field" before the seed has sprouted, so God knows the righteous heart that will, by faith, yield the fruit of righteousness.

James 2:14-20, refutes the shallow concept of an empty faith. God's promise of imputed righteousness was clearly validated when Abraham offered his beloved Isaac on the altar in response to the command of God. In response to "faith only" doctrine, James replies that even the devils believe - and tremble. This implies that the demons may have a better grasp of God's requirements than many "cheap grace" Christians do.

Now let's come back for another glimpse of grace. We say that grace is unearned favor with God, and so it is. The grace of forgiveness is ours, only because Jesus paid the price of it.

But the same grace package carries a twin aspect. Some say that grace makes up the shortfall; the difference between what a Christian should do versus his actual performance. But grace is almost the exact opposite. *It is the unearned power to live lives that are holy, righteous and God honoring.* When Jesus paid for our forgiveness, he did it with the larger view of our very transformation. He who has the *"power on earth to forgive sins"*, commands us to *"go and sin no more"*. The evidence of saving faith is the life that brings forth the fruit of righteousness. The Christian call is to abide in the vine, which is Christ. Those who abide in Christ do bring forth fruit. Those who do not abide, do not bring forth good fruit. Those branches will be cut off and cast into the fire.

Beware of being deceived with the idea that God plays some kind of word games, and that he wears rose-colored glasses, so that we may slip past him in our sins, through the pearly gates. Grace is not so cheap as to justify sinners in their sins after being so costly that Jesus Christ died on the cross *to save his people from their sins.*

GOD, GENESIS AND THEOLOGY

Did you ever hear someone reflect on the vast wealth of another and say, "If I had his money, I could throw mine away?" Sadly much of the church has thrown away the authority of Scripture on the assumption that the "wealth" of scientific evidence displaces the Genesis account of the Creator and the creation.

However, if your belief in God is founded on a literal acceptance of the Genesis record, you already have a solid background for understanding in both science and theology. You will have no need for the ongoing, ever changing, guessing games of evolutionary debate. In fact, there is no reason to even have an evolutionary debate. Why debate how a chicken got its feathers, if you haven't settled the score of how the chicken got its breath? So the question is not about evolution. It is about life. I say this as kindly as I can. He who does not believe in God, doesn't have a clue. So let's get on with the credentials for God, because the declaration of God's glory in creation provides compelling evidence for the very person and character of God, (thus for theology).

The first lesson in Genesis theology is that God is powerful. How powerful? *In the beginning God created the heavens and the earth.*

When my wife bakes a cake (I wouldn't know how), she doesn't say "let there be cake." She does combine the right basic ingredients, then slips the mix into the oven for the right amount of time.

But God didn't do it that way. For example, He didn't assemble basic raw ingredients for light. What He did do was say, *let there be light.* The basis for creation was the power of God's word; Nine times in Genesis we find *And God said . . .* typically followed with - *and it was so.* If you are about to laugh at my naivete, let me remind you of one thing, and then ask you a question.

This is the reminder. We know that all matter consists of molecules, and that molecules consist of energy, of electrons, protons and neutrons. Trees are not made of sawdust bonded with a resin, but of energy. Water is not some liquid dropped upon us from some other place in the cosmos. It is created of energy. Everything in the universe is packed tight with energy. (Sardines in a can would be the ultimate in roomy comfort by comparison.)

Now for the question: how could anyone account for such an incomprehensible quantity of energy, apart from the Almighty God?

But — we have another problem apart from God. The transfer of matter into power is not a problem. It is as easy as a lightning strike in a dry forest, or lighting a match at a gasoline spill. In fact, we deliberately convert millions of gallons of gasoline into many millions of highway miles daily. In warfare, bombs are turned into horribly destructive forms of energy. But neither time, nor chance (the evolutionist god), nor human intelligence, is able to convert energy back into matter. The factory smokestack never produces a gallon of paint. The burning inferno of a forest fire, never leaves a new house in its wake. The energy expended on highway miles never produces a single shiny new automobile. The bomb that is dropped never produces a new city.

By the way, a process that would compress energy into planets, stars, dogs, cats, trees, mice kangaroos, apes, and people would not be a "big bang." It would be the exact opposite; the compression of a colossal amount of energy. That is why the "big bang" must forever remain an adult fairy tale, only useful to people who have closed their minds against God. But God is not merely the only sufficient answer. He is the only answer that doesn't make a fool out of me.

Do you fear the power of lightning, of the tornado, or of the hurricane? If we find the release of energy, fearsome, how much more should we fear God, the ultimate source and controller of power?. The cause is indeed far greater than the effect. And the ultimate cause is God.

The second lesson in Genesis theology is that God has purposeful order to everything. He divided light from darkness, and arranged our solar system with days and nights, and with season following season, always in the same predictable order.

In the world of living things, God ordered that everything would reproduce *after its kind*.

If men were wise, they would cease trying to claim otherwise. The fossil "evidences" that would trace slime into simple forms of life and apes into man have come from vivid imaginations and sometimes from cruel hoaxes. Know this, that true science cannot be separated from biblical theology because the God of Scripture is also the God of nature. Science is nothing more or less than an accurate assessment of created things. It is knowledge derived from repetition of the same consistent results. Thus science is science only in being true to what exists in nature, where dogs remain dogs and babies are human beings from conception. Science is established in certainty, not in guessing games. But where Genesis is rejected, guessing is the only game in town.

We live every day in a world of absolutes, a fact that the evolutionist cannot embrace, but one that defines the very nature of God.

The third lesson in theology is the revelation of the majesty and glory of God. The Genesis description of creation is that *it was good*. In fact, *it was very good*. Who could argue the point? Even though creation has been in growing-old mode ever since sin entered into the world, it is at once both functional and beautiful. It is obviously made to be enjoyed. There are no superlatives sufficient to describe the wonder and beauty of birds, trees, flowers, or starry heavens. How can anyone study science and biology and fail to see the glory of these things on every hand? Truly, creation is the grand display of the goodness and glory of the Lord. Before you leave this lesson behind, take a good look in a mirror. First a reminder of what you don't see.

Call it "gross" anatomy. As living, functioning, humans, we are filled with organs and glands that we don't want to see. So what did God do with these functional yet ugly insides? First, he gently padded us with fatty tissue, to cover all the sharp edges, and then covered us in skin. He shaped ears, noses, and lips in right proportions (that can widen in a smile), added color and expression to the eyes, and added hair, finger nails and toe nails. And what is the result? God did such a wonderful job that vain people actually hold beauty contests.

And God knew that we needed to eat. He supplied the pastures with cattle, the peach trees with fruit, and various stalks with various grains. But how to get us to eat the stuff? No problem. He made our stomachs to complain with pangs of hunger (whatever that is). He gave us a sense of smell, and added taste buds to convince us that these things actually taste good. In fact, he even threw in negative buds, (the *yuk* factor), to keep us from eating at least most of what is poisonous, spoiled, or rotten.

The fourth lesson in theology resolves the questions of human and animal order. We are not our own. The Creator is the owner and director of the created. People may deny God, and refuse his instructions, but the absolute nature of what he has made is ringing testimony of his authority. And how does Genesis spell this out? God made the man in his own image and likeness. Then he appointed Adam with authority in his own right, as CEO of Eden, and as superintendent of the animal kingdom. Animals can be true only to instinct, humanity is responsible to the commandments of God.

The fifth lesson is the divine order of authority in the human family, the origin of male and female, and the establishment of marriage and family. These doctrines are clearly and liberally taught throughout Scripture, and have their source in God from the beginning. When Jesus was questioned about marriage and divorce, he referred his listeners right back to Genesis and original intent. God made them male and female. One male and one female are joined together in marriage. They become one flesh. They furnish the context of family. They replenish the earth. *"What God has joined together, let not man put asunder"*.

We need one more consideration from Genesis theology. After sin came into the world, and death by sin, Adam and Eve sought to cover their shame with fig leaves. But God was not satisfied. He clothed them with animal skins. Our culture today, has cast off both the shame and the protection of modesty in clothing (churches mostly included). Satan uses this departure from modesty, and the resulting sensual display, against sexual purity, fidelity in marriage. and the gift of reproduction.

If we would return to the theology of Genesis, we could be restored to the favor of God. But if we refuse to obey, we suffer the cultural consequences inherent in the blindness of evolutionary beliefs.

DISOBEDIENCE AND THE DECLINE OF SOUND JUDGMENT

We address this article to a culture that is long on equality, personal rights, and democracy (everyone gets equal say), and short on the wisdom of obedience and submission to authority. Far from being immune to the problem, Christianity in the West seems hopelessly mired in the same misguided ideals. Thus a culture where attempted answers merely multiply the problems.

Recently, I asked a few jail inmates for one-word descriptions of sin. The answers —drugs, alcoholism, lust, sexual immorality. Not a bad description. I wasn't expecting such a stark admission of sins that strike so close to home.

But there is a deeper reason for raising the issue. The Garden of Eden had every kind of tree needed for good food. Yet, through the tempter, Eve came up with three *logical reasons* to eat of the only forbidden tree in the whole place. (Your children are experts at that, right?) 1. Good for food. 2. Pleasant to look at. 3. It would add to her intellectual status.

But in eating, and then in Adam doing the same, they bartered both the wisdom of God, and the relationship with God. These losses form the common denominator of disobedience to all legitimate authority. It may be as simple as youthful shenanigans that at once blames the strictness of parents for the problem, even while the act of disobedience proves that he had no wisdom of his own. On the other end of the spectrum, are brilliant evolutionary scientists who gaze fixedly at old fossil bones in search of non existent evidence that God does not exist.

In either case, the most tragic loss is the severing of the relationship lifeline. This is so because the act of rebellion necessitates overthrowing (in their minds), the authority figures standing in the way. The youthful critic and rejecter of parentage, will carry his scowls and his cockiness over into every authority relationship. Not initially, of course. Being persuaded of the justice of his own case, he expects his new apartment landlord, or the new boss, or his pastor, to quickly rally to his cause. When that doesn't happen, they too get written off. This leads him to bond deeply and dangerously with those who are mirror reflections of himself.

In the case of the scientist, I suppose that many did expect that fossil analysis and space exploration would indeed provide justifying evidence for an anti God stance. But the utter complexity of the universe and of all living things has turned back the hope that the telescope and the microscope would be friends to their cause. I believe this readily accounts for the spate of vitriolic anti God books that have been published within the past five or six years. Like teenagers in rebellion, these atheists of academia, are not about to bury the hatchet (against God).

But, we are ahead of our story. Adam and Eve didn't need perfect understanding. Obedience would have saved them. Logic apart from God, turned them as sheep, to be fleeced by the devil. God did not require that they understand, but that they obey. Thus the greater definition of sin. *Sin is the transgression of the law of God.* It is the claim that I know better than the God of the universe. This is arrogance on the level of a three-year-old demanding equal voice in his father's business decisions.

I suppose that most "Christians" give grudging assent that the Bible should be believed and obeyed, though there is too little evidence that this actually happens on a wide scale. For many, who live in the darkened corridors of lying, cheating, or committing adultery, the transgression of Adam and Eve wouldn't amount to a blip on the radar of conscience. Yet, that single transgression opened the gate to everything that is evil.

This same truth holds on a personal level. The tragedy of rebellion is, that it does indeed open the way for all kinds of sins. It is as though the spiritual immune system is breached, lowering the resistence to temptation.

The testimony of Scripture is clear. Apart from obedience, and thus the transmission of grace and peace, there is no relationship with God. The plea of Jesus is clear: *"Why do you call me Lord, and do not the things that I say"?* And in another place: *"If you love me, keep my commandments"*. And the difference between the wise man who built his house upon the rock, and the foolish man who built upon the sand? The foolish man heard the Word of God, but didn't do it, while the wise man heard and did the will of the Father in heaven. To the many who profess to know God, yet fail to submit their lives in obedience, Jesus says, *"Depart from me, ye that work iniquity"*.

There is yet another hurdle to cross. Perhaps we are ready to concede that God is indeed to be obeyed. But we tend to forget that the authority of God is over us every day, in very practical, very human ways. Following are examples of God's authority — the father and mother in the home; the husband over the wife; presidents, rulers, and kings; the sheriff and the highway patrolman, and the boss on the job.

By now, I suppose, we will either cringe or mock. Or, perhaps we could still consider obedience so long as these authorities are of good character, and providing that the instructions given are of Eve-like reasonablness, such as *pleasant to our eyes, good for food*, or *desired to make us wise*. Sorry, but submission is not tested on wether authority is agreeable to us. It is measured on whether we are agreeable to authority.

Now, obedience to authority is not to lead us into sin. But those who dwell in divine wisdom will understand when obedience to human authority would amount to disobedience to God. As a Jewish captive in Babylon, Daniel knew that King Nebuchadnezzar's meat and drink would defile his conscience. Thus he refused it. Later, under King Darius, he knew full well that faithful worship to God was the path to the lions' den. But in the need to disobey, he did not rebel against these kings. Instead, we see Daniel continuing to cultivate a truly caring respect with both of these kings. There is no other way these pagan kings would have been led to acknowledge and worship the God of heaven. The believer can render such respect, not for the goodness or justice of authority, but because of the grace and love of his own heart in God.

As a culture, we are ever so bombarded with the defense of our "rights" to forbidden fruit. While in the West, we are enamored with the right to do as we please, we actually undermine our institutions of democracy and freedom. The greatness of a nation is not defined by voting rights and individualism, but by integrity and respect for authority, in the context of godliness. In fact, "democracy," is more dependent on the personal integrity, and the righteousness of the people, than any other form of government. What we see today, is that the conditions that would maintain our nation and culture are fast eroding, and heading to eventual collapse under the weight of the moral failures, inherent in the rejection of divine order.

Rebellion is always the path to chaos. Its energy is wasted in confusion and division. Subjection, on the other hand, is unifying and constructive. It is in harmony with the Spirit of Christ in the Believer, and magnifies our God. We may be tempted to think of subjection as the function of weak character. The opposite is true. The lives of the greatest of men, such as Noah and Moses, were marked with following God's instructions, *exactly.*

God would spare us through repentance, and with a return to the wisdom of his word, obedience to his commands, and subjection to authority.

FOR THOSE WHO WOULD TAKE BACK THE GOVERNMENT

We bring confusion and shame upon Christianity and the name of Jesus, with a misguided notion of a special permanent relationship between God and America. Over the last thirty years we have seen "evangelical Christian" presidents preside over ever lower legal and moral standards. It also appears that moral and ethical failures ensnare "Christian" politicians at about the same rate as their non Christian counterparts. While we can be sure that God has not changed, we cannot claim the same for the so-called Christian west. Just to reflect that change - there was a time when evangelical Christians would have wanted their women to stay out of politics. Also, in my growing up years, a divorced/ remarried man would have little chance of winning the presidency. Yet by 1980, the *favored candidate of the "moral majority"; was swept into office by the "conservative right."* If *"till death do us part,"* is so lightly taken, is it surprising that all moral values become negotiable? Is there really some substitute moral foundation that can take the place of keeping our marriage vows?

With due respect to men who established the nation on great biblical principles, I question just what it is the evangelicals mean when they talk about the need of "taking back" the country. Do they want the return of Sunday "blue laws' that close stores and businesses for the Lord's day? Is it the laws against public profanity and indecent exposure (immodest dress)? Is it the good old days when divorce meant an actual court battle? Is it to roll back *Roe* vs. *Wade*? Or would we break new ground with legislation banning TV time for school children?

If this is what we want, we don't need the government to do it. We Christians can take Sunday to remind ourselves that God created the world, that he is a Holy God, and that ultimately his word prevails. We are also perfectly free not to go shopping, dining out, or even to visit the newly opened

Creation Museum on Sunday. And since we Christians will answer to God for profanity and violence, we can shut down the device(s) that endlessly spue this awful stuff on us and our children (thus agreeing with God concerning things he hates.)

It gets even better from here. We, who are married, can refuse to become fools, by keeping the vows made at the first marriage altar. We can give our children the security of knowing that father and mother will never divorce (*Moses, for the hardness of your hearts suffered you to put away your wives, but from the beginning it was not so . . . What God hath joined together, let not man put asunder).* Pastors will perform a vital role by refusing to perform marriages for those with a former partner still living. Why have we opened the gates that Jesus himself firmly closed? *(If while her husband liveth, she be married to another man, she shall be called an adulteress.)*

We also can move to take back church youth groups to actual biblical standards: (*But fornication . . . Let it not once be named among, as becometh saints.)* This clearly calls for churches and parents to provide a controlled atmosphere of modesty and reserve, with a code of conduct conducive to keep youthful lusts in check. We cannot reveal the body in ways that should be concealed. (If I'm reaching concerned mothers in the readership, I have heard of online sources that specialize in modest clothing). We must not break down the sacredness of sexuality for entertainment or pleasure. We need to restore healthy reserve between young men and young women. Many have taken vows of chastity, only to break them later. However sincere, Christian youth groups lacking the full compliment of Christian standards, will suffer serious losses.

The following statics as given by a psychologist, spell out the magnitude of the responsibility we face in the present youth environment:

- The average young person watches 41/2 hours of TV daily. There is no way parental teaching can compete against the moral filth and violence portrayed as normal.
- American teens are the most violent in the world. In the U.S., 50% of all felonies are committed by males 15-21 years of age
- 80% of high school seniors have been drunk.
- 50% of seniors have tried drugs
- The number of sexually active 15- year old girls has doubled since 1990.
- 10% of 15 to 19-year old girls become pregnant every year. U.S. teen pregnancies and abortions are the highest in the world.
- The suicide rate has doubled since 1970. It is the second leading cause of death among teens (after car crashes).

The same psychologist bids us, (not exact quote), "remember the days when young men were taught skills and trades in preparation for courtship and marriage? The girls learned their own set of responsibilities. They could cook a meal, keep the house, and plant a garden. Both sexes knew that life and love and marriage and children were a challenge. They took it on, were equal to the task, and were fulfilled in doing it. The church and community culture supported this system".

In those days, there really wasn't much to "take back" from the government or anywhere else. That was in the days before we had given it away. In contrast, the present moral climate results in two things. It teaches young girls that they are throwaway commodities of pleasure with neither the value nor the holding power for the lifetime commitment of responsible men. It leads young men into the moronic pursuit of instant gratification at the expense of real manhood, marriage, and fatherhood (in that order).

Our young people have been duped. According to a recent poll reported by the St. Paul Pioneer Press the biggest factors of happiness for people age 13- 24 are good relationships with family and friends, and faith, and on the negative side: booze, drugs, and sex.

I think it is us as elders (including church elders), who are responsible for the confusion. We chose to make temporary the marriage God made permanent. God did this for good reasons. Those reasons are Tony and Tammy and Marsha and Kristina and Chad and Craig and Will and James and Jered and Micheal and Troy and Christopher and Austen and Ricky . . . Yes these are real people with their real names who have fallen through the cracks. These are just a few of many I have known. Their numbers are in the millions. They are the reason I am passionate about this subject. The church may not be directly responsible for many of these. But the breakup of marriage and family surely is. And to whom should people be able to look for examples, if not to those who claim to know God?

In summary, there is indeed a taking back that needs to happen, but it is not first the government. It is one that begins with humility and repentance, for letting go of godly standards that alone can keep a culture on track. It proceeds with my commitment, my integrity, and my fidelity - and yours. Only then, can we impact the next generation - and the government. How else to answer to God?

We end up paying double for despising the law of God. We pay a fearsome price in the loss of the next generation.

Unless we turn, we pay yet again when we face judgment before an angry God. *Come, and let us return to the Lord, for he hath torn and he will heal us. He hath smitten, and he will bind us up* (Hosea: 6:1).

The challenge is not to politically take back the country. It is for us who name the name of Christ, to depart from iniquity.

EVOLUTION AND THE DISCONNECTED CULTURE.

In an industrial accident, a piece of flying shrapnel severed a nerve in a young man's shoulder. It left an otherwise perfect arm hanging worse than useless, in a disconnect with the rest of the body, severed from communication with the brain.

As a parallel to this illustration, I am proposing that the acceptance of evolutionary dogma is a disconnect from our divinely created origin. Thus disengaged from the mind of God, we lose our way, mired in confusion and misinformation, tossed about by problems that have destroyed our peace and that threatens our very existence. This is inevitable, as Darwinism severs from the divine creative mind, to be joined to . . . nothing.

The damage is so widespread, because this disconnect has not been stayed by the church. In the past century, prominent clergymen and mainline denominations proudly joined the Darwinist hype of evolution. The claim imposed on impressionable minds, in schools and churches, is that people are accidental products of chance. The data clearly show that this disconnect devalues humanity, and is punctuated with devastating losses of wisdom, integrity and of morality. In its place, we embrace shameful and destructive behaviors.

We follow the lesson of the useless arm for yet another reason. From it, we can show that evolution is scientifically impossible, that Darwinism is a futile attempt to bridge an impossible divide in living systems.

To proceed with this claim, let's be sure we understand that there are two separate systems to our existence, yet functioning perfectly as one.

The first is the command center. The human arm does not come with self-contained instruction for its functions. It is wired to the command center (the brain) and works in conjunction with the rest of the body. Had the shrapnel not come at the speed of a bullet, the command center would have ordered the body to duck. The command center provides the dynamic of being alive. It is the seat of consciousness and intelligence. Greek philosophers referred to this as *Logos.* I just read the scoffing remarks of an atheistic scientist against religion. He dismissed the idea of the human being having a soul, based on the fact that dissecting a human brain fails to yield a soul and spirit. In that he is right, of course. But he fails to realize the simplistic nature of his argument. That is on par with doing an autopsy to find out the person's last words, or taking a computer apart to find the password. By the time science examines the cadaver, Logos has fled. Logos (along with soul and spirit), is not dead but alive.

The second system is *Sarco;* also from the Greek, is the flesh. This is the physical body. It is the perfectly matched host for Logos. A mismatch would be worse than useless. As with a computer, the software (logos), must be compatible with the operating system(sarco). In fact, the incompatible operating systems between animal species rule out random selection and survival of the fittest as tools for the development of new species.

In this discussion, I will use the term *sarco* interchangeably with the physical body and also in illustrations of inanimate objects that play host to information. I will use *Logos* as a proper noun as pertains to life and consciousness, information and intelligence.

We can illustrate the relationship of Logos and sarco with Scrabble game letters of the English alphabet. Let's follow two options. First you could lay out the letters blindfolded. But, as with ink in a pen, communication flows only if directed by an intelligent mind. Blindfolded, a random, readable word or phrase, (I love you), conveys nothing at all. (Call it a false positive.)

The silly argument I've heard, that a monkey randomly hitting typewriter keys over eons of years, would finally produce something meaningful, is absolute nonsense. The communication of genuine Logos is only from an intelligent host to a recipient with a compatible system. The monkey question might as well be; how many million years would it take a solitary, jabbering monkey to learn to speak only in perfect English? The easy answer is NEVER! The possibility lies outside of the monkey command center.

Your second option is to select and arrange those letters to convey the intended message, (will you marry me?) In this illustration the letters represent sarco. The intelligent arrangement represents Logos. The letters are mere carriers of intelligence. There is no point in examining individual letters under a microscope. There is no inherent Logos in them. In light of this, Darwin's "survival of the fittest" as the mechanism of evolutionary ascendency is not merely dead on arrival. For lack of Logos, it never got started. Randomness is blind. Starting with randomness yields only randomness. It has no access route to either Logos or Sarco. Like shrapnel, if powered at all, it is uncontrolled power. And like shrapnel, it may kill a living man, but it will never raise a dead corpse.

The science of DNA reveals encoded information (Logos). It defines every detail of sarco, leaving no areas to chance development. Supercharged growth of sarco, jumping the bounds of programing, does happen. Darwinists would call this evolution. We call it cancer (sarcoma).

Strange that evolutionary dogma persists with a life of its own in what is marked as a day of scientific enlightenment. The self - entrenched theorizing of many scientists along strictly materialistic lines, blinds them to the backward, unscientific nature of the evolutionary model. It ignores completely the hard science of biogenesis — only life begets life. Some (like Francis Crick), speculate that life was introduced to earth from another planet. Which answers nothing. How did life get to *that* planet?

Survival works because living things are already fit. It works because all the ancestors of things alive today always were wonderfully fit, with sarco matched perfectly to the right Logos. This points to the divine copywriter, mapping out the information in Logos, and matching the sarco to run precisely on that information. No worry about early, simple forms of life - born in primitive, oceanic soup, strong enough to raise dead matter to life, yet deadly enough to keep it from happening. God provided incubators and intensive care stations in the wombs and nesting habits of created-to-order adults.

The "survival" theory would speculate that an automobile battery could mushroom into a full-blown Mercedes, or that a single Scrabble tile would develop into a complete Scrabble game. Actually, even to illustrate, we allow the evolutionist too much rope, since the battery and the tile were patented by Logos, not by randomness.

Thus to claim that a random assembly of chemicals could beget Loges and sarco, through time and chance, is the antithesis of science. On the other hand, to claim that life on earth must spring from the preexisting, living God (LOGOS), is more than a religious statement. It is a statement compatible with hard science.

Evolutionary dogma bravely attempts to track human development through reptiles, birds, fish and ape-men, even though the operating systems are incompatible.

Now get this: a physical chain of evolutionary development (ameba to man), would require a parallel, double evolution of logos and sarco, with logos showing the way. This fits the science of DNA and of creation perfectly, but runs off the radar of evolutionary probability.

For example, the intelligence for a bird's hollow wing structure and intricate feathers must lead the way in the development of the wing. But, the bird needs not only the sarco (the physical body and capacity to fly), but the specialized, distinct, bird-only information, perfectly matched to what its sarco can support. Bird Logos covers myriad for-birds-only information. Along with bird sarco, bird Logos must map migration patterns, teach bird song and nest building, and what and how a bird feeds its young. So when did the "ancestor" reptiles start singing, migrating, and building nests? It is not enough for a mouse to chance into bat wings. With mouse logos, wings would hang useless. The mosquito must not only have the complex equipment to draw blood, but also the logos to use it. If randomness could order complexity, it would leave us with a lineup of creatures hopelessly trying to use equipment they no longer have, or having equipment they don't know how to use.

The understanding of Logos and sarco also clarifies other confusing issues. Contrary to Darwin's day, we now know that there are no simple forms of life. Every form of life, even if microscopic, is complex beyond comprehension. What we have is a vast array of living forms, every one of them fit to survive. All have their unique aspects to their operating systems and checkpoints beyond which they cannot develop. These are barriers science cannot span. If you thought that man is the pinnacle of evolution, remember, there are millions of things that a man cannot do. This is not lost abilities. The man was simply not encoded with spider logos, to spin a spider's web, or with chicken logos, to lay a chicken's eggs, nor with monkey logos, to swing through jungle trees. (For that I am grateful). However, the man is indeed at the pinnacle of creation, in a special relationship to receive instruction from the mind of God (the divine Logos).

The fallacy of the evolution of man from the primitive into higher races, obviously yields a darker side, that of primitive men and inferior races. Though polite society has muted prejudice against Australian aborigines and blacks, racism is both the native and natural fruit of the evolutionary tree. Again, special creation gets it right. Racial differences are superficial, as all humans come from the same original pair.

The information highway joining Logos to sarco is evidence for an infinitely wise and powerful LOGOS (Jesus Christ as Creator God, John 1:1-4).

Like a bird losing its nesting or navigational skills, humanity, sundered from God by evolutionary dogma, loses both its moral dimension and its purpose. Such a culture goes into spiritual self-destruction mode, by denying the life-giving LOGOS (God).

The clergy and church should never have catapulted to theories conceived in scientific dark ages, and hatched in agnosticism. Those who are anchored to the love of truth, beginning with the Genesis creation model, may also access the redemption model, the coming of Jesus Christ into the world to save his people from their sins.

THESE UNCERTAIN TIMES:
THERE IS A CAUSE

BEYOND BELIEF

This was the bold headline of our newspaper the day after 9/11 (September 11, 2001). Shortly thereafter, from Ground Zero, the President declared that the terrorists who brought down the Twin Towers can never destroy the foundation of America. But what is the foundation of America? And what hath Washington to do with prophecy?

Fast forward to 2008. Now for the biblical version of **BEYOND BELIEF**: *No man buyeth their merchandise anymore . . . For in one hour is so great riches come to naught.* (Revelation 18). On and since September 29, 2008, on Wall Street, many trillions of dollars in paper wealth have come to nought. Thus the Bible prediction of sudden catastrophic meltdown is understandable today in ways that the biblical writer (two thousand years before Wall Street), could only have known by inspiration from God. From loftiest heights of wealth, glory, and power - into chaos and destruction — one of these times the bell may be tolling for us.

Today magnificent structures of granite and glass, housing our great corporations and financial institutions, have become a deceptive facade, masking compromised policies that have drastically altered the old status quo of sound business policies and lending practices.

In every natural tragedy, there is a cause. There is a reason when a train jumps the tracks or an airplane falls out of the sky, or a space shuttle disintegrates.

The same principle applies to the internal workings of politics, energy policy, and in the housing and financial markets. Sustainable institutions of the past, were governed by tried and true principles in management and operation. Bounded by ethics and integrity, these stayed the course, making minor corrections as needed, just as a capable pilot maintains his flight pattern - with minor adjustments of a few degrees. When a pilot resorts to desperate or contradictory maneuvers, the flight is in danger.

The evidence of economic peril surrounds us. The unprecedented rise and fall of the stock market, the housing market, and of crude oil, and the incredulous salaries of top executives and sports figures, the enormous wealth gained in speculation, and the culture given over to lotteries and gambling — these all attest to an economy out of control.

We have gone quite mad. We throw billions in borrowed money after bad money in the financial markets — as though the way to fix a leaking reservoir were to pump more water into it. We run ahead of science, pursuing energy policy and global warming concerns with questionable science, but with blind fervency. We embrace false balance sheets and rigged computer models. We despise fossil fuels, and do a belated repentance of dependence on foreign oil. Yet we have known since the embargo of 1973, that the advantage goes to those who develop available reserves, not in cutting production and neglecting refining capacity, as we have done.

We speak glowingly of renewable energy sources that in total combination come nowhere close to sustaining us, or that pose an even greater threat to the environment. We balk at offshore and arctic drilling, but we plunder thousands of acres of the best crop land for fuel, putting both food price and food supply on the line (not good for poor and hungry people around the globe).

We do well to be self -critical in relation to consumerism. We have been fixated with material goods and material goals in a tradeoff of greed over integrity, and in taking instead of giving. This unprecedented lavishness and luxury will continue to cost us down the road. But the newest demands on containing global warming, and preserving energy will certainly punish us without resolving our problems. We cannot turn back the global thermostat even while the major populations of the world industrialize, unencumbered by clean air standards. Yet we are poised to radically cut carbon emissions (regardless of effectiveness, costs, or negative consequences), on the assertion that the narrowest margin of human-caused contribution of carbon dioxide is the cause of global warming. (Carbon dioxide is not a pollutant). This ignores the possibility that warmer trends may cause rising carbon dioxide levels, rather than the other way around. It also overlooks the cyclical differences in solar trends (solar winds, cosmic rays and sunspot activity or lack thereof), as the controlling factor in pronounced warming and cooling trends that go back over known history. Indeed, some scientists now predict decades of cooling based on present calming down of solar activity.

So why does this longtime Anabaptist pastor address political, economical, and environmental issues?

THE SOLUTION IS NOT WHERE WE THINK
If we would survive at all, or survive other than a crime - ridden nation of warring factions, we must deal with the underlying cause. We have departed from our historic world view — the persuasion that God overrules in the affairs of men (to quote Benjamin Franklin). We have denied unchangeable divine law, for the low ceiling of conflicting opinions of men. Though this shift hasn't yet brought on an official profession of atheism (as it did the self-collapsing Soviet block), it does leave us on the same self-destructive slope. It leaves us to govern, to make decisions, and do business, as if God no longer existed.

But the Almighty does not change. We can merely trade off his mercy for his wrath. His commandments forever qualify the laws and constraints by which men may be justly governed and live securely. Without this law of God, we destroy our moral foundation, and our cultural foundation with it. Confusion reigns. Our differences mushroom, fueling hotter debates, and leaving us swamped in social and criminal problems beyond solution.

The new dogma insolently betrays and persecutes the old. This is America pursuing barbaric policy, where criminal acts now take on legal protection. This is not a land of the free and home of the brave, but one of forced toleration and inclusiveness. Ironically, such a culture loses patience with those who dare to frame sobering questions, or demolish politically correct strongholds. The result is this frozen, denial-of -God atmosphere, where conscience is fettered, and truth is bartered for corruption.

The liberal left with its jealous monopoly on public education, put God on furlough a long time ago. Equating a boy with a dog — or a snail — as an evolutionary accident, has had its negative impact far beyond any classroom where Darwin is revered. So why wouldn't the brightest students in class make the easy decision to cheat their way through exams? They graduate into adulthood and go into law or politics, but without a stabilizing moral compass. Or - they become powerful figures in large corporations or on Wall Street. They are a law unto themselves. They live in a vortex of greed. The effect on others, and even the corporate health of their companies, doesn't register on their radar. And because greed knows no limits, the system is finally over heated. The result is an economic meltdown. The solutions are beyond the pale of financial gurus and governments solutions.

Now back to the same classroom — the fellows meet the girls. They make the easy decision that bypasses marriage. This behavior is reenforced through reproductive clinics and abortion mills (very like no down payment mortgage deals for unqualified buyers). It has altered the social landscape. It has procured monstrous bailout programs of welfare as a replacement of absentee fathers and breadwinners. The children are deprived from birth of half their parentage. But these substitute programs only assure that fathers become social misfits by escaping rightful responsibility, and that the sure foundation of marriage doesn't get rebuilt.

The Christian right differs from the liberal left, but mostly in rhetoric. They believe that the U.S.A. has favored nation status with God. Thus many of them seriously believe that the nation can be taken back for God by political means. I will be bold enough to say — it will not happen in a thousand years. Why? The kingdom of God advances by power of the gospel of Jesus Christ for the redemption of sinners. This turns lives and morals toward righteousness. Favored status belongs only to those *who do the will of the Father in heaven.* (Matthew 7:21). Yet the Christian right tends to embraces an empty faith that brings reproach into their personal lives and chosen political fields. They too are caught in spin and corruption and scandal. They divorce as readily, and their children are about as cravenly worldly and immoral as the liberal left. What standing do they have in the day when Jesus Christ shall judge all people according to the gospel?

Had we not forsaken the foundational dynamic of righteousness, we wouldn't be asking moronic questions about what constitutes marriage. We would be taking instruction on marriage from the God who created male and female, endowed with reproductive capacity, and entrusted with responsible procreation. No alternatives are needed to live well, responsibly, and securely. Small wonder that the Bible posts stern warnings against tampering with marriage - this only sufficient cornerstone of civilization.

The hallmark of civilized culture (as in our national history), is uncompromising regard for human life. Yet we have traded this prized gift from God for the bizarre notion of a "woman's right to choose." But what standing has murder under state sanction with the High Court of God?

We present this as a valid apologetic against a corrupting cultural shift. This has happened inside Bible defying denominations, Ivy League academia, the courts and legislatures, and in economic and corporate institutions. Thus we face the vengeance of the God of rejected moral absolutes and neglected Christian teachings.

Finally, this is neither threat, nor phobia, nor coercive measure against anyone. It is the claim that all valid ideas have their basis in the wisdom of God as revealed in Scripture, and that the average person can know and embrace simple truth. Welcome to the voluntary response of a renewed conscience toward the truth, and the invitation to choose life. God's invitation stands: **Look unto me and be ye saved, all the ends of the earth.**

A PROBLEM OF PACKAGING

Know ye not that the unrighteous shall not inherit the kingdom of God? Be not deceived, neither fornicators, nor idolaters, nor adulterers . . . shall inherit the kingdom of God. (I. Corinthians 6:9,10).

Know ye not that ye are the temple of God, and that the Spirit of God dwelleth in you? If any man defile the temple of God, him shall God destroy; for the temple of God is holy, which temple ye are. (I. Corinthians 3:17).

Unto Adam also and to his wife did the Lord God make coats of skin and clothed them. (Genesis 3:21).

Now examine the above passages again. What do coats of skin have in common with preserving the temple of the Holy Spirit, and with sexual purity?

Recently, evangelical leaders have been sounding an alarm. One book, *"Already Gone,"* shares the grim statistics of losing many youths from our churches even before they reach college age. The research shows that young people are not properly grounded in the authority of Scripture and with the creationist world view. This leaves them an easy target for all kinds of diverse and confusing ideas. The obvious answer then is to instruct them and ground them in biblical information. Right?

In fact, the problem is more complex than that. There are two fronts to the issue of turning this tragedy around. One is indeed training in biblical truth, and Christian principles. Lack of respect for the Scriptures and the authority of God through the Scriptures, does indeed leave young people mired in unbelief. To such, the church becomes irrelevant.

But there is a second reason, perhaps more powerful reason the church becomes irrelevant. It is unlikely that any other culture in the history of the world has ever been so bombarded with opportunity to be mesmerized and over-

226

come with evil, as is the present young generation. There is nothing to be imagined, that is not available at their fingertips through technology. There was a time when the worst technological influence you could imagine, was the teenager with his own TV in his own room. Not anymore. Through Face book, chat rooms, texting, sexting, and the likes, everything is possible. Many of this generation can and do share filth and lewd photos of themselves and others from anywhere, including church hallways and auditoriums. This young generation knows this, is bombarded with it, and many fall prey to it. This doesn't mean that they are especially bad. Simple curiosity, and sometimes goading by others, can take them where they never should have gone. Wherever the moral fiber of church youth groups is compromised, doctrinal truth from the pulpit on creation and salvation, will have little impact. They are indeed, *Already Gone* . . .

Why? Because they lack the moral "coats of skin" protection, with which God himself clothed Adam and Eve. This is the lesson of the coats of skin. Adam and Eve need this covering for their shame, as they must now navigate their way through a fallen world with a fallen nature. And that is why the church needs a lesson from the packaging industry. It's not just knowledge of truth that young people need. They need the preservation of chastity, a way to block unobstructed access to wrong thinking, pornography, and sinning with their own, or the opposite sex. They need boundaries that provoke them to flee youthful lusts, rather than encouraging licentiousness. Nothing less than thorough application of practical godly standards will enable them to escape the destruction of sexual immorality. Those youths who are truly preserved as vessels of chastity and honor will want the protection of the faithful church.

We could take a lesson from the banana industry. You could have the best contacts with banana brokers in Central America, and the best and fastest possible shipping arrangements for importing them to the states. But if some broker decided to peel those bananas to save on space and weight, and ship them in bulk to save on boxes, the best production practices would avail nothing. Those bananas could not be saved. There would be 100% spoilage. And that is the lesson in packaging.

Packaging is a huge industry. Billions are spent every year on crates, cardboard boxes, packing materials, shrink wrap, and strapping tape. Yet packaging is also a lowly industry, for packing things in crates and cartons is not an end in itself. Packaging is devoted to a single purpose - delivering valuable goods to their destinations, without damage or spoilage. Much packaging material is discarded after single use. Packaging for transport is for utility, not for show. Those banana boxes don't come gift wrapped. Packaging will usually conceal, rather than reveal, the value of content. Where gift wrap is used, it is a paradox of sorts. It has no power over value within. The removal of the wrap may bring gladness - or even keen disappointment.

But packaging is expensive. True. The cost is a necessary expense. It sustains our economy, and even our lives as food, (including those bananas), is distributed from afar.

Inadequate packaging goes back as far as Adam and Eve in their vain attempt to cloth themselves. It was God who clothed them sufficiently. Modest apparel is still the gift of the merciful God, for those who humble themselves to receive it. The lesson, though non optional, is reserved for those of a teachable spirit. But this is also the very realm in which the Spirit of God ministers, to magnify and to preserve the great treasure of godly character and purity of heart — the only claim of the Christian to being the temple of God.

The packaging must be sufficient to "keep" believers in a world at enmity with God, a world boldly sold out to all kinds of evil and deviant behavior. As already implied, Christian "packaging" is not only just a clothing thing. It applies to everything needed for the preservation of sexual purity and personal holiness. The temple might look good outwardly, only to be inwardly corrupted in the high tech exposure to the sensual and perverted "norm." It must preserve the godly values we pursue, what we do for entertainment, the music we listen to, and define our dress code (a high calling indeed, in the midst of a crooked and perverse nation, where we are called to shine as lights in the world).

The very scarcity of teaching and writing on outward standards is evidence that the church is blind to the negative impact of this mass voluntary exposure to the works of darkness. As a result, the Christian community loses the dynamic of the Spirit filled life and victorious living. Spiritual fruit spoils in shipping, as the church neglects defining sanctifying limits for Christian living. When believers, parents, and churches default on their responsibility, it simply becomes nobody's business how sensually or lavishly people may dress, or how defiling is their entertainment. For many growing up in the church, the damage and loss is never recovered.

Many Christian authors' personal appearance, on glossy covers, in Christian bookstores embody the popular embrace of *Your Best Life Now.* The Tele-evangelistic community has also given us an eyeful of examples, not only with lavish and even seductive wardrobes, but also with Rolls Royce, Rolex, and an air-conditioned dog house for Rover. Thus even writers and leaders shamelessly mimic the gaudy gift wrap and packaging of the ungodly - often with the same excesses — and with the same ungodly results. Whoever is clothed shamelessly, without regard for godliness, modesty, and chaste behavior is easily brought to shame. As these things transpire in the churches, the Spirit of God is grieved into retreat.

Consider for a moment the efforts among evangelicals to stem the tide of fornication among young people with virginity vows and chastity ceremonies. This is no trivial concern. The spiritual life of church and family is nothing amidst the moral washout of believers. That is the encouraging side of the effort. But these virginity vows are shown not to be very effective. Why? Because the promise of the lips requires the backup of consistent packaging. Chastity requires a heart well insulated with an outward appearance and a personal environment deliberately chosen to protect the treasure of the purity principle within. The vow of the lips is no match for sensual appearance and questionable standards of entertainment, music, and conduct.

We may not know the whole of what transpired in the fall. But we do know that right through our present time and experience, Satan would clothe every attractive female in gift wrap, as a sensual goddess, with the singular goal of leading men like oxen to slaughter. But this comes at the expense of marriage, of family, and of one's own soul. The book of Proverbs clearly labels the house of the sensuous woman as the doorway to hell.

God's provision of modest clothing was and is an act of mercy, closely entwined with the blood of animal sacrifice. The image of God in humanity requires the preservation of biblical morality. The pure in heart who will see God will gladly subject outward personal choices to the inward goal of living in the grace of God. Whatever gets in the way — from entertainment, to music, to wrong influence from friends, to improper clothing, or undue familiarity between the sexes must go. There is no *keeping the heart with all diligence,* apart from taking the protective measures God has made available.

Proper clothing is beneficial not only for believers. *U.S.A. Today,* did a survey before and after school uniforms in the Long Beach CA school system in the early '90s. They tracked ten categories of problems. Every category showed marked improvement — after school uniforms. Vandalism showed the least improvement — down 18% — sexual offenses the most — down 74%. This is not claiming that decent clothing has power to change the heart, but it does confirm that indecent clothing does incite evil tendencies.

The dwelling of God is in two locations. First is the high and lofty place above the heavens which is his throne. The second is in within the humble and contrite heart on earth. He utterly rejects the proud of heart with their outward trappings. Perhaps this is the day to start applying these principles, beginning with your wardrobe. For you, Christian, yet unprepared to follow such an order, the question is actually — what makes you think you are following Christ at all? Jesus warns us that it is better even to sacrifice an eye or a hand, than to have two eyes and two hands, and to be cast into hell. Packaging plays a vital part in this equation. Your future good and your eternal abode will surely be worth it.

So what to do with the *Already Gone* syndrome? I personally believe that the best possibility of success may not begin with the foundational ABC's of doctrine, but with the XYZ's of moral guilt and moral ruin. This means addressing the guilt, the sinfulness, and the lostness of sexual immorality directly to the conscience. This is accomplished through peaching and teaching that engages youths directly, right to the heart of the need. This type of conviction of sin, bypasses the immediate need for full doctrinal understanding. If I could preach to a thousand youths whose houses were on fire, I would go for the fire extinguisher, before exposing the missing foundation of their belief system. In their relief that the fire is out, (and the peace of forgiveness is in), I think they would accept our help with the foundation.

ENTITLED TO RUIN

When they knew God, they glorified him not as God, neither were thankful, but became vain in their imaginations, and their foolish heart was darkened (Romans 1:21a).

Thanklessness toward God crosses a line that sees the role of the Almighty God through a distorted lens. This distortion assumes that the ways of God come short in meeting the needs of humanity. It is the idea that God needs our help for the best arrangement of our circumstances. It assumes that the commandments of God such as *love not the world*, and *lay not up for yourselves treasures on earth*, and *love your neighbor as yourself,* are best disregarded. A tradeoff happens, wherein earthly substance is trusted, hoarded, and even worshiped, above the Creator who provides these things. The assumption is, that earthly gain is always good, and that losses are always negative.

However, cash is an insufficient keeper of the soul. The love of money inevitably loosens the bands of integrity and stabilizing morality (*the love of money is the root of all evil*). Thus the transfer of security in God into the lust for things, turns human wisdom into foolishness, and ends upsetting every ethical/moral absolute. This leads to a culture seeking answers to perplexing problems and finding none, because the underlying madness defies solutions. (For a current example of such moral, financial, and social chaos, we need look no further than U.S.A. 2010).

While our biblical text could trace various cultural missteps down into the same pit, we will retrace a line that has changed our mentality dramatically over the past one hundred twenty years, yet evokes little concern across America, not even in the churches. It is the idea that personal financial means may be maintained on the backs of other people or institutions. It often operates on a lottery of sorts, but instead of buying chances to win, it's buying chances to lose. In the lottery, the risk associated with a small outlay, "entitles" the winner to make it big. But in our fears of losing what we have already, we buy entitlements called premiums. This small outlay then, is the protection against the day of loss, whether fire, theft, illness, or act of God.

The tragedy may start innocently enough, but becomes profound. It takes people from the realm of cheerful givers who care about the needs of others, and transforms them into grabbers and takers. The greed virus eventually finds its way into all things monetary and blossoms into social programs. It bleeds what succeeds to cover abject failure. In so doing, it also guarantees that failure survives and that ever greater resources will never be sufficient, which describes the state of our economy today.

Recently, as I finished a kitchen project, this respectable customer of many years pointed out that he was writing the check to me personally, rather than to my business. At first, I was baffled as to his intent. I found that he was suggesting that this was like paying cash. "Cash," he said, as he now quoted someone else, "is the small businessman's only friend." Surprised at the suggestion, I assured him that the method of payment made no difference, that all our income is reported.

It would be enlightening, I think, to pursue his philosophy to a logical conclusion. Could he tell me at what income level would I no longer "qualify" to under report my income? And could a "small" businessman, cash in on other advantages as well? For example, Walmart is a huge corporation. It is also in much better financial shape than the U.S. government. People have ways of "under reporting" the merchandise going out the door (it's not called stealing, just shoplifting). But at what level would one no longer qualify for "free" merchandise from Walmart? In fact, the notion that the genuinely poor are entitled to shoplift, providing the retailer is sufficiently prosperous, was recently floated openly by a clergyman, (to the embarrassment of his denominational leaders). In any case, stolen merchandise and employee theft is a multibillion dollar problem quite apart from what follows.

Let's peer into the present financial near-meltdown. It is triggered by, but not limited to, a not-so negative sounding term called entitlement. The American dream has long dictated that we are "entitled" to own our own homes. But in recent years encouragement to ownership was greatly expanded by suspending sane lending practices in the mortgage market. The rest is history. The attempt to put many more Americans into their own homes has resulted in the exact opposite - the loss of homes and jobs for millions of Americans.

Unfortunately, the entitlement mentality is so entrenched that it was the only lens through which the damage could be viewed, so the same mentality that brought on the crises, also dictates our long ongoing recovery attempts. This led to personal stimulus checks; bailouts for selective defunct institutions (too big to fail); cash for clunkers; tax breaks for first-time home buyers, and huge infusions of cash to save or to create jobs. Never mind that the cost of these programs far outstrips any possibility of long-term benefit.

At this writing, instead of careful analysis of where all this is headed, the focus goes to yet another entitlement; affordable health care for everyone. Yet the real tragedy in health care is not that millions of us are uninsured (many of us by personal choice), but the idea that health insurance is a personal necessity, and the only viable option for the average American. It appears that way only because it's more glamorous to go into debt for McMansions and Lincohn Navigators than for medicines, appendectomies, or other surgical repairs. The drain of medical costs may indeed impede status for a generation that believes life really does consist of the abundance of things possessed. I challenge that notion. When health really is at stake, of what use are the unaffordable toys. Further, the best of health care plans, cannot cover for careless or self-destructive habits, neither do they deliver from accidents and terminal illnesses.

(Ten out of ten Americans will die). This *I'm not responsible for -my -bills* mentality, is accompanied by the continued shrinking of the collective American spine, perhaps at a rate comparable to the shrinking of the Arctic icecap.

The fixation on entitlements and insurances, along with the search for quick riches through malpractice suits, is the major cause of skyrocketing medical costs and then attempts to conceal them. We are easy prey to promises of painless ways of doing things. We seemingly never learn that painless (as in insurance and socialist programs), breaks the vital financial link between medical provider and patient. It provides a "free zone" of irresponsibility that leaves costs unchecked. Finally then, "free" ends up costing the most, even while robbing us of character.

But now we are way ahead of the story. Up through Grover Cleveland's presidency, it was understood that the financial support of the people was not the function of government, but that the people supported the necessary expenses of government. President Cleveland was very adept at stern lectures to those who thought otherwise. He made clear that the plight of poor and needy Americans could be faithfully entrusted to the generosity of their "sturdy fellow Americans." In this Cleveland was clearly defining the case for limited government. If government had continued to function in the realms of order, justice, and security, "we the people" could have continued to arise to the occasion and find the means to support both the government and the excessive burdens of our neighbors. As it is, the system is long broken down in government overload (there are already "Bridge Out Ahead" postings for Social Security and Medicare), as bureaucracy ends up swallowing the camel.

Wise old Grover could have said it one better, had he explained that this truly is the legitimate, permanent, separation of powers between the Church and the State. Indeed, it wasn't long after Cleveland that State started playing Church. To be sure, the state should have been free at any time to charge the church with dereliction of duty if the church failed to perform. Instead, it took over and displaced Christian duties such as family support and giving to the destitute. As it is, both church and state suffer for the switch. The bankrupting costs to the government of entitlement spending is tragic. But so is the resultant milk toast character of church people relieved of stewardship responsibilities in our communities. Not only are we Christians now free not to reach out to the genuinely poor among us, but the sheep of the church are themselves guilty of overgrazing government pastures. The great tragedy is the mentality that has transformed us from being a church of compassion and giving, (part of the essential nature of the gospel) into to an "owes me" culture of takers and cheaters. And what can we say of the damage when the fat of our wealth is then squandered in empty diversions into short-sighted pleasures and wanton materialism?

If only we could grasp the fact that our distraction with things that pass away, robs us of joy and gratitude in God for things that truly last, such as with houses not made with hands, eternal in the heavens.

Why not . . . ?

- Consciously dedicate everything you have to God.
- Prepare for accountability to God by assuming the responsible role as stewards of earthly things, as gifts from God.
- Assume responsibility for total integrity in earning, buying, selling, and giving.
- Reject the thought of having the right to the labors and resources of others.
- Take the long view of the love of giving. It is the way of laying up treasures in heaven.
- Reject the idea of pursuing personal rights by suing our fellow men.
- Remembering: *We brought nothing into this world, and it is certain we will carry nothing out.*

STARLIGHT, TIME, AND THE AGE OF THE EARTH

This is one vast universe. At 186,000 miles per second it takes millions, or even billions of years for starlight to reach the earth. For many scientists, and old-earth Christians, this proves that the universe is billions of years old.

Now hold it just a minute. According to USA Today (March 17-19, 2006), the "Big Bang" lasted for a trillionth of a second. So in the teeniest fraction of the blink of an eye, the universe went from marble-size to billions of light years across. I hope you've absorbed this startling revelation.

If scientists have not shot themselves in the foot on this one, then they have surely shot the starlight/time theory between the eyes. Clearly, you can't judge the age of the universe by star light and light years after all. Perhaps light does travel at a present constant of 186,000 miles per second. Yet in this supposed "big bang," you have just cancelled any light years argument for the age of the earth. You are suddenly confronted with light catching a piggyback ride on matter, hurtling through the universe at *billions of light years in a split second.* Or did light not get out of the starting gate at the same time? If it didn't, were the stars themselves dark for millions of years?

Now this doesn't mean that I have actually resolved the starlight/time issue. I just wanted to point out that scientists mean to get by with the sort of incredible theories that would make me blush, if I proposed stuff like that to get God off the hook.

By the way, how is it, that God; infinite, omniscient, and omnipotent, could not possibly have created the earth in six days, whereas "big bang' could do it inside of a second? Who struck the match for the "big bang.?"

As we have explained elsewhere, the formation of matter should call for an imploding of vast amounts of energy, not the other way around. Now we don't have ways of formulating matter, but we do have lots of ways of releasing it. The explosion is always proportional to the transfer of matter into energy.

I would say this, to old-earth Christians who seem obliged to dance with Darwin. The millions (or billions), of years theory would lend itself much better to extinction and annihilation. The law of entropy simply takes too great a toll to think that gradualism could survive and thrive over a period of millions of years. That would be asking an awful lot of this solar system. What we do have on this earth, teeming with life and beauty, fits much better with a still vigorous, young earth.

It works a bit like this. If you claimed your Chevy has a million miles on it, I'd say, Umm... "remotely possible", but if you said the Chevy you're driving today is a million years old, I wouldn't believe it, even if GM had been around for so long.

And thou, Lord, in the beginning hast laid the foundation of the earth; and the heavens are the works of thine hands: They shall perish, but thou remainest; and they all shall wax old as a garment; and as a vesture shalt thou fold them up, and they shall be changed: but thou art the same, and thy years shall not fail (Hebrews 1:10-12).

Think on these things.

IS YOUR MARRIAGE WORTH SAVING?

Have ye not read, that he that made them in the beginning made them male and female and said, For this cause shall a man leave father and mother, and shall cleave to his wife: and they twain shall be one flesh? Wherefore they are no more twain but one flesh. What therefore God hath joined together let not man put asunder (Matthew 19:4-6).

Please give careful heed before you head for that tragic chasm called divorce. Whether or not you consider yourself a Christian, there is probably much more at stake than you realize.

Our word must be our bond. Marriage is such a bond. It is a vow that carries across the uncertainties of life; for better or worse, in riches or poverty, and in sickness or health. It is a vow of personal performance, saying in effect; *I will always be there for you and with you, quite apart from your performance.* Though marriage is for time, and does not extend beyond death (Matthew 22:30), it is grounded in Scripture as being permanent on earth. Marriage is God's idea and his planning in the context of a lifelong union. He made the woman from the man, and presented her back to the man. Adam, upon seeing Eve for the first time, recognized her immediately as being uniquely his own. *"This is now bone of my bone, and flesh of my flesh"* (Genesis 2; 21-24). How does one divorce his own body? Permanence of marriage was established from the creation and confirmed and sanctioned by Jesus Christ. *"What therefore God hath joined together, let not man put asunder."* Thus the biblical teaching is clear. Marriage is "until death do part."

In essence, God owns the rights and the terms of marriage, and then offers franchises to those who will commit to it. Since the terms and conditions are his, the contract never changes. Getting married means giving up the right to all other options. (Don't try to pursue a McDonald's franchise, when you already have one from Burger King.) For those who are comfortable with breaking their word with a spouse, let me remind you that God keeps his word and woe be to us, if we don't keep our word.

Marriage was not designed to be a burden, but as a fulfillment of human need. It comes with God's sanction and blessing (even on those who did not ask him). The sheer delight of newlyweds in each other is every married person's rediscovery of what Adam found when God presented Eve to him. Though believers are not to marry unbelievers, God has and does sanction the right of unbelievers to get married. The marriage of unbelievers is not a relationship of sexual sin. But neither does unbelief excuse breaking the marriage vows.

There are two things concerning marriage that are especially outstanding: First is the factor of physical intimacy. Now obviously sex, in itself, cannot hold a marriage together. But taken seriously in the context of a lifetime commitment, it reenforces the marriage bond. It is an unspoken message of enduring love and togetherness through the best and the worst that life can offer. This is so because in marriage alone, it is true to the context in which God gave it. It is very private, yet very right. It is free from the shame, regret, and guilt of wrongdoing.

Secondly, marriage is a trust of life-producing proportions. To this union of male and female is entrusted the reproduction and the future of the whole human race. In becoming "one flesh," they become at the same time, an integral part of the chain of generations. Who can argue against a God who orders that all conception, childbirth, and child training should be confined to the permanent relationship of marriage? God designed the family tree to be intact and orderly, rather than disordered and confused. The statistics are in. The high numbers of broken homes and illegitimate children bode ill for the generations to come.

There is no great mystery as to why God is so unyielding on sex outside marriage and on adulterous relationships. Uncommited sex is not love. It is false to its very essence.

That which God planned as a lifetime bond is now lived out in the context of cheating. (It is as though you didn't have the patience to wait for an inheritance of millions that is to be your's, so you go out and commit a crime instead - you rob a bank). In the context of cheating, there is the sowing of mistrust and confusion. Sinning partners shortchange themselves and their partners. Guilt and shame make for rocky relationships, and frequently end up driving the couple apart. Thus they destroy the good foundation that might have been.

God is not permissive about divorce. There are occasional cases, based on the wrong doing of an unfaithful spouse that may leave the partner in a divorced state (a state of aloneness). Such a divorced person need not be rejected of God. The instruction is clear. Either remain single, or be reconciled (I. Corinthians 7:11.)

But God is not at all permissive about remarriage (while the first partner still lives). *"If, while her husband liveth, she be married to another man, she shall be called and adulteress"* (Romans 7:3.) Divorce is the act of being severed from your legitimate marriage partner. When a marriage partner dies, the survivor is single. But divorce leaves a severed relationship, not a single state. But divorce does not end the desire for sexual fulfillment. Most divorced people seek new mates. Yet the only obvious exceptions to the taboo of remarriage were for Old Testament times only. Jesus explained it this way, *Moses allowed divorce and remarriage for the hardness of peoples' hearts, but from the beginning it was not so.*

I don't write this without feeling. I have many friends in such a plight. Some of them doubtless will read this. Yet I must share this for the spiritual peril of those who choose to remain in a remarried state, and for those who are even now being lured into divorce court, with the temptation of starting over again with someone else.

To you, I ask the question. Do you remember the delight your marriage partner once was? Why do you now see that same person through eyes of lovelessness and hopeless-ness? After divorce, have you considered that someone else will likely come along to claim your castaway as the greatest prize ever found? So why not *reprize* (to coin a new term), the one you already have?

Obviously, the feelings of love toward our mates are not permanently engraved in our hearts. If they were, we would not now despise the one that we once thought we couldn't live without. Even so, love need not be permanently lost. The same kindness, attention, and thoughtfulness you practiced in winning your mate, will go a long way in reclaiming what was lost. Is staying in a difficult marriage worth it? Are you really responsible to quench a new flame with a new lover? If reconciliation is still an option, should you reconcile? Yes, to all three questions. You will not be setting up yourself as an enemy of God. You will do your posterity a tremendous favor by maintaining a consistent family tree. You will likely keep your children from becoming social menaces and free-loaders. You will bless society with a good foundation for times to come.

But what if the case is beyond reconciliation? If one will indeed live a godly life, nothing and no one can prevent that. Yes, for some this narrow way of life will mean living alone. The marriage institution is always greater than the individual, which means that the rules of marriage hold sway over the desires of the individual. Ultimately the price will be worth it. Would you pursue your own desires at the loss of your soul?

And for those who are married: you must be man enough, or woman enough, to reject the divorce option, and to maintain absolute marital fidelity. You need to shut down whatever channels would tempt you otherwise. You must be the person who exercises responsibility and integrity. While you are at it, research the biblical manual. You will find that husbands and wives are designed to fulfill differing, yet com-plimentary roles. You will also find that children are a great blessing to the marriage. They are a worthy part of a man's diligent provision, and a mother's career as a homemaker.

Except the Lord build the house, they labor in vain that build it: Except the Lord keep the city, the watchman waketh but in vain. It is vain for you to rise up early, to sit up late, to eat the bread of sorrows: for so he giveth his beloved sleep. Lo, children are an heritage of the Lord and the fruit of the womb is his reward. As arrows are in the hands of a mighty man; so are the children of the youth. Happy is the man that hath his quiver full of them: they shall not be ashamed, but they shall speak with the enemies in the gate. Blessed is everyone that feared the Lord: that walketh in his ways. For thou shalt eat the labor of thine hands: happy shalt thou be and it shall be well with thee. Thy wife shall be as a fruitful vine by the sides of thine house; thy children like olive plants round about thy table. Behold, that thus shall the man be blessed that feareth the Lord. The Lord shall bless thee out of Zion: and thou shalt see the good of Jerusalem all the days of thy life. Yea, thou shalt see thy children's children, and peace upon Israel (Psalm 127 and 128).

THE CASE FOR SEPARATION

Biblical separation is possibly the most neglected teaching in Christianity today, especially in the West. Through sheer neglect (or unbelief), the life of the Christian is reinvented as a mere statement of belief apart from any change of life, and where nothing changes in relation to a world of ungodliness. The gospel is reduced to this: One accepts Jesus into his heart. God forgives. Heaven is sure. That's it. But nothing has changed. The new Christianity does not usher in the divine grace of transformation that breaks the old sin patterns and brings forth a life ordered from God. Instead, it has invented a divine blindfold, where God no longer sees the sin of the Christian.

But God is not mocked. Heaven is reserved, not for those who profess Jesus as Lord, but for those who do the will of the Father in heaven. ("He shall save his people *from* their sins.) Salvation results in single minded devotion to God, producing a separation from the powers of darkness and from the defilements of the world. Believers are the unique treasure of God."*Know ye not that ye are the temple of God, and that the Spirit of God dwelleth in you? If any man defile the temple of God, him shall God destroy; for the temple of God is holy, which temple ye are"* (I. Corinthians 3:16,17). Separation then, is the necessary fortitude against anything that would defile this treasure, indwelt by the living God. It is the principle of holiness, whereby Christians live "*in the world without being of the world".* Separation serves as a divinely prescribed respirator, sparing every godly person from the toxic effects of sin that dooms the multitudes on the broad way to destruction. Rather than adopting the defiling ways and values of the world, children of God of necessity receive their orders from God. They make careful and faithful applications to biblical commands and teachings.

The history of separation goes all the way back to creation. In the beginning God separated natural light from natural darkness, without which, there could be no life on earth.

Spiritually, he applies the principle of light versus darkness as the litmus test of all who claim a relationship with God. *"If we walk in the light as he is in the light, we have fellowship one with another, and the blood of Jesus Christ, his Son. cleanseth us from all sin. If we say that we have fellowship with him and walk in darkness, we lie, and do not the truth."*

With no exception, the lifestyle choices of godly people in history were regulated by the command of God. Noah, moved with fear, built the ark to exact divine specifications, and separated himself and his family from the plight of the ungodly. Abraham, (the spiritual father of all the faithful), at the command of God, deserted the idolatrous city of his ancestors. He left his world behind, to dwell in tents, in hope of inheriting the eternal city of God. Moses made the early choice to reject temporal worldly pleasures, in order to embrace the hardships of the godly. He faithfully received the ordered ways of God for his people. Sacrifice, worship, dietary instruction, wardrobe, giving, sanitation, principles of marriage and of justice - no details escaped the notice of heaven. This obedience created not only a pronounced separation from other nations. It also provided a divine shield against warring enemies, and stood as the sole protection against becoming like the nations who had long departed from the ways of God, and who were now slated for judgment and destruction.

The ultimate purpose of Israel was to honor God as a control group. They were to be the standard by which the wisdom, the glory, and the fear of God would be shown to the nations. In fact, Israel's own failure in separation turned them from the favor of God, to be castaways themselves: a principle that is still in effect today.

Separation has an eternal future. In the Day of the Lord, all people, of all generations, will stand before God in judgment. All will be judged, not by profession of Christianity, not by miracles, prophecies, or good works, but in doing the will of God among men. In that day the sheep will be forever separated from the goats. The righteous will inherit the kingdom prepared for them. The wicked will be turned into hell, and all the nations that forget God.

The contrast could hardly be more striking. The pursuit of worldliness is temporal and meets a horrific end, for the friend of the world has made himself an enemy of God. Separation unto God is good for the present life and for eternity. It is the only permanence available within a temporal system. *For the world passeth away, and the lust thereof, but he that doeth the will of God abideth forever.* Strange, isn't it, that we should be so enamored with the "forbidden fruit" of this world, the lust of the flesh, the lust of the eyes, and the pride of life, which all are to pass away? Equally strange, isn't it, that questionable things, and the deeds of darkness of the world should be preferred to the glorious light of the commandments of God?

Billy Graham made the striking point in a message at a mission conference in Urbana Illinois in 1987. Graham addresses 18,000 people (mostly college students) and recalls a message by one Donald Grey Barnhouse, a message Billy had heard in a similar conference in 1948. After thirty - nine years, Billy said, "I'll never forget his message on separation from the world."

Now quoting again Dr. Graham, *"We have gotten away from that. We have moved in with the world and allowed the world to penetrate the way we live. So things we used to call sin are no longer sin. Things that we would have abhorred a few years ago, we accept as matter of fact today, not realizing that they offend a holy God."*

Earlier in that same message Graham referred to TV content, . . . *it's almost embarrassing to turn on the television set. We do not realize how this offends a holy and righteous God. We act as if it doesn't really matter how we live or what we think or say because God will forgive us anyway.*

Thus Billy Graham exposed the heart of the matter. But have we made any kind of a turnaround? The indicators of acceptable Christian culture and practice indicate that we have not. **We are no longer afraid not to do the**

will of God. We seem bent more than ever to rejecting the redeeming commands of our Creator/ Savior, preferring to blindly copy the degrading cultural practices of the world. Thus the signals come, not from God, but from deniers and haters of God. *He who would be the friend of the world, is the enemy of God.*

Typical Mr. and Mrs. Christian (and their offspring) are largely imitators of ungodly culture. Yet they would be shocked at the idea of being enemies of God. The result is what we have repeatedly reflected upon in this column. Many people in the churches reflect the same failure of basic standards as their non-Christian peers. This includes the loss of integrity and truthfulness, it portrays personal shamelessness and immodesty, (marked by exposure of the body), music that banishes the echos of tender conscience by glorifying lawlessness and sexually immorality, and broken homes. In this way the "church" is in affinity with a world at enmity against God, aligning with the multitudes of those who "treasure up wrath against the day of wrath, and the day of perdition of ungodly men."

But what saith the Scripture? *"Be ye not unequally yoked together with unbelievers . . . and what agreement hath the temple of God with idols? For ye are the temple of the living God . . .* **Wherefore come out from among them and separate yourselves, saith the Lord, and touch not the unclean thing; and I will receive you, and will be a Father unto you, and ye shall be my sons and daughters, saith the Lord Almighty"** (II. Corinthians 6:14-18).

THE END OF CERTAINTY

Charles Darwin's 200th birthday is widely celebrated this year with many special events. Even many churchmen who take Darwin's words over God's Word are caught up with celebrating "Darwin Day."

Atheists are putting on their own push with advertising on billboards and buses such as this one:

> ## THERE'S PROBABLY NO GOD
> NOW STOP WORRYING AND ENJOY YOUR LIFE

These people must believe that an actual God in the universe is something like a cancer that would keep you from enjoying your life. But if I was trying to shed my faith in God, I wouldn't find any reassurance in such advertising. If you had symptoms of cancer, but your doctor said you "probably" don't have cancer, wouldn't you want a biopsy, or at least a second opinion?

In fact, these people do not understand the tradeoff. God over the universe is the system of certainty and security. We have it in nature. The certainty principle in natural laws allows us to plant and to harvest, to travel and explore, to build, to experiment and invent, all within the security of those laws. But we have so much more than function. Our senses are assailed with beauty. We enjoy innumerable wonders on constant display in the heavens and the earth "*The heavens declare the glory of God, and the firmament showeth his handiwork* (Psalm 19:1). The law of certainty also gives us the promise of a bountiful earth. *While the earth remaineth, seedtime and harvest, and cold and heat, and summer and winter, and day and night shall not cease.* Such is the promise of the living God. And from this springs the confidence, that in sowing and planting, we will ultimately reap. On this principle, life on earth not merely survives, but thrives.

There is likewise a parallel certainty in spiritual law, as revealed to us in the Holy Scriptures. *"The law of the Lord is perfect, converting the soul: the testimony of the Lord is sure, making wise the simple* (Psalm19: 7). So, as in the natural, it is in the spiritual. Whatever we sow, we will reap. To ignore certainties, in either the natural or the spiritual, is to invite confusion, and great troubles. Free choice is our's. But we cannot choose the resulting consequences.

So what is the legacy of Darwinism? It is the denial of the principle of certainty. If it were in accord with science, Darwinist claims of evolution would have been resolved a long time ago. Scientists are good at proving things in accord with nature and finding ways to get things done. They don't do a pitiful plea that because they say so, the earth is round, or that the sun is ninety three-million miles away. They simply wield the evidence. They don't speculate that men could be sent to the moon, or that megabytes of information could be stored in silicon chips. They explore, they engineer, they invent, and they do test flights. All this falls within the confines of the certainty of natural law. No intelligence or ingenuity can overcome what the laws of nature cannot support.

But Darwinism is embraced as the Holy Grail of the learned, not as a science, but as a philosophical foundation of a belief system. It violates the principle of certainty. This is an awkward way of saying it, but simply put, Darwinism is a belief system to destroy belief systems (think computer viruses). It embraces false science, for the promised release from the moral/ ethical standard that comes from God to man, to which all people are accountable. It promotes the notion of doing what you please without consequences. Theoretically, the thing that counts is personal choice — doing what you want to do.

This is the lie that goes all the way back to Eden. The theory could be tested with a hundred unsupervised children, five to ten years old, on a playground. Darwin's "survival of the fittest" quickly comes into play. Only the bullies "enjoy life." The rest have plenty to worry about.

But don't we grow out of that as adults? Absolutely not. In reality, those who write their own rules are forever infringing on the rights of others. That is why we lock up murders, rapists, thieves and robbers. Darwinists in America have not learned the lessons from Stalin, Hitler, and others who elevate themselves on the corpses of their own people. Thus what we didn't see coming was the sophisticated in-your- face lawlessness and scandal now permeating our culture, and even the whole world. It threatens our peace, our economy and our very existence. It has found its way into the highest levels of financial and political power. Honor has given way to scandal and dishonor. Policy, and power are increasingly vested in the few who make our choices for us. Thus the cultural landscape has morphed into an unstable monster that could not have been imagined even fifty years ago.

Christian teachings and Christian moral principles long dominated Western thought. People got married, stayed married, carried their babies to term, worked hard to pay their bills and their taxes, applied effective discipline when their children misbehaved, taught them a vocation, ran the schools without cops, or metal detectors, prayed and read the Bible in the home (and school), and took the whole family to church.

Why did they do this? Because they believed in the certainty principle — that God made heaven and earth in six days, that he made people in his image, that honor and integrity trump pleasure, and that punishment of wrong in homes and courts was but a prelude to hellfire for those who ultimately wouldn't settle their accounts with God.

Within those bounds of personal responsibility and morality, Americans did enjoy freedom — freedom of press, freedom of speech, and freedom of conscience, and freedom from oppressive rule. But with Darwinist uncertainty going mainstream, and conscience not informed with God-defined morality, we thought that wasn't freedom enough. We wanted to expand sexual liberties. Thus the rush into hedonism, and the likes of the Beatles, Elvis Presley, and Michael Jackson becoming gods to us.

We altered freedom of press and of speech, to make vulgarity acceptable, and pornography undefinable. And we had to redefine even the right to life to exclude millions of inconvenient babies, thus adding murder to an acceptable lifestyle package.

Yet any culture that lives for kicks and thrills, because of the law of diminishing returns, must of necessity ramp up the dosage and thus the harm done. Licentiousness prevails at the expense of marriage and home and a solid upbringing for children. Sexual wickedness runs aground, and has no place to turn, but to feed on itself, male with male, and female with female. The Bible describes such cultural reversal as being *"against nature,"* and transpiring in the context of *"evil men and seducers waxing worse and worse,"* and also as people who . . . *"treasure up wrath against the day of wrath and revelation of the righteous judgment of God."*

Thus the battle lines are newly drawn. The degrading elements of human passion that we were once expected to curb, we are now expected to embrace.

This turns to haunt us in ways we did not expect. One of the goals of Darwinism was to escape moral judgments. The effect though, is the loss of all sound judgment. The only thing left in the unbeliever's toolbox is man-made dogma, "Truth" is whatever world leaders and men in power make it, along with coercive regulation to enforce it. It's an awful thing to cut the reins of certain truth from the Almighty, only to vest those powers in unstable demigods.

Yet we pin our hopes on the same. Even science takes the back seat in the ideas on fixing the economy, climate change, or even health care. Today, major, costly policy can be implemented on less research, development, and scientific certainty, than goes into a single new model rolled out of Detroit. There are reasons for this, of course. The world quickly rejects the problems with a machine on four wheels, with a motor. But deeply flawed social or economic policies, are not so easily identified.

Darwinism delivers nothing of, "*don't worry, simply enjoy.*" There is plenty to be concerned about, in the men, and the policies, that take over for God.

Besides Darwinism, we have raised a second barrier against returning to God. We take to the notion that all belief systems are equal and acceptable — excluding the one of moral certainty — once inscribed in stone (The Ten Commandments). The exclusive righteousness of biblical Christianity is repackaged to fit as an equal player with the other major religions of the world. We now see religious diversity as a thing to celebrate. But the casualty here is the same as that of Darwinism. Truth itself is lost, as the line between good and evil is erased. Christians have been among the chief offenders, living contrary to truth, exchanging faith as the responsible way to live, for a bogus ticket to heaven. Thus like Israel of old, we have bartered away the *fountains of living waters*, only to *hew out for ourselves broken cisterns that hold no water* (Jeremiah 2:13).

But in fact, certainty does return to exact vengeance - that of misery and suffering and judgment from God.

THE PRICE OF REDEMPTION: PRICE VERSUS PENALTY?

The following is a response to what I believe is serious error promoted from time to time on the manner of Christ's atonement for our sins. This centers on the idea that in his death on the cross Jesus was tainted by our sins, and that as a result, he was rejected of the Father, and suffered torment as a result. The letter that follows has been slightly expanded for the understanding of the general reader. Note: I received no response from presenting this concern. This letter was dated 10/12/08.

"For the life of the flesh is in the blood: and I have given it to you upon the altar to make an atonement for your souls; for it is the blood that maketh an atonement for the soul "(Leviticus 17:11).

"Behold the lamb of God, which taketh away the sin of the world "(John 1:29).

I'm responding with concern to an article from your latest newsletter. The case in point is the misrepresentation of the role of Christ and his sacrifice for our sins. Your article presented a shrieking Jesus, damned of his Father, damned forever, (words almost too shocking to repeat). By your own testimony, you weep over this, and bless others who perpetuate the error. If this is any consolation, you are hardly alone. Similar ideas continue to come up. One evangelical leader claims that it was God who killed his Son, whereas Peter says, *"ye have taken, and by wicked hands have crucified and slain"* (Acts 2:23). God doesn't have wicked hands. What God did do was raise him from the dead (verse 24). The same leader claims that the cup that Jesus was made to drank, was filled with the wrath of God. Now Jesus told the sons of Zebadee that they would indeed drink that he drank of. So did these apostles, James and John, also drink of the wrath of God? The cup of the New Testament, in his blood, is a costly one, not a wrathful one.

What you brethren are doing is misinterpreting a few passages of Scripture into something really wild and wooly, far beyond the pale of Scripture. You are confounding the **price** paid for our redemption, with **penalty** for sin. As to **price**, *only* by the shedding of blood is the remission of sin. As to **penalty**, the wages of sin is death, followed by eternal damnation. In fact, the Savior paid the **price** (the shedding of his blood), so that the sinner may escape the **penalty** (death and damnation).

Now we might have imagined that the two would have been the same. That God would have decreed that his Son be "lost forever" for our redemption. Someone else recently claimed; the Jesus was a robber, a murderer, and an adulterer, and guilty of every other sin ever committed by the human race. But this is not justice. In fact, it is a doctrine too gross to even contemplate. In such a case he would indeed face the wrath of his Father and go into perdition in our stead. Thus, price and penalty would be one and the same. Certain saints (Moses and Paul), appear to have actually volunteered to bear the penalty of perdition for their unbelieving peers. But that was never heaven's way, and never was the way of salvation.

If we witnessed a righteous man stepping forward to be executed in the place of a wicked man, would we attribute the deeds of the wicked to the righteous, and turn on the righteous man in wrath? That would be unthinkable. Why then would we think that God would wrongly attribute sin to his beloved Son?

(In this writing, I will be referring to certain Scriptures, without noting the specific references. You know the Bible well, and will recognize the biblical grounds for what I say.)

The Old Testament animal sacrifices were a type of atonement for sin. These sacrifices covered the cost of atonement, not the penalty. The sacrificial lamb was not tainted with sin. Neither was it damned, nor sent to perdition, for the sins of the offerer. Rather the lamb pays the price. The blood of the dying lamb is itself the atonement; the "cover - over" for sin. The New Testament moves us from the type to the reality. The old Testament lamb was a yearly cover - over. The New Testament lamb is the washing away of sin (once for all), by the blood of the perfect Lamb of God.

Let's take a natural example of **price** versus **penalty**. We could insist that the only just way to rescue a drowning man is for one to jump into the same water, and save the drowning one by drawing the water from his lungs into the rescuer's lungs. In every case the rescuer would need to die, the victim of the very water the other had ingested. That would be *penalty*. We could take penalty a step further. The now dead rescuer would go to hell if the one rescued had not been saved from his sins. True, the very thought is atrocious; but no more so than the idea of imputing our sins upon the dying Lamb of God.

In contrast, *price* is not about punishment. It is about the sufficiency of the act. In the case of drowning, the price of a rescue could range anywhere from throwing out a lifeline, to risking life, to giving up life to save life. If the rescuer ingests water, he is not in a position to save anyone.

Indeed, the Father did not kill his Son. The *princes of this world* did this to the *Lord of Glory*. Only *wicked hands* would crucify the Son of God. The cup was not filled with wrath toward the Son. It was filled with this hour and this agony, wherein the sinless Son of God would become - *not a sinner, but the offering for sin*. This is the hour wherein the grain of wheat would fall into the ground to die. It is the hour from which Christ could not be spared, because to this purpose he came into the world.

Have you heard of cases where onlookers at some natural disaster could not bear the suspense of watching the outcome? Could we not identify with the Father disengaging himself from the scene as his Son is suspended on the cross to die as though he was the vilest of the vile? Was the Father scarce restraining himself from breaking through in wrath once for all against the perpetrators in this worst rebellion in history? He had, after all, broken through in wrath upon offenses much less than these. Would we attribute the revolt of nature that day, to abhorrence toward the one on the middle cross? Was not the natural rampage rather due to the horrible specter of Creator/ Savior/Righteous One, dying on that tree?

To be sure, to be crucified denoted a curse. Thus was the Son of God shamefully strung up that day, as though unfit to live. But, was anyone at the scene that day taken with sudden revulsion that the Christ on the cross had been transformed into the epitome of wickedness and violence? No not one. Was his face suddenly shadowed with hatred and his mouth filled with bitter words or blasphemy? God forbid. Even the hardened centurion (and those with him), could not stifle their own heart cry: ***truly, this was the Son of God***. And even as he died, it was with; ***Father, into thy hands I commend my spirit.***

Can we not see then the only proper biblical use of "damnation" is limited to impenitent, hardened sinners, trampling the blood of the Son of God? Be it far from us to assign such a term to the Lamb slain from the foundation of the world, paying the price so that we might escape damnation.

Because he died the sinless One, he arose again in righteousness, and is set down at the right hand of the Father. May his name be blessed forever. Amen.

A CONVENIENT CAUSE

We've become a rebel culture. As a result, the rejected underpinnings of the Judeo-Christian absolutes leave us with no consensus of morals and values.

Perhaps it feels good for a time just to do what you want with endless rounds of partying, drinking, and sexual flings, and cheating in any way you want (things the Bible says we ought to be ashamed of).

However, the human spirit is made of sterner stuff than that. Being deprived of fulfillment in legitimate challenges leaves us character orphans, looking for a cause. For the young, it is living on the edge in violence and gang activity. The more mature find challenge and fulfillment in more worthy causes. Bill Gates and Warren Buffet have found that charitable giving and supporting various causes feels good. It may even do some good.

But it also goes awry. For example, in the search for sacrificial causes, many have lost sight of the fact that forestry and commerce both do best in harmony. Careful management and harvesting is simply that best answer to having timber products today, and the best possible resources for the future. The same applies to most anything in nature.

Only thirty years ago we were being warned about a new ice age based on a slight dip in temperatures from about 1944 to 1972. There were dire predictions of crop failures with the resulting starvation of millions of people. One far -fetched idea was if we could find a way to melt the polar ice cap (the very thing we now fear), it would help stabilize global temperatures. But is the globe now warming? To be sure, urbanization, with added mile after mile of concrete, asphalt, and steel will raise local temperatures. There will also continue to be changing trends both in climate and temperature. Regional severe flooding and severe drought are both vividly stamped on childhood memory. But people have been attributing the drying up of our local Shue's Pond, to global warming. (It has nicely recovered since).

Yet, this sort of thing has had its versions all over the globe. So have mild winters and severe winters (and frozen citrus in the deep south.). However, in the present politically correct climate, every unusual weather pattern is attributed to global warming.

We are being "trained" by politicians, accounting firms, CEO's, "Christian" evangelists, and film makers, to reject absolute truth. Thus it is truly amazing that we should suddenly find absolute truth and noble cause in *Inconvenient Truth*, the agenda - driven film on global warming.

We note that our "sacrificial" causes are usually geared to having others do the sacrificing. We can be persuaded to dim our neighbors' lights, ensnarl traffic by driving under the speed limit, make everyone pay an extra buck or two in gasoline taxes, and cut national carbon emissions by about a third, thus ensuring poverty and inadequate food production.

It's interesting that it should turn out this way. As deniers of moral absolutes, we could shrug off the responsibility to be generous toward the needs of others, and to strive for the general welfare of our fellow church members and neighbors. This has turned many of us into self-indulgent and overindulgent consumers. In yet another turn, the cost of supporting the resultant bloated economic system, costs much more in higher taxes, than it would have through church offering baskets. Finally, as enlightened rejecters of godly absolutes, we have fabricated substitute causes, whereby we can deprive ourselves quite handily. May we find it fulfilling.

BORN AGAIN: A BEGINNING OR A DESTINATION?

What follows does not in any way detract from the need of the New Birth. Jesus himself declared that unless a man is born again, he shall not see the kingdom of God (John 3:3). We must preach the same with all authority.

One of the great tragedies in modern attempts to see people converted to Christianity, is a narrow focus on *how to* be born again. It is a subject that the Bible spends little time on, and for good reason. Until people know the sinfulness of their hearts, and the lostness of their souls, majoring on how to be saved is counterproductive.

This is like going around the country, teaching people how to plan the perfect wedding. Such an effort would change nothing for the multitudes who do get married and then proceed to break every rule of success. Most couples do commit to the perfect plan for the wedding day, yet miss the needed commitment that engages the couple in working out the rules of successful marriage and family. Such a wedding is like an elaborate entry door, fit for the most beautiful mansion in the land, only to be installed on a run - down trailer in a decrepit mobile park.

For parallel reasons, we also need a shift in focus from a "getting saved" formula, to one that plumbs the depth of human need, and so prepares one to deny himself, and take up the cross to follow Jesus Christ on the narrow way that leads to life. Again, of what point is it to cross the threshold of the Christian life, only to bring reproach to Christ and fellow Christians, in refusing the yoke of obedience to the Christ who is Lord and master?

To explore what must happen in the "new birth," we will observe two laws that define the lives of all people, apart from the grace of Jesus Christ. These two laws are described in Romans chapter 7, as a desperate struggle to do well, yet miserably failing to accomplish our good intent.

A third law, with the actual power for living the Christian life is described in the beginning of Romans, chapter 8.

The first of these laws appears in verse 7:23, as the phrase, *the law of my mind.* If you back up one verse, you find what this law of the mind is like. *I delight in the law of God after the inward man.* Some will surely say, "Not me. I'm no Christian. I don't believe in God." But in fact, this law does pertain to everyone, whether they know it or not. Romans 2:15-16 addresses unbelievers as having the law of God written in their hearts, and that their conscience bears witness to the truth. It happens all the time. Unbelievers affirm the kindness of the neighbor who brings in their mail, waters their flowers, and reports any suspicious activity while they are away on vacation. This law of the mind also causes them to trust emergency room staff in a strange city when the planned vacation has taken a tragic turn. In fact, it is this law of the mind that still keeps many, many people from becoming murderers, adulterers, thieves or rapists. And even among those who sin grievously, you will still find some admirable traits. It turns out that those who go totally upside down are actually quite rare. This law of the mind serves as a control factor on the side of decency, and is clearly a carryover from being made in the image of God.

However, there is a negative side to the "goodness" programming of the conscience. It is the notion that this level of goodness should satisfy the righteous standard of God. It goes so far as to question the justice of God for not going along with this man - centered analysis of good. It is a mistake to conclude, as many do, that the degree of goodness displayed makes us good people. It does not.

There is another law present in my members warring against the good intent and the actual good that is accomplished by the law of the mind. It is called *the law of sin* (Romans 7:23), and it resides in every human body. It has its own opinions, will and emotions with an exceedingly high demand for what it wants. Its focus is on immediate pleasure and on shortcuts out of challenging situations. In so doing, it promotes interests absolutely contrary and even deadly to personal well-being. It permeates the mind with wrong, and builds the desire for evil and breaks through the defenses of a mind wanting to do what is right. What we perceive as people who have it all together, such as the good neighbor, or the emergency room staffers, are caught up in the same struggles you face. It is really quite simple. Sin breaks through the facade of goodness and respectability, leaving us struggling, frustrated, and defeated. We find ourselves powerless over this, because the law of sin ultimately dominates and defines who we truly are. (We are not the good person we meant to be). It marches a relentless course of spiritual death because of the dominant, contaminating nature of evil. The otherwise perfectly good hamburger from your favorite fast food place is no match for the trace of salmonella. The same holds true for the sin of the "good" person. *He that keeps the whole law, yet offends in one point, is guilty of all.* Paul says it well in raising the question that echoes through the condemned conscience: *Who shall deliver me from the body of this death?*

In summery then, we have the mind to do well (I witness this repeatedly even among criminals), but are brought to defeat and despair by a sinful nature beyond our power to control.

There is only one sufficient answer - only one course of Christian victory. In our natural world, thousands of travelers illustrate this principle every day. They board jetliners they don't own. They couldn't move them an inch, much less get them off the runway. Yet they fly! All they need is a boarding pass that entitles them to a seat. Then they sit back and trust the airlines to fly them from Detroit to Amsterdam, or from New York to Los Angeles, mocking gravity all the way. Every successful flight meets the following conditions; aircraft designed to the laws of aerodynamics, safe flight patterns, mechanical soundness, and sufficient quality and quantity of fuel. Cutting corners is lethal. Why expect short-cuts in becoming children of God?

The one sufficient answer to the defiling power of the flesh, is from Romans 8:2. *The law of the Spirit of life in Christ Jesus hath made me free from the law of sin and death.* This law produces the sufficiency and the enabling power of life in Jesus Christ, who shed his blood and suffered death on the cross for the remission of sins, that we who were dead in trespasses and sin may now live unto him who arose from the dead. This holds a standard to which other religions, and a compromised version of being saved cannot attain.

To substitute a shallow "accepting Christ" for genuine repentance from sin, restitution for wrong doing, and unreserved faith and loyalty to Jesus Christ, mocks the God who owns the spiritual "airlines" and books passage to victory in Jesus. The scandals that frequently haunt the ranks of the saved, blocks the testimony of the church in society, and discourages some who might otherwise be sincere seekers after God.

For to be carnally minded is death, but to be spiritually minded is life and peace, (Romans 8:6). **Ye must be born again.**

TO END DOMESTIC VIOLENCE

My goal is to be a Christian, a faithful family man, a minister, and a furniture manufacturer, in that order. These may seem like far-flung goals. Yet, these are not at odds. For example, there are times when the manufacturing part of me simply confirms what I have already been taught as a Christian, from the knowledge of the Word of God.

At the heart of success with furniture is bonding. Bad joints and mismatched materials can never be overcome with the best of glues or joining methods. But even with good joinery, bonding materials must not be applied carelessly. Good adhesive, carelessly applied, makes for a costly cleanup.

Similar absolutes apply to sexual issues and domestic violence. Obviously, sex is powerful. As an advertizing tool, it sells anything from magazines, to automobiles, to liquor, to indecent apparel. As an entertainment medium, it has broken down discretion and sacred inhibitions, and has molded the way a whole generation thinks. That is why, today, sex is considered just another pleasurable or recreational activity. Going to bed together is on par with eating pizza with a friend, or jogging with your neighbor.

But sex sells something else. It sells the private and priceless, as a cheap public commodity. It sells the body, as unworthy of high morals and permanent, sacred trust. It sells youthful innocence and freedom into the bondage of crippling diseases, vices, and the gratification of vile individuals. Last, but not least, it sells another generation of babies down the river.

Sex as a gift from God is, in its very giving, the exclusive bonding material for marriage only; biblically speaking, two become *one flesh*.

However, in the case of sex before marriage or as an aside to marriage, that glue is being applied indiscriminately. Where this bonding happens, objectivity concerning the character of the partner is never established. It blinds the sexual partners, not merely to annoying personality differences, but even to horrendous and dangerous character flaws. Too late, the one attempting to cut the bonding becomes the object of violence or even murder. Behind *every case* of domestic violence is either careless bonding with bad material or the too-soon bonding that threatens to destroy suitable material.

Any woman who would not be used for male gratification; and then abused; who would not live in terror from a former live-in, or a jilted husband, must not offer bonding, ever, to the uncommitted male. If you get a "good" domestic partner by sleeping around, it is only by chance, not from the high ground of clear-minded evaluation. The only certainty of finding true love, is to marry a "waiter," and then to have him wait (as in marriage certificate).

We need to revise our view and practice of sex. We must understand that moral looseness cannot be configured into the safety, happiness, and security of this, and coming generations. Nothing will change that. No hand-wringing over domestic abuse, and no posturing against violence, will ever sanitize recreational sex.

Now for these changes to happen, we also need a change of mind on what constitutes suitable material for entertainment and reading. If you can join the theater crowd to be entertained with nudity and unwed sex, or succumb to the immoral allure screaming from the newsstands, you are at risk for violence. And one more thing. It does make a difference how you dress. If in appearance, the body appears to be bait, you need not be surprised to find yourself among wolves.

No wonder the Bible portrays sexual sin as transgression against one's own body, with negative consequences too numerous to mention in this space.

Why not join a full-scale revolt against the sins that bring us low, for a return to the high moral ground of the permanent bonding of marriage, with the blessing of God?

WHICH WAY?

THE GOSPEL ACCORDING TO THE READER'S DIGEST

While out of town on Monday morning, Oct. 11, 04, I dialed up the news on my cell phone. Christopher Reeve had died just that weekend. This news brought me into sober reflection. It was only after Reeve's riding accident, ten years earlier, that I learned about this man, or even recognized his name. But I became personally interested in this once Superman actor, now wheel chair bound, and in his humanitarian efforts.

Only days before his death, I had read with keen interest the October '04 feature interview with Reeve in the Readers' Digest. I was especially intrigued with Reeves' explanation of his newfound Unitarian faith.

...The Unitarian believes that God is good, and believes that God believes that man is good. Inherently. The Unitarian God is not a God of vengeance. And that is something I can appreciate.

Let's compare this supposed goodness of man with other fare from this same issue of Reader's Digest.

1. Binge drinking among young women now rivals that of young men.
2. A career woman, on lunch break, is attacked right on a busy sidewalk, and viciously dragged into a side street. The tragedy of this story goes far beyond the criminal actions of one thug in broad daylight. It highlights the indifference of fellow pedestrians to the plight of this woman and her lone rescuer, both in obvious mortal danger.
3. "Crime Pays," details the tremendous cost of free medical care for inmates, much of which would be financially unavailable to law - abiding citizens. This includes priority status for organ transplants, and even pricey sex -change hormones for prisoners miffed over their inherited gender.
4. Hollywood knows the minds of terrorists, and uncannily constructs (on film) terrorist acts before they happen.

5. The author of detective stories writes about the homicidal binges of two serial killers who snuffed out the lives of at least 36 and 48 women respectively.

Now this ought to raise questions already to the claim of inherent human goodness. Reeve's claim that God *and* people are good highlights the tension of the issue. Is God good? Are people good? Can both be good?

If people are good, then doing good should come naturally. In fact, the more "natural," the better. The purest good should spring from human nature, unrestrained and uninhibited.

But this doesn't square with unrestrained human nature. Why doesn't "inherent goodness" translate into integrity in business and government, and a general gravitation toward moral excellence? Wouldn't a good person be good 100% of the time? (Would you buy a cheeseburger with just a little spoilage, or peanut butter laced with just a bit of salmonella?) Try taking this *good* person through the Ten Commandments (try this for yourself). He should not have broken a single one of them - no lying, stealing, coveting, no committing adultery, etc. Keeping nine out of ten commandments is not goodness. Yet truthful evaluation will show that we have broken the commandments of God, and that we are not good.

This is not to say that the human race is without good attributes or good deeds. Even in a fallen world where evil threatens our peace, and even our very existence, there is still a lingering agreement of heart and conscience with the righteousness of God. The fact that sin came into the world, and into our lives, has not allowed us to sever all moral responsibility to our Creator. This sense of right and wrong puts constraints on evil, and keeps much of the population from becoming murderers, arsonists, armed robbers, or rapists.

However, in respectable society, we justify evil with reasons to fudge on our taxes, cheat the employer, spend inappropriate time with someone other than our spouse, or claim that a lie really is the best response to a particular situation. Thus we deceive ourselves by denying the defilement of our sin, and convincing ourselves that we surely don't deserve the judgment of God, and that hellfire would be unjust punishment. But in this, we already invent a religion that gives permission *not to do the good that we ought to do, but to do the evil that we should not*

I am not questioning Reeves good intent. He puts into words the idea of millions around the world who erroneously deflect moral judgments as the way to cover for the power of the sin nature within. But obviously, we only pave the way for more evil by denying its existence.

Mistaken claims of human goodness get in the way of understanding both ourselves and our God. When we accept the sale-priced version of human goodness, we expect God to deliver us from the pain of our wrongs, to cater to our whims, to honor us, and to set our little world at right again. When this doesn't happen, we raise the wrong questions* (see appendix). *Why do bad things happen to good people? Where is God when innocent people suffer? What did we do to deserve this? How could a good God allow so much evil and suffering in the world?*

It is only in an undefined context of the righteousness of God and the supposed goodness of people, that anyone can claim a sugary goodness for both. Even this quickly breaks down because God is perceived as failing good people. This forces a real dilemma. To our own confusion, we would have to conclude that God is not good, or that He is powerless over the terrible injustices that occur in our world every day. How much better to gain an accurate conception of God, and to acknowledge the propensity of people to fill the earth with wickedness and violence.

THE SEARCH FOR TRUTH ABOUT GOD

In a debate held between an atheist and a Christian, the atheist claimed that to know an unseen God in a totally natural world would be impossible. In contrast, his Christian counterpart referred repeatedly to his own spiritual rebirth as proof for God and Christianity. Let's probe both of these claims, considering them in the present religious climate.

The pressure is on in these days to concede that all religions are good, even equally good. *Why shouldn't every individual have the right to his own religious ideas? Who dares to claim that one religious lead is better then another, or especially that mine is better than your's?*

But in fact, religions are many, and religious experiences come easy, because religious higher powers are an easy invention in the human mind. I encounter an ongoing flow of people with a mixed religious bag; beliefs assembled out of a personal wish list of what God should be like. But let's zero in to the obvious. When religions are concocted in fertile imaginations, then there is no real difference in whether one puts his faith in some vague "man upstairs," in a lavishly sculptured block of marble, in the full moon, in virgin forests, or even in a door knob.

All these are essentially doors to nowhere. To be sure, you can build costly shrines over dead men's bones, or spend large money on elaborate temples, mosques, and cathedrals, and assemble thousands or even millions of followers. But let's cut to the very basic question from the Bible: *Can men by searching find out God?* (Can man figure out God?) The answer is no. The ease of inventing religion is matched exactly to the folly of doing so. That the human brain is equal to the challenge of creating acceptable religion is one of the greatest myths of all time. The greatest human minds are not equipped with "God Discovery" hardware. These "gods" of the people are simply bogus. There is no truth in them now, and they will not save in the end. Some people know this intuitively, and carelessly dismiss *all* religious experiences out of hand.

There are other problems with man-made religions. In celebrating religious diversity, truth itself becomes the casualty, and the line between good and evil is lost. Believing as we please, leads to doing as we please - while still claiming to be good. Cultural moorings are lost as upside - down belief systems spew a rising tide of contradictions and non-answers to social and economic problems, and introduce new lows in human misery.

But there is a way by which we can truly know God. Though we could not find God, he knew exactly how to find us. It is the Bible that reveals what we could not invent. The teaching of the Bible is God's way of making himself known to us. Thus the path to knowing God was laid out not from earth to heaven by men, but from heaven to earth, by Jesus Christ.

So the real audacity is not in believing in only one way to God, but in claiming that false is as good as true, and that all God claims are valid. And the question finally, is not whether the Christian debater is or was saved. It must rather be whether Christianity came from God as a package of definable, unchanging, and historically grounded evidence that such salvation is possible, and that it works the miracle of forgiveness of sin and salvation for everyone who will commit to it. (It does.)

The natural shell that the atheist claimed would keep God out of the universe (and out of his life), was never real in the first place. He must assume (falsely), that the natural world couldn't possibly have had a divine cause, that his own ancestry is slime rather than human, and that the Jesus who fed the hungry, healed the sick, raised the dead, then died on a cross, and rose from the dead could not have been the Son of God . He must also believe that his denial of God will suffice to deliver him from rising from the dead, and ulti-mately save him from answering to the Almighty in the day of judgment. In the meantime, he must also maintain that a world that is so wonderfully designed and well ordered, is just an incredibly lucky roll of the evolutionary dice.

THAT WE MIGHT BE SAVED:
THE GOSPEL ACCORDING TO THE HOLY SCRIPTURES

The Bible declares the truth about God

God is God over all. There are no other gods. God is eternal. He is self existing, having neither beginning nor end. His character is intrinsically good. He is morally, ethically, and absolutely righteous. God created the heaven and the earth, and everything that is in them. Likewise, he upholds all things by the Word of his power, The present, the future, and the end of the world are equally under his control. To Him belong all things: the kingdom, the power, and the glory forever. Amen.

The Bible declares the truth about humanity.

God made us in His own image, and set humanity apart and over the rest of creation such as mammals, birds, fishes and reptiles. The first man, Adam, was commanded not to eat of the tree of knowledge of good and evil. He was fore-warned that death would result from the sin of eating the forbidden fruit.

Adam's disobedience to this commandment, was the first cause of both sin and death in the world. As a result, the descendants of Adam (that's all of us), are directly subjected to a sinful nature, to physical death, and to eternal separation from God.. *There is none righteous, no not one. For all have sinned and come short of the glory of God.*

The Bible confronts us with the consequences and the judgment of our sin.

The wages of sin is death. We must all appear before the judgment seat of Christ to receive according to the deeds we have done, and to be judged according to our works, whether good or bad.

The wicked shall be turned into hell, and all nations that forget God. Those who at judgment are under the curse of sin, are doomed to everlasting fire, prepared for the devil and his angels.

The Bible teaches that there only one way to be saved from sin.

Salvation is the result of godly sorrow for sin, with faith in Jesus Christ as personal Savior and deliverer from sin. This results in peace with God, when our sins are forgiven, and held against us no more. *If thou shalt confess with thy mouth the Lord Jesus, and believe in thine heart that God hath raised him from the dead, thou shalt be saved. He that believeth and is baptized shall be saved.* Salvation is a change of loyalties. The new life calls for open identity with Christ, and with God's people in the church through baptism with water. The believer testifies of his faith in Jesus Christ. This is an effective witness for the salvation of others.

The believer is not self- righteous, but he does have a comforter and a guide through the Holy Spirit. The righteous-ness which is by faith prevails over the former lusts in which he lived. The teachings and commands of Scripture form the path of life. He accepts adversity and trial as necessary components of his growing faith. He is careful to walk in the will of God. *Not everyone that saith unto me, Lord, Lord, shall enter the kingdom of heaven, but he that doeth the will of my Father which is in heaven.*

Neither is there salvation in any other, for there is no other name under heaven, given among men, whereby we must be saved.

RECONSIDERING OUR CONCEPT OF GOD

Before we blame God for terrible injustices and tragic sufferings around the world, we need to revisit where and why things went wrong. The Bible allows us to do exactly that.

The disobedience of Adam and Eve, in eating the forbidden fruit, brought sin into the perfect world which God had created. It scrambled everything. This world is like a house, damaged, but still standing, after an earthquake. The integrity and safety of the house was compromised. Sickness and death invaded our world and our bodies. Human nature changed. We gravitate toward doing the wrong things. That is why we load human history with horrible tragedies. We stoke our self-inflicted problems though sexual immoralities, violence and murders, drinking and partying and all sorts of excesses. Even nature is now locked into age and decay mode. It goes on rampages with floods, droughts, famines, earthquakes, fires and tornadoes.

It is commonly argued that a good God would stop evil. But unlike the instinctive nature that controls the animal kingdom, God created people with a conscience and with a free will. The will was to be subjected to God our Maker. Should God override our freewill and turn us into robots? Should God have stopped the murderous rampages of the likes of Adolph Hitler? Should he have stopped people deliberately flying planes into the World Trade center? Should He stop an evil step father from abusing a little child? Should He stop murderers, thieves, and rapists? The next time you choose to do wrong, should God stop you? Are we wiser than God?

In fact, God does have a way of stopping evil. He doesn't do it by overriding personal choice, but by the inward transformation that comes by faith in Jesus Christ. It is his way of stopping lying, stealing, and adultery, as well as suicide bombings, school shootings, drunkenness, abortions, divorce, domestic violence, and homosexual activity.

Probably the first thing that comes to mind for most people, is that God is supposed to be loving. He is. But if we believe that love is the only attribute of God, or even the most important, we end up taking offense at God.

In fact, the loving God, is above all else, the holy God. He is just. He is right. This is His unchanging nature. So the revealing of His love will be according to what ultimately is just and good and right. Amazingly, the love of God was best revealed in the day of the darkest deed in the history of mankind. It was the day Jesus Christ was nailed to the cross for our sins.

Perhaps by some stretch of the imagination, you could visualize a circuit judge who so loved criminals that he would throw every case out of court and set every criminal free. But that would make him an accomplice to every criminal act. He would not be anything like Jesus who loves righteousness and hates iniquity. Nor would he be like a good shepherd who loves sheep and hates wolves. Such a judge could not also be good. If he were good, he could not possibly ignore the damage of criminal acts either to society, or to the lawbreaker himself. In fact, you would soon realize that his professed love for murderers and rapists proves that this judge does not love the righteousness of the law. Nor does he love those who live by the law. He has come down on the side of evil. In so doing, he promotes lawlessness and perverts justice.

On the other hand, the good judge will love justice and will impartially impose the righteous standard of the law on every case that comes before him. As you followed the cases of this judge, you could observe the justice of his work. In the case of a remorseful thief, the judge will levy a suitable fine, and order full restitution. Justice is served, and the thief goes forth to steal no more. Another defendant (same court, same judge, in a state that doesn't allow capitol punishment), gets six life sentences for murder with no possibility of parole. The judge is not unloving. He is accurately applying the law to the heinous nature and the just consequences of the crime. This murderer has forfeited his freedom forever.

Now in the day of judgment before the Holy God, it is not the measure of greater or lesser sins that determine the outcome. All sin spells condemnation. In that day a serial killer could be justified because he repented and forsook his sinful ways, whereas the petty thief (because he denied his sin), may be banished from the presence of God forever.

This exposes the great degeneration of western thought. We want God to give us a long, pain- free life, the privilege to do as we please, plus lots of things to make us happy (along with a happy hereafter, in case there is one). Apart from that, we would rather have God undefined and out of the way, and surely not one who would punish sins.

Even our physical death challenges this mentality. Death bears witness that sin is as deadly as it is portrayed in the Bible. Death may seem a long ways off. But death finally claims every last person of every generation. Even as I write, death rattles her sabers, snatching another 140,000 people away by the end of the day. And those unprepared will rightly face the terror of eternal judgment.

Yet the invitation of the loving God still beckons : ***Look unto me, and be ye saved, all the ends of the earth.***

Breinigsville, PA USA
21 February 2011
255963BV00002B/2/P